Echoes from the Oasis

A R Tirant

Copyright © Rosie Tirant 2010
Writers' Copyright Association
Registration #C103722

ISBN-13: 9780992808600
ISBN-10: 099280860X

A.R.Tirant asserts the moral right to
be identified as the author of this work.

All characters and events in this publication,
other than those clearly in the public domain,
are fictitious and any resemblance to actual persons,
living or dead, is purely coincidental.

All rights reserved. No part of this publication may be
reproduced, stored in a retrieval system, or transmitted,
in any form or by any means, electronic, mechanical,
photocopying, recording or otherwise, without the prior
permission of the publishers.

This book is sold subject to the condition that it shall not,
by way of trade or otherwise, be lent, re-sold, hired out or
otherwise circulated without the publisher's prior consent
in any form of binding or cover other than that in which it
is published and without a similar condition including this
condition being imposed on the subsequent purchaser.

Cover: Anse Georgette, Praslin, Seychelles

*In memory of my Mum and Dad, Maryse and Marcel Tirant.
I am eternally grateful for your guidance and integrity.
You shaped my life.
Rest in Peace.*

Acknowledgements

First, I should like to thank my dearest friend Marie-Helene Layton for believing in me, and for being there during the highs and lows whilst this book emerged. Thanks too to Noreen and Terry Collins for listening with enthusiasm and joy as I read them the latest chapters. You were both an enormous help, and looking back now, it was great fun too…

Thanks go to my nursing tutor, Patricia Revera, whose passion instilled in me the love and rewards of nursing. I shall never forget you, nor my hospital family and PTS colleagues of 1975. It was a great honour to have worked alongside you all, a memorable experience that still echoes today.

Moving on to the present, and to the others who have helped me achieve my dream. To Jan Carney, Anna Stephens, Doris Walker and Annette de Saulles, thank you all for your patience and enthusiasm. You were my lifeline. To my daughter-in-law, Lisette Morel and my sister, Wendy Baralle, your help was precious, thanks. To my dearest sister-in-law, Margaret Moran and her extremely kind husband, Pat, a big thank you to you both for your invaluable input and assistance when I needed it the most.

Finally, a special mention for my husband, Stan Longhurst, who deserves an enormous and heartfelt 'thank you' for all his patience and support. Life with me must have been tough for you, particularly when my characters and I traversed those emotionally difficult periods of 1912 to 1914. Thank you for your understanding and patience, mon chéri, it was my longest journey.

Contents

	Prologue	ix
1	The Birth of Eliane	1
2	A Journey Begins	16
3	Mermaids in the Moonlight	35
4	Personal Drama	45
5	A Little White Sand Crab	56
6	The Little Mermaid	85
7	General Gordon's Connection	103
8	The Mauritian Visitors	118
9	A Dark Cloud	130
10	A New Dawn	168
11	The Silhouette of a Sailboat	205
12	Suicide and Rewards	217
13	The Roar of German Metal	238
14	The Aftermath	248
15	A New Life	298
	Epilogue	345
	Glossary	347
	About the Author	351

PROLOGUE

A Day in July

It was the year of 1912 and the heat was overpowering. Its menace and malevolence permeated everywhere and everything.

Anna Savy, just sixteen, a wisp of a girl, angrily threw the cleaning cloth onto her neatly-made bed. Then, tears streaming down her clear, pale face, she ran from her room and the house. Her bare feet struck heavily on the packed dirt path leading up from the compound. Her long black hair hit in waves and ringlets over her shoulders and back. Beneath the starched cotton of her print dress, her trim, boyish body was changing. The swell of breasts had begun to develop. Her hips had taken on the slightest flair. Downy hair had begun to shadow her girl parts. She was, on that hot and humid day, on the very brink of womanhood. In her heart and soul she was still an innocent girl. But her eyes and mind saw only too clearly the fate awaiting her, a young Catholic girl coming of age. And that vision stole her breath from her. *How could they? How could they?*

The air in her house had been stultifying. The atmosphere too painful to bear. She needed the safety of the only sanctuary she believed in - nature - soothing, wild nature. Already she felt her young life in the close-knit Catholic community gathered in the valley was over and gone, lost to her. The daily rites, with their deeply-intoned prayers and shadow light, the stiff, formal and strict ritual, the incense perfumed air of the church…it suddenly all seemed as alien to her as it must have to those African natives when they were first led inside to be saved by the missionaries.

She only wanted to be free of it. Before she knew what she was doing, she was running. She was up into the dense vegetation, pushing branches apart with her thin arms all the while high-stepping the tall grass that tickled her legs under her long dress.

As she ran, her mind was in turmoil. Had everything she thought was true and good been a lie? Had everyone who professed to love her lied?

All the dark whispers, the secrets passed along with glances and nods, the frightened eyes, the sad expressions, the unspoken words, the things that warned her that this day would one day come, suddenly came together in a vision so clear in its cruelty that she could barely stand it. *If only I were a boy!* Yes, if she was a boy, then she would have a world to look forward to, a never-ending horizon of experience and opportunity. But she was not a boy and the world promised to her was dark and closed off.

Of all the betrayals, her mother's hurt her the most. She could not understand how her own mother could want such suffering for her. How could *she* of all people talk to her about a *wedding proposal*? Had she really thought she was doing the right thing to prepare Anna for that horrible future?

Anna paused. Her breath came in harsh gulps of air. She turned and looked back at Beau Vallon, the picturesque seafront village that had been her home since she was born. How many times had she paused at this very spot and looked back at this very same village? How delightful and beautiful it had seemed to her then. How often had she traced the curves of the northern coastline of this island of Mahé? How often had she taken comfort in the church of Saint Roch dominating the far end of the bay? Here, where Albert and Therese Savy had raised Anna and her six siblings in a small, thatched cottage on the hillside overlooking the beach. The cottage resided on the immense estate of the du Barré family for whom Albert worked as an overseer.

Now? Now, everything had changed. She turned and continued her climb, wishing she could leave it all behind forever. As she climbed, she trembled as her mother's cries of agony echoed in her ears.

Adding to her distress was this oppressive, unnatural heat. For months on end, the island had suffered. Temperatures soared. Humidity soared. The elderly were reduced to listlessly seeking a cool wisp. Children played only in the early morning hours or after the sun had set. The heat seemed malicious, the discomfort it caused personal and vengeful. The waters of the bay, normally rippling in the island air with white caps, had become flat and languid. Like the bay, the sea beyond had lost its roar and its power. Life itself seemed to have lost its energy and vitality, and only the broad beaches, painted by swathes of powdery white sand, seemed untouched. The sand sparkled in the harsh sunlight, as if millions of diamonds had been scattered among the fine grains. A beauty so natural, yet so overwhelming, with the power to mesmerize.

Anna continued her climb up the hillside from the valley. She was more than halfway up the slope now, much further than any of the older people could ever climb. Below her, the Indian Ocean seemed to stretch out forever. The church of Saint Roch seemed to be little more than a doll's house in the distance. The heavy vegetation of the jungle kept most of the valley hidden from her eyes. She leaned against a small bolder to catch her breath and shivered as the cool of the boulder pressed against her overheated and sweaty body. Here, high up on the hillside, the air was cooler.

She had climbed through the heavy, hot cloud that had settled upon the valley. She wrapped her arms around herself and enjoyed the feeling of the cool stone. But still she could not shake off the feeling of being cursed, cursed as a woman, cursed by this oppressive heat.

She shifted her gaze upward, into the endless blue sky and the heavens beyond. *Lord, what have we done to deserve this?* She lowered her head and dropped her arms. *Why must there be such sadness and pain?*

With her 'God's-eye view' above the valley, the fullness of the calamity that had befallen it was both plainly evident and curiously veiled. If she believed in those rumours circulating the village, she would think that an evil spell had been cast upon the graceful valley. But she did not. What did she have instead? Truth? Reality? She shivered again, only this time not from the coolness of the boulder, but from something deep within herself.

She took to her climb again. As she did, she tried to convince herself that perhaps things were not as terrible as they seemed. *There is still all this*, she reminded herself, taking in the brilliant beauty of the jungle around her. She knew that the sanctuary she was still able to find in these high reaches of nature would become more and more important as her fate closed in around her. Anna was not the only one to take the heat personally, nor to recognize evil in its presence.

"It is a bad omen, you mark my words," Gaston Hoareau bellowed.

Gaston was neither a pious man nor a young girl. He was a mountain of a man, the village's blacksmith, and not given to senseless proclamations. But there was something about this heat that had got under even his skin. "Bloody terrible," he added, shaking his head on his massive neck. "Nothing good to come." Gaston's message had been unchanged for months. Anytime someone stopped by his forge as they made their way through the village, they were regaled with the same, distressing words. "This is unnatural heat," he stated.

Gaston knew heat intimately. His blacksmith work guaranteed that his bald pate was always shining with sweat. The perspiration poured down over his face and into his thick beard, down his furry chest and back, finally settling in the waistband of his old grey trousers and filthy apron. So, if he felt that the heat was unnatural...then it probably was.

Despite his concerns, he continued his difficult work, keeping the metalwork of the village in order – knives, axes, hoes and spades, and soldering watering-cans, bedpans, pots, kettles, and various other utensils on demand. Like his father before him, Gaston had devoted his life to the hard labour at the heat of his anvil. In doing so, he had gained the respect and admiration of all the villagers, and made his forge central to daily life.

The place that Gaston occupied owed itself to both to his hard work and to the forge's geography; it was located in a central position alongside the main road, the small *malbar* grocery shop, and the beach.

The open veranda of the forge proved to be an ideal place to gather and chat, to smoke a hand-rolled cigarette or a pipe, while observing the various comings and goings of the village, not to mention all the activities on the waterfront. What a sight that beach was! Fishermen pulling in mackerel and sardines in their huge nets, all the while being directed by the screaming voice of the unseen 'Commander' in the top branches of one of the massive trees bordering the beach.

"Dwat! Dwat! Gos! Lans!" From this vantage position at the top of the tree, he marked the movement of the fish and guided his colleagues in the correct manoeuvring of their nets. Of course, if it was something other than mackerel or sardines that tempted the palate, one needed only engage in conversation at Gaston's for a short while before the *lansiv* sounded that one of the black pirogues had returned ashore with its daily catch.

Commerce. News. Gossip. Anyone looking for any or all had to look no further than Gaston's forge to get his fill. Nevertheless, the past weeks had found the conversations dominated by a single topic – the heat.

While some shared Gaston's perspective that the heat was an unnatural omen, others held differing views. For some, it was a natural occurrence. To others, it was a disturbance caused by what was likely a hurricane on the other side of the globe. Still others saw in it the hand of God, finding displeasure in some aspect of the villagers' daily lives. Over time, with the heat wave becoming more and more relentless, even the most rational of the villagers had begun to attribute it with supernatural qualities. Its oppressive nature, the very heaviness of the air, the way it sapped the strength from even Gaston's powerful muscular biceps, had put everyone on edge. The elders of the village were at a loss to explain what was happening. As the weeks turned into months of unremitting heat, tensions rose, patience was sapped. A sense of dread accompanied the rising of the sun each morning.

Not far from Gaston's forge, a small group of shirtless fishermen sought shelter under the shade of the massive *takamaka* trees bordering the beach. Dressed in old khaki shorts and wide-rimmed, straw hats, they mended their nets or wove bamboo strips into fish traps. They worked reflexively, long years of practice making their task second nature. Despite the shade of the trees, the heat seeped into every nook and cranny.

Even as they hummed along, doing their work, with the half-smoked cigarette hanging between their lips, their thoughts were on the cool of sunset, when they would push their pirogues from the beach and into the silent bay. From there, they would row out towards Silhouette Island to bottom-fish.

"Heh, heh," they hummed and chuckled, dreaming of the boatfuls of *bourzwa* and *vyey* they would bring back to shore before the sun rose on the following morning. These fishermen did not debate the heat wave nor indeed much of anything else. They were simple souls, unlike the grey-haired, time-worn elders who were able to call upon their memories of long ago, when the island was young. They had many years to live before they could be counted amongst the elders. For the time being, they would tend to their nets and their fish catching and let others worry about the ominous heat. What was curious was that while the elders wrestled with all manner of holy and divine reasons for the heat, considering too, supernatural and sorcery causes, they remained blind to the one obvious reason for their dilemma.

From the beginning of time, the Islands of Seychelles had always been nurtured by the gentle favours of mighty Mother Nature. Perhaps this giantess of great care and passion also harboured, in addition to her sometimes vivid temper, a dark and fearful character. Perhaps there was a side to the great mother that the islanders had never witnessed until now. Perhaps they had simply failed to show their gratitude for all that Mother Nature had given them. Compounding this sin, their seeming determination to see a greater cause in the heat wave might simply have exacerbated her anger.

Certainly, there had not been cause for alarm when it first began. The breezes, usually evident on a daily basis, disappeared. No one noticed the eerie quiet their absence left for several days. Then the sea grew lazy and tired. It flattened into a gel-like lake, too weary to toss up even the most modest whitecap. There had been no rain, turning the grass and plants into golden sticks. As the days and weeks slouched on, the soil grew parched and cracked. The streams began to dry up. Soon, every aspect of life was affected and even the youngest on the island understood something had gone wrong.

As bad as the endless sunshine had become during the day, the nights had become even worse. The heat lay upon them like a heavy blanket, one that could not be easily thrown off. Sleep was fitful and unsatisfying, and dawn arrived with everyone feeling less rested than when they had laid their heads down the night before. For all that was wrong in Anna's life, she still felt a greater sense of injustice because of the heat.

As Anna gazed towards the Indian Ocean far in the distance, she felt the oppressive weight of this catastrophe, and of her fate. Even at the far edges of the horizon, where the ocean drew a thin line of blue against the sky, she saw no sign of hope. She lowered her head. Her shoulders sagged.

Everything was becoming worse. Perhaps, she thought, the heat was a punishment for the more personal of these terrible events. After all, it was several months before that her mother had laid out her future for her. Then the heat wave came. Could the two be connected? Could cosmic forces at work be punishing both Anna and the village? Or were they both merely pawns in some larger design? Even with hope failing her, Anna could not help but gaze out in the direction of the ocean, and dream of being able to escape on one of the steamers that plied her currents.

There *had* to be more for her somewhere out there! How easy it would be if only she were a man! A man wishing to see the world and make his fortune had only to join one of the crews to earn the well-wishes of his family and friends. Alas, a woman could entertain no such wish.

The culture of the islanders of Mahé wrestled with the beneficence and punishments of Mother Nature in one way. However, as the good Catholic missionaries had imposed their worldview and belief system upon the island, more and more of the islanders viewed calamities such as the current heat wave as a test set before them by the Almighty. The good Catholic response, practiced by Anna and her family, as well as everyone in the village, was to recite prayers and perform vigils. The people asked *What curse has God placed upon us?*

The missionaries and good Catholics had no answer. What curse *could* God have put upon them? And for what purpose? Had Job himself known any greater despair than they? The Holy Book had no answer. As the weeks and months progressed, everyone on the island experienced powerful doubt in the faith they had always held dear, from the youngest of the good missionary families to the oldest of the grey-haired elders. Anna could see how the blanket of heat diabolically allowed the sun's heat *in*, thereby increasing the suffering, but then refused to allow it *out* at the end of the day. And so the heat built up and up.

How often Anna had sought sanctuary up upon this hill; here where nature, her dearest companion, offered her comfort and safety. She recalled her first visit to this place, at another time when she felt the burden of her world pressing down on her. On that day, she had been particularly brave and had roamed higher up the hill, following the river, determined to find its very source.

The elders warned against such ventures. The origins of that river, the source of life to the village, was sacred. Her mother, for different reasons, had cautioned her about forays into the jungle. "A young lady should not be out on her own," she had observed with a knowing look.

So, on that first day, Anna decided that the adventure would be her own secret. Even when she stumbled and fell as she climbed higher amongst the slippery vines, she remained determined.

Her zeal had been rewarded by that first view of the vision before her now, the wondrous and mesmerizing beauty of the island beneath her.

Hills cascaded down, elegant and mysterious, dotted with dark, giant grey boulders and emerald-green canopies of trees and lush vegetation. And colour! What colour! Flaming reds and deep burgundy, with the occasional white canopy of the *albizia* tree, offering golden shoots of fire though the colours. It was all so startlingly beautiful.

And far below, the array of thatched roofs of the village, peering from between the trees, each marked by a small rising strand of grey smoke from the outdoor kitchen. At the time, the image had been both breathtaking and soothing. Beau Vallon Bay. Beautiful. Awe-inspiring. Home. Safe. No more.

She turned and headed higher up the hillside. That first day, her adventure had ended only a few hundred yards further along, with a discovery so startling that it had taken her breath away. It was that day that she had chanced upon a small camouflaged garden that filled her with such a sense of wonderment and contentment, that she thought that she had stumbled upon the doorway of Heaven itself. Like Moses before the Burning Bush, she realized she had come upon a place of holiness, maybe the place where life itself had started?

As she approached that sacred spot, Anna felt herself draw back. A shiver went through her soul. *No! Not here as well!* Even here, she could feel a sense of apprehension, a tremor of doubt and disquiet. *Not here!* she cried aloud, stamping her foot on the flattened grass and branches. Now she knew beyond any doubt that God had turned His back. *How could you?* she wanted to cry to the heavens. *How could you be so cruel?* But she remained silent. Words failed her. Suddenly, she began to run, as if by running she could outrace the evil that was overtaking everything she held dear. She swept the vegetation out of her way with her arms, the tears building up in her eyes causing her to run blindly. *I must get there before it is too late!* She was in a race with her own innocence itself, and she was losing ground much faster than she could ever make it up.

On that first day, she had come to a sudden stop when she had first heard the sound of the waterfall. Even over her ragged breaths, she could now hear it, snaking softly at the bottom of all the intricate passages that years of heavy monsoon rain had carved into the hillside, until it finally cascaded over the boulder jutting out from the side of the hill where she was standing.

It dropped ten feet down, in the middle of the dark and dense oasis, splashing on polished rocks and white gravel. Ah! The music of that falling water, even here a distant echo of the melody further downriver. The music of these falls had been so seductive, drawing her closer that first day as she had sought out the place of perfect refuge.

Today she stood there, transfixed. Her dress was glued to her body by her sweat, and even her hair was drenched by her efforts to get to this spot. She looked down at her hands and saw that they were bleeding. She squeezed them into fists, wincing at the effort. The hurt made her feel alive but even the throbbing in her hands and bones could not wipe away her despair at the events of the day. Her mother's cries of agony still resounded in her mind.

She stepped forward, the ground beneath her wet from the splashing water. The vegetation was succulent and dense, the colours dark emerald. Then she parted the bushes and entered this new, dark world that existed under the thick canopy of the huge *bodanmyen* tree. Her very own secret refuge! She closed her eyes for a moment, then opened them slowly so that she might be able to see more clearly. Everything looked content and full of life, thriving even. So unlike what was happening below in the valley. Here, the beautiful plants and flowers were still safe, far from the blazing sun. Exotic ferns competed for space with big fan-shaped leaves of wild yams.

The snaking creepers entwined around the cinnamon bushes were laden with puffs of snow-white petals, perfuming the air with their delicate fragrance. Mists and sprays of cinnamon scented the glen, embracing her. Comforting green arms seemed to reach out to her, welcoming her to their peaceful sanctuary. Overhead, tiny slits of sunlight penetrated the tree canopy, merrily playing in between the sprays of the waterfall, dancing around the droplets, with their sparkling light like diamonds in the cascading water. They seemed to emit a mysterious, enticing power, an alluring force.

Drawn by the seductive beauty of the cascading water, Anna slowly peeled the sweat-soaked dress from her young body. She was desperate for its hypnotising comfort, desperate for a respite from all her pain. Naked, with the signs of her budding womanhood apparent, she stepped into the falling water. The sheer luxury of the cool waters was simply amazing. Caressing, stroking, and soothing her senses, it washed through her black hair and over her snowy shoulders, over the small buds of her breasts, down over her hips, past her womanness and down her slender legs.

Small frogs and birds gathered in the glen and watched this beautiful nymph. She was aware of their presence and felt herself blush knowing that they were seeing her this way. Two small frogs joined her then, leaping from rock to rock, croaking happily in unison, adding their harmonious tune to the magical aura of this special place. Her long black hair was painted to her creamy-white shoulders as the waters cleaned away her sweat and blood, her fear and her tiredness. She closed her eyes and turned her face up to greet the flowing water, immersing herself in the comforting and protective power of the water and of nature.

I am sixteen years old today, she said out loud, smiling as she said it, for the water seemed to wish her a happy birthday. *Sixteen.*

Suddenly, her smile faded and her joy evaporated as sadness enveloped her again. Even in this magical place, there was no escaping the reality of her fate. The message her mother first delivered months earlier still held true.

The family had gathered in the sitting room to relax after dinner. Her father was in his favourite armchair, puffing contentedly on his pipe. The children were engaged in reading or playing, or some manner of occupying themselves. Mother was sitting in a canvas armchair in the corner of the room, next to the flickering candle. Without lifting her eyes from the needle work on her lap, she spoke as if to no one in particular.

"You will be sixteen years old soon, a *big* girl. When you finish school at the end of the year, you will have to start working on your trousseau."

Anna felt her heart catch in her throat.

"It is always good to be ready early," her mother added, glancing up and catching her daughter's eye. "You do not know what God has reserved for you."

There was silence in the room. The only sounds were of her father's gentle puffing on his pipe and a sudden rustling alongside Anna. "Maman," Chantal said softly, "does that mean that Anna is to be married?"

Anna could not describe her emotions at that moment, when her little sister had given voice to the harsh reality of her mother's casually-presented words. Anna felt sickened. Betrayed. Hurt. Were her feelings not to be considered? Was she merely a possession, like a piece of furniture, to be passed around on a whim?

Anna had not taken a breath. Chantal laid down her favourite copy of 'Histoire Sainte' and stared expectantly at her mother, awaiting an answer.

How could she? Anna thought, her face colouring in shame. *How could her mother make her seemingly idle comment so publicly to the family?* Of course, there should have been no surprise at her mother's observation. Anna knew that much in her bones. Her mother had only given voice to what was expected of any young, Catholic girl by her family, society and church. Therese turned her attention to Chantal. "We hope that with God's grace, Anna will not have to wait long for a good marriage proposal." She sighed. "It is not good for a girl's reputation if she passes twenty-one years without a good marriage proposal. It is also a bad reflection on her family."

Anna felt the heat burn in her soul. Was she expected to speak? To stay silent? Was she expected to be *glad* that her future was being planned out for her? Was she expected to feel honoured that her destiny was to be fulfilled without so much as her say so? She twisted her hands in nervous agony, but remained silent. Beneath the horror of her feeling was the deeper shock that her mother, her very own mother, was so blithely placing her on the sacrificial altar, without so much as speaking to her!

Anna shivered under the waterfall, her body now covered in goose pimples. That evening was as immediate to her as if it was happening right now. She felt the same betrayal, the same outrage. *Have I no say in my own life?*

Sadly, she knew how her family and her religion and her village would answer that question. She was little more than property, belonging to her parents. Turning sixteen felt like the beginning of the end of her life, rather than the beginning of a wonderful life. Why was being born a girl such a curse? It was not just marriage that she dreaded. No, that was only part of it. She had heard her mother's labour agonies. She had been at the cottage during her sister's birth today. Those ungodly screams, the blood…it was too much, too much…and now I am to be expected to endure that same agony!

The stream water mingled with her tears. The weight of her bleak future engulfed her in total helplessness. The cascading diamond waterfall flowed continuously as she sank to her knees, hugging her body. There was just so much comfort and peace nature could bestow.

The frogs stopped leaping and hugged each other too, covering their faces. Softly they croaked, in unison with her sobs.

CHAPTER 1

The Birth of Eliane

The cycle of life seemed especially cruel to Anna on this particular birthday. For it was not only *her* birthday. At the dawn of this very day, Saturday, the first of July 1912, her mother had awakened knowing that this would be the day. After feeding her children breakfast, the very-pregnant Therese gathered the six youngest of them under the veranda of their small, thatched cottage. She gazed upon her children, and between teeth-grinding contractions, smiled at them.

"Go along, my children," she said, edging them toward the path. "Mère Monia is awaiting your visit. Go along".

The children hesitated. They could sense that something was different. Perhaps it was the way their mother would suddenly stiffen and grit her teeth as another contraction passed through her. "Go on," she urged them, forcing a smile before another contraction came. They were becoming more powerful and urgent and she wasn't sure how much longer she would be able to focus on her other children.

"Oui, Maman," they said, putting on brave smiles and faces themselves. They turned and made their way down the footpath leading to the main road. The two older boys, Antoine and Maxime, were carrying their bouncing younger brothers, Joseph and Didier, aged four and two respectively, upon their shoulders. The two girls, Chantal and Maryse, were holding hands, capering and lagging behind their brothers. Although they were troubled by their mother's soft groans during breakfast, the morning felt like a big adventure. They were off to visit their grandmother. "Au revoir, Maman," they shouted when they were far down the footpath. Joseph and Didier waved without turning about, their delighted laughter filling the morning air.

Therese took in their farewell with tears brimming in her eyes. Her children were everything to her and already she felt their absence powerfully. If it were up to her, she would not send her children away ever. "Oh," she groaned, a sharp breath leaving her. Her knuckles turned white as she gripped harder at the veranda post, trying to breathe through another sharp contraction.

"It is not good Christian behaviour to have children around the house when their mother is going through labour and delivery," declared Madame Monia Savy, Therese's mother-in-law, before Therese had even given birth to Antoine. As was usually the case, when Madame Monia Savy declared something, it had the weight of divine law.

So began the practice of sending the children to their grandmother for each childbirth. Mère Monia, as the children had fondly named their grandmother, lived with her elder son, Lionet Savy and his family in Saint Louis, a thirty-minute walk from Beau Vallon. Therese did not agree with her mother-in-law about this, or indeed many other things, but she felt it was her duty to obey her respectfully. Therese waved one more time to the now-empty path. The children had already disappeared into the cinnamon bushes and coconut palms.

Lionet Savy was a prosperous man who had earned his prosperity working his way up the ladder to his current position of Clerical Officer, a position that commanded respect. He served His Majesty's Service in the Queen's Building, situated in the centre of Victoria, the capital of the Seychelles and the official seat of the British Colonial Government's administration.

Even more than other government workers, Lionet wore his pristine white cotton trousers starched to perfection, with distinctive ironing lines that ran all the way to his ankles. A white, long-sleeved cotton shirt completed his daily ensemble.

He wore his uniform and his position with pride. He was part of the mighty British Empire. Far from resenting the colonial powers, he was an unreserved Anglophile. His love of the Empire and the Crown defined every aspect of his life, right down to where he would secure his bicycle each day - 'Reserved for HM Servants Only.' He was a very blessed man and he knew it. Not only in his position but in his personal life. His wife Florence had been one very big blessing; marriage to her in 1880 had meant the inheritance of a big house in Saint Louis, a convenient ten-minute downhill cycle ride to Victoria.

Ten years later, he was promoted to Clerical Officer. Yes, he was a very blessed, and very self-satisfied man. Nothing like his younger brother, Albert.

Lionet and Albert were separated by six years and grew up in a little thatched cottage perched on the hillside overlooking Beau Vallon beach. Their father, Maurice Savy, was the overseer on the du Barré family's vast estate. Maurice and his wife, Monia, were descendants of French tradesmen, the first whites from Europe to colonise the Seychelles. Forming only five per cent of the Seychelles population, the whites tended to band together. The handful of very wealthy white landowners on the Seychelles islands relied on people like Maurice and Monia to oversee the working of their estates.

Lionet despised his father's job, feeling mortified every day of his life to be the son of a *mere* overseer. Albert, however, loved it. Whenever he could, he tagged along after his father, asking question after question each step of the way.

Then, in the evenings, Albert would bore Lionet with his stories of how cinnamon is processed, what happened to patchouli leaves before the oil was extracted, how to maximize copra yields, and so on and so forth.

Being regaled by such wisdom drove Lionet to distraction. To his great relief, he got his job as Office Assistant the year after he left school, and he was ecstatic. Then, in 1880, he left the little thatched cottage behind, moving into the big house with his new wife. Lionet could not leave the plantation and the small, thatched cottage – *that tiny hovel* – fast enough. For his part, Albert was happy to spend the rest of his life there. When Maurice passed away, Albert became the du Barré's overseer. After twenty years, he married. He had not been driven by passion or circumstance in deciding to enter the state of matrimony, but by the nagging of his mother.

"Yes, mother," he said. "I will settle down."

"When?" she demanded.

He rolled his eyes. His work had always been his passion. He had stepped comfortably into his father's shoes at seventeen, building on the knowledge that his father had passed on to him. Under his oversight, the du Barré's business prospered. Albert was well-respected as being hard-working, competent and above all a fair and impartial overseer. He had instituted assigning 'foremen' from among the black labourers to lead small teams on specific jobs, and this radical move had produced outstanding results. His management strategies in the copra and cinnamon industry were often copied by many plantation owners despite the fact that these same owners had initially ridiculed his every effort.

"Watch him," they counselled du Barré. "This business of elevating black labourers above their station is sure to cause problems."

Christophe du Barré had stood by him unreservedly, and had been rewarded with ever greater success. Rather than cause problems, Albert's method of giving command and responsibility to some of the labourers had caused them to view him in a positive light.

This had not only benefited du Barré, but lessened any simmering tensions that might have existed on the plantation. However, the other landowners were not completely misguided in their fears and criticism; while the practice of giving authority to a black man had been unheard of in the history of these islands, Albert Savy's first steps had set a precedent for the future of the black population of the Seychelles.

Albert was a man in his element; an Adam in his garden, but without the conscious need for a companion. "It's unnatural for a man of your age to be without a wife," his mother insisted.

Finally, he could no longer bear the constant nagging – or the feeling of disappointing her. So, at age thirty-seven, Albert married Therese Beaudouin, a virgin spinster of thirty years and a devout Catholic who also worked for the du Barré family.

Orphaned at six years of age, Therese had grown up in the household of the owner of Silhouette Island, Monsieur Paul Duval. At age twelve, she became the personal maid to Genevieve, Monsieur Duval's daughter, his only child. Service was comfortable to Therese. Although she had a naturally fiery nature, being an orphan and a maid, coupled with the teachings of the Church, had tamped down that nature and made her sweetly subservient. When her twentieth birthday came and went with no marriage proposal in sight, Therese's faith helped her come to terms with what she believed to be her fate – a life of service to others.

She was twenty-five years old in 1888 when her mistress, Genevieve Duval, married Christophe du Barré, the only son of Francois and Marie-Antoinette du Barré. Together, both Therese and Genevieve moved from Silhouette Island and took up residence in du Barré's big family house at Beau Vallon, on the island of Mahé.

Of course she knew of Albert. Everyone on the du Barré estate knew of Albert. He was spoken of highly and with genuine affection. During her first five years at Beau Vallon, she might see him on an almost daily basis. Still, his sudden marriage proposal had come as a complete surprise. At thirty, she had resigned herself to her station and had even grown contented in her place. Of course she respected and admired Albert, everyone did. But marriage? She was left in a daze by the proposal. *Why now?* she asked God. *What kind of test is this?*

"Stop being so silly," Genevieve teased her. "You should be honoured to get such a good marriage proposal at the age of thirty." Therese knew Genevieve, in the guise of teasing, spoke the truth.

Although she had resigned herself to being a spinster, marriage to Albert turned out to be what Therese had been waiting for all her adult life. She found herself in complete bliss, and the little thatched cottage reflected the happiness of its new mistress. Her joy was evident everywhere, in the sparkle of the polished wooden floors, in the ironing details of Albert's khaki trousers that hung next to his sun-bleached white shirts, in the mouth-watering dishes prepared daily from hand-picked fresh fish, in the beautiful flowers adorning the front of the cottage…everywhere.

She had not understood how liberating it would be, how joyful, to no longer be a maid or a spinster. Now, she commanded respect. She was the *wife* of the overseer. The black labourers would remove their straw hats when they wished her a good day. Like a prayer, she would occasionally whisper to herself *'Madame Therese Savy'* just to hear the sound of it. She considered herself greatly blessed, and got down on her knees daily to thank God for the blessings and happiness that He had provided.

She vowed to always be Albert's loving and devoted Catholic wife for as long as she lived. No longer an orphan, no longer a maid, no longer a spinster, her marriage increased her faith and devotion to the Church.

Therese now attended mass with her husband, and each Sunday morning she came into the church on his arm and with her head held high. She was now a full member of the *krinol hats* and *zouven shoes* Catholic ladies club. Which is to say, she was respected.

On the first of July 1896, two years after Albert and Therese married, she gave birth to their first child, a baby girl. She was named Anna after Therese's late mother. To have a child! This was a blessing beyond blessings! In truth, Therese had not expected to be blessed with children at all, given her age. But she gave birth to Anna, and then the babies kept coming. Every two years, there was another, then another, then another. Now, eighteen years into her marriage, Therese was about to give birth to her eighth child.

Madame Yvette Letourdie was the island's best midwife. Having delivered hundreds of babies over her twenty-five years of midwifery, she had known many losses of mothers and babies during difficult labours. After all, childbirth is a perilous time for both. However, she had delivered all seven of Therese's children safely, without any complications, and looked forward to delivering this, the eighth.

"Take this now, Madame Savy," she said gently, giving Therese the herbal infusion that she gave to all her patients. As always, it began to work quickly, quieting the natural agitation that Therese felt accompanying her labour. From the time her children had disappeared from her sight earlier in the morning, Therese's contractions had increased in both frequency and intensity. She had sent Anna to get Yvette who lived at the nearby village of Glacis.

"I am not feeling well, I need the nurse," she told her daughter. Anna had helped her mother get to her bed, and then she had run off to get Yvette, who had returned with her immediately.

"All is good, no need to worry," Yvette said to both Therese and the worried Anna. "Get me some hot water please." With this statement Anna was dismissed from what was now considered as *granmoun* affairs. Young girls were not privy to anything that would, 'open their eyes' to the adult world, and the delivery of a baby was definitely one such adult-only affair. Therese's contractions grew strong. She was soon fully dilated. "It won't be long."

But it *was* long. Terribly, horribly long. For the next four hours, through excruciating labour, nothing happened. Therese screamed in agony until she was exhausted. Bringing yet more clean linen, hot water and tea for the busy midwife, Anna trembled in fear at what was happening to her mother, and what was causing her so much pain. Yvette dismissed her each time with a knowing adult look. She was not allowed in the bedroom. She was not an adult. Anna hated it.

But no amount of pushing brought the baby forth. As the clock continued to tick away, real fear seemed to descend on the small cottage. It had combined forces with the heat wave, and was lurking in every corner. Yvette could no longer hide her own concern. She had long before ceased sending Anna to make her another cup of tea, which had stopped Anna from doing just that. One cup of tea after another.

Yvette knew that Therese needed to be in the hospital in Victoria, but moving her now was out of the question. She would never make it there alive. Hundreds of deliveries, many complications. Every birth is different, but there were lessons to be learned from each. Yvette focused on the matter at hand and considered her next, dramatic move.

Therese was laying naked in her wooden four-poster bed, which had been a wedding present from Lionet to his younger brother and new bride. She was in a pool of blood, her pale skin wore a deathly sheen of oily moisture, and her black hair was soaking wet from the heat and her exertions. Her still very-pregnant stomach looked enormous, her skin striped with the stretch marks of seven previous pregnancies. Her large, sagging breasts flopped to either side of her body.

In truth, she was a horrible vision. And yet, amidst this gruesome scene, in her exhausted and pained expression her turquoise eyes shone with a fierce, determined brilliance. It was a clarity so profound that it transcended pain and called to mind one whose beliefs let her know she was not alone. God was in that room with her. Even as she bled out and stained the white cotton bed sheets, Therese's faith never wavered. If God willed that she should give up her own life, then she would. But on one condition - that she first bring forth this new life safely into the world. As the fingers of her right hand fingered the beads of her rosary, she implored God to grant her this final blessing. Her lips moved in prayer, and in the middle of a 'Hail Mary' she screamed in agony, as yet another contraction racked her body.

Yvette Letourdie prayed too. In the outdoor kitchen, Anna gripped harder at the door post, tears streaming down her face, wishing she could do something to stop her mother's agony. Yvette knew that there was precious little time left. The situation was now as desperate as it was hopeless. She had to turn the baby around, and she had to do it now.

"Aaaaaaahhhh!" "Aaaaaaahhhh!" Therese screamed as Yvette's hand and forearm reached up her vagina and into her womb. Twisting slowly, Yvette pressed forward and upward, ripping and tearing, searching for that obstructive posture. Outside, Anna pushed a clenched fist into her own mouth to stop herself from screaming too.

Then a very long, eerie silence followed. Anna hugged herself as she sat trembling on the kitchen stool. *She is dead. My mother is dead.*

After much negotiation, Yvette finally gripped a soft and rounded posterior, and the ten-pound baby girl accepted having her buttocks pulled all the way into this new world. Therese, who had fainted in the final attempt, was oblivious that she had another daughter.

"Anna, Anna, I need your help in here!" Yvette shouted, breaking with protocol and the strict rules. After all, were rules not made to be broken?

Wiping her eyes, Anna rushed into the cottage. The scene looked like a horrifying nightmare, but was only too real. Her mother lay naked and spread-eagled in a blood-soaked bed, a mass of tangled and bloody afterbirth rested between her legs. Anna felt the room swirling, her knees shaking uncontrollably. *She is dead! My mother is dead!*

"Over here." Yvette called out to the pale-faced young girl, "Your sister needs help."

A dark blue, tiny crinkled bundle was being wrapped in white linen by Madame Letourdie. She did not resemble any baby Anna had ever seen. She was not making a sound. She looked dead too. Then something strange happened. In the depths of her soul, Anna felt something stir, something that was commanding her next action, something that was taking over. "What can I do to help?" she said to Yvette.

They all but ignored the unconscious Therese as they engaged in a desperate attempt to resuscitate the newborn. Tick. Tick. Tick. The seconds passed. Be it God himself, or her overly-sensitive motherly intuition, but in her dark world Therese could sense the danger, and knew she had to fight back. Her eyes suddenly opened, and she watched as the Angel of Death hovered over her, ready to engulf her yet again in its big black arms. It descended closer and closer. She knew she only had seconds left. Reaching deep down within her heart and soul, she summoned her last remaining ounce of strength and whispered. "Holy Mother, please spare my baby's life."

The art of carrying two metal pails full of water along a winding hillside path, manoeuvring round stones and pot-holes, required a lot of balancing action which Anna had mastered beautifully. As she left the river, the martens had already begun their sunset songs. In two hours, darkness would fall. Her brothers and sisters would soon return and they were sure to be famished after their long walk back from Saint Louis. She hurried her pace, careful not to spill any of the water from the buckets. As she arrived at the cottage, she found Yvette freshening her patient and the newborn baby. She looked up at Anna. "Well, girl, I am ready for a cup of tea." Anna's eyes widened. *It's amazing how many cups of tea this woman can drink!*

"Right away, ma'am."

But first, she had to gather things for dinner. From the vegetable garden at the back of the cottage, Anna picked a small white pumpkin, a couple of tomatoes, a Chinese cabbage spinach, as well as some thyme and parsley. Soon the aroma of fried onions and garlic mingled with the songs of the martens. The sky had turned into a palette of oranges and reds, and like a giant fireball, the sun was soon to set and ready to sink into the ocean beside Silhouette Island.

Anna's dinner was ready: fricassee pumpkin with fried fish, seasoned with fresh herbs, garlic and ginger; steamed rice, and sauté spinach with fresh tomatoes, as well as a purée of red lentils.

"Bonswar, Msye, Madam."

Anna looked out from the kitchen to see that Tonton Lionet's gardener, Guyto, had arrived at the cottage with a message from Mère Monia.

"Yes?"

He delivered his message. Mère Monia had decided to keep the children overnight at Saint Louis. Anna laughed out loud from sheer tiredness and relief. She could already picture her nicely-prepared dinner floating in the pig's bucket. *Won't that fat pig be happy tomorrow!*

Therese opened her heavy-lidded eyes and scanned the room. For a brief second, everything looked as it always had. Perhaps she had just been dreaming…but then she remembered everything. The dull ache throbbed in her womb, the burning pain around her vagina was still intense. Her heart lurched. My baby! She looked down at the bed beside her and there, curled in the contours of her abdomen, between the layers and folds of a tired, forty-eight-year-old belly, her newborn daughter slept the sleep of angels.

"I see you are back with us," Yvette said with a warmth in her voice.

Therese smiled weakly as Yvette walked in, parting the curtain that hung in the doorway of Therese's bedroom. Then her expression shifted to worry.

Yvette shook her head. "Do not be concerned. You are both fine. Although," she added, her face becoming serious, "you had me worried earlier."

In the bedroom, there was no sign of all the pain and suffering Therese had endured. Her bed had been freshly made up with white cotton bed sheets. Her long hair had been combed and plaited into two long tresses, and a clean white nightdress was decently covering her down to the ankles. Therese was exhausted, but refreshed.

"A breech?" she asked Yvette softly.

The midwife nodded. "I will get you a nice cup of tea, then, afterwards you can have an early dinner. You have to rest. Do not worry about a thing." Then she glanced over her shoulder in the direction of the kitchen. "She is a very good cook, your Anna."

Therese smiled, thinking of her eldest child. Then she reached out with her hand and stroked her baby's soft skin, her youngest. Oldest to youngest. Both born on the same date. She felt such a deep sense of blessing and grace. With her eyes on her baby, she sighed. "We should be eternally grateful, God spared us both." Suddenly, she became aware of a shooting pain in the palm of her right hand. She shifted her attention from her new daughter to her hand.

As clear as day, a cross was deeply imprinted in her flesh. She let her head fall back to her pillow. By God's grace! She had been clutching her rosary when her daughter was being delivered. Her rosary was on the bedside table where Yvette had placed it. Therese reached out for it and brought it to her lips. With deep love and reverence, she kissed the tiny silver cross. It smelled of dried blood.

From the wall across the room, the Holy Virgin Mary, immaculately dressed in a light blue robe and long white veil, looked down at Therese and her newborn infant. Her eyes full of love and affection, she was standing on the globe of the earth with her own baby Jesus in her right arm, and beneath her feet, the crushed head of the evil snake. Two dried palm branches jutted out from behind its wooden frame, a remembrance of the previous Palm Sunday. "Thank you, Holy Mother," Therese whispered, her eyes on the holy image, "for sparing my baby's life."

All the drama of childbirth had taken place outside of Albert's awareness. The drama, the danger to his wife and his newest child, all of it. Therese's contractions first came long after Albert had left the house. By five o'clock that morning, he was already behind his desk in the warehouse. It was loading day, and loading days were always long and busy.

Why would he even spare a thought to those women's things? After all, seven times before Therese had given birth, and seven times before all had been well. Not since the miracle of his first child, when Anna was born, had he devoted any real thought to the actual birthing of a baby. So, on this day, he was at his desk in the warehouse, which was located in the courtyard at the back of the du Barré family home. It was brimming with bulging sacks of copra, cinnamon, patchouli and salted fish – all ready to be transported to Port Victoria.

Albert looked at the stacks of commodities and saw there the culmination of two long weeks of hard work from over one hundred labourers and fishermen. He felt a deep sense of satisfaction. The fortnightly rhythm was vital if the products of the estate were to be moved in an efficient and profitable manner.

The scent of Marie's morning offering made her presence known seconds before she actually came into the room. Two big mugs of freshly-brewed coffee and piping-hot bread. Albert glanced up from the paperwork on his desk and smiled. Marie had been with the du Barré family for as long as anyone, since before the days of Francois du Barré. She had known Albert's father very well and had watched as young Albert grew up.

Albert had always shared a special relationship with Marie. She had been a rock for him always, especially after his father's death when the task of running the estate fell completely to him. Over the years, they had developed a morning ritual that they both looked forward to – her bringing in morning coffee and bread, then spending some time listening to his concerns. For Albert, there were few better, or more trusted counsellors than Marie, and in Albert, Marie found a friend who respected and valued her not only for the things she did on the estate but as a person.

As he smiled at her, he marvelled at her seeming agelessness. Even as he had noted the years carving their wear on his own face and body, she remained unchanging. A sweet, round ebony face under a white head scarf, unlined by time or worries. Over her printed floral dress, she wore a navy cotton drill apron which was always dusted with white flour from her baking duties.

More than baker, she was the head-cook and she ruled her kitchen with warmth and authority. She had not earned her reputation as one of the island's best cooks by allowing herself or others to do anything less than their best. She saw to it that her larder was filled to bursting with the delicacies of the varied Creole cuisine. She catered to the favourite dishes of every member of the family and their friends, and prepared meals to satisfy every taste, palate and occasion.

Christophe and Genevieve du Barré admired and respected her greatly but their two sons, Henri and Louis, simply adored her. And she, them. She spoiled them as if she were their born grand-mama. She had done nothing less when Albert was a child.

The rich aroma of the coffee mingled with the tangy smell of cinnamon and patchouli to make the warehouse a bouquet of richness.

"It looks like the Alouette is going to be full to the brim today," Marie noted, glancing at the gunny sacks filling the warehouse. Albert let the rich, hot coffee linger in his mouth, then he swallowed the liquid. "Yes," he agreed, as he reached for some fresh bread.

Not far from the warehouse, the graceful Alouette was anchored in the calm waters of the bay. Even with her sails down, she was an impressive schooner. Her hull was pure white but for the wooden inlay running two gold strips through her middle, from bow to stern, and her bow was graced with her namesake bird, the Alouette.

She had only been launched eighteen months earlier, but she was already indispensible to the operations of both the Beau Vallon Estate and Silhouette Island.

Albert rested his cup on his desk and breathed in the smells of the warehouse. At home, Therese was about to give birth to another child.

All is well in my world, he thought to himself.

CHAPTER 2

A Journey Begins

When Paul Duval died in 1905, Genevieve du Barré, as sole heir, became owner of Silhouette Island and all of her father's riches. But riches can sometimes also be a burden; with her immense inheritance came the task of managing and maintaining the third largest island of the Seychelles.

A continuing challenge for her was transportation – of goods and people. The seafaring Benezet family had provided schooner services between Silhouette and Port Victoria on Mahé for years. But poor business decisions, coupled with a lavish lifestyle, had resulted in the progressive disrepair of the schooners and the worsening of service.

"It is unacceptable," Christophe complained one evening at dinner, "that service should suffer and we should be held hostage to ever more exorbitant price increases!" Genevieve shared her husband's frustration.

"There must be something we can do."

"Why don't we simply get our own schooner?" suggested Henri.

At first, Christophe and Genevieve were flabbergasted by their eighteen-year-old son's suggestion. But the more they considered it, the more obvious it was. Having their own schooner would make them master of their own fate. So, the Alouette was commissioned and launched two years later, on the first day of December 1909, under the strict supervision of her Sailing Master, the highly reputable seafarer, Captain Frederic Francourt.

Henri du Barré was almost twenty years of age when the Alouette was launched. His suggestion to have their own schooner had not been merely academic. He was one of those young men who loved the sea from their first memory of it. Although he had many responsibilities on the estate, he managed to assist Captain Francourt from the outset. He had seen Alouette take shape, plank by plank. He knew her more completely than any lover ever knew his beloved; he knew her every curve, every stitch in her wide white sails.

He stood alongside Captain Francourt at the helm of her maiden journey, and on each and every run since. He was, as Captain Francourt noted, a natural sailor. As such, the ancient seafarer was happy to bestow upon the young man the benefit of his many years of knowledge and experience.

"The sea can be a cruel mistress," he said. "Below her beautiful surface, there can be danger. She is capricious, sensual and seductive. And sometimes deadly." Then he laughed. "Like any other woman."

Henri laughed with him, entranced by the weathered captain's manner and salty charm. For the first six months of Alouette's service, Henri apprenticed himself humbly and diligently, soaking in every lesson, every current, every aspect of the sea and the running of a ship upon her. As they made their way across the waters one day, Captain Francourt turned to his young charge. "Henri, son, what else can I teach you?"

Never taking his eyes off the sun-glittered waters before them, Henri shrugged. "I am constantly amazed at what you teach me, sir. I can't imagine you ever running out of lessons that would be beneficial to me." The captain smiled. Henri's answer was nothing less than he would have expected from the young man.

"You're a good lad, a special lad. But the truth is, you are ready for a better teacher than I."

Henri glanced quickly at the captain, a look of horror in his eyes. He could not imagine who could be a better teacher than Captain

Francourt. "But, sir...please don't suggest that you are not going to continue to instruct me in the ways of the sea." The old captain smiled. "I would never abandon you, son. But experience is a better teacher than I could ever be." With that, he relinquished the helm to the younger man.

"But..." Henri began to protest.

"You are ready," Captain Francourt said simply.

And so he was. Although tentative at first, Henri's natural command took hold and he was quickly piloting the Alouette as if he had been at sea for half a century.

Captain Francourt had no sooner handed over the helm of the schooner to Henri than he recognized a new dilemma on the horizon. Henri was not the only one of Christophe du Barré's sons with a love of the water. The same passion that had glowed in Henri's eyes also burned brightly in young Louis's eyes each time he had accompanied them. Captain Francourt recognized another born sailor. On the one hand, such recognition filled the old sea dog with a great deal of joy. On the other, how could he tell the father that *both* his sons, both the heirs to the du Barré's fortune, were more passionately at home at sea than on land? How could he tell the father that his two sons stood ready to abandon the land in favour of the sea?

Albert instructed that the first pirogue be loaded with sacks so that it could row out to the waiting schooner. The process went smoothly. Load one pirogue and send it off on the water, while he then supervised the loading of the next. Unlike other operations, Albert did not have to raise his voice. By virtue of the respect he accorded his workers, they respected him and toiled fully and efficiently.

The workers moved in brilliant synchronicity. Two straight lines, up and down the white beach, the black labourers moved the hundred-pound sacks, their bare muscular chests and broad backs glistening with sweat.

At the end of each line, the last worker waded knee-deep in the water to reach the black pirogue and offload their cargo, then away to the warehouse again for another load. Over and over, sack by sack, from early dawn until midday, the labourers went up and down the beach, heaving their loads to the pirogues, and then the pirogues went to and from the Alouette. When Albert had first seen a similar operation overseen by his father, it made him think of a beautiful dance, with all the dancers moving to a rhythm and beat unheard in the world, like the ticking of time that continues in the absence of a clock.

At midday, the church bell of Saint Roch chimed softly from across the bay. Each man in his spot, from Albert to the lowliest worker, crossed himself and scurried away to find a shaded spot and their lunch bowl, happy to enjoy a well-deserved break away from the heat of the scorching sun.

That midday found the du Barré family – Christophe, Genevieve and their two sons, along with Albert and Captain Francourt – in the wood-panelled dining room of the du Barré estate. The room was a favourite of the family, seemingly always infused with the sweet fragrance of frangipani blossoms. The walls were panelled in the soft natural colour of *kalis di pap*, while in contrast her wooden floor was of a rich, glossy mahogany finish. The ceiling covings with carved details in matching mahogany, edged around the four sides, lending a gentle sophistication to the room.

Sparingly furnished, the room displayed the family's focus on quality rather than quantity. A long dining table with eight matching chairs stood in the centre, whilst on the two opposite sides of the room, two finely-turned, traditional sideboards with intricate carved designs reflecting the subtlety and depth of their craftsmanship, completed the furnishings.

On this day, a soft peach damask tablecloth laid on the table, its pastel shade emphasising the bright cherry tone of the *sandragon* wood. A large vase filled with white frangipani blossoms sat delicately on the white crochet cover on each of the two sideboards. Despite the heat, the room was pleasantly cool and fresh, the benefit of the wide veranda running across the whole frontage and the three sides of the house, thus shading its interiors.

Christophe had taken his place at the head of the table, and his wife, Genevieve, sat at his right along with Louis. Henri, Albert and the Captain sat on his left. Gazing upon the tall jugs of freshly-squeezed lemon drink, the bottles of French wine, and fresh coconut water in between the bowls and platters of this delicious Creole lunch, Christophe smiled. "It looks as if Marie has created another marvellous meal," he said.

And indeed, she had. Charcoal-grilled red snapper, chicken curry prepared with fresh coconut milk, and steaming rice. A *rougay* of salted pork sausages, cooked with fresh tomatoes and green beans, was in between the bowls of fresh lentil purée and sauté of aubergine platter. A large dish of seabird egg salad with fresh watercress and red onions completed the sumptuous spread. Along with, of course, Marie's homemade fresh bread.

They ate in silence for several minutes before Christophe tapped his glass with the side of his fork, getting everyone's attention. "I have an announcement to make," he said, a tiny smile playing happily at the sides of his mouth.

Genevieve looked at her tanned and handsome husband, nonplussed. What could the announcement be? It was not like Christophe to surprise her this way, but it was clear he was relishing the moment of suspense.

Even so, as she always did, she found herself taken by her husband's physical presence. Sitting at the head of the table, he exuded confidence and gravitas. His tanned face with high cheekbones and piercing black eyes, the same colour as those last hours of night, was complemented by an impressive black moustache. Even as the father of two young men, his thick, curly hair reaching the base of his neck was still jet-black. In truth, he looked more like a handsome Spaniard rather than a French descendant.

Christophe would have rejected both notions. Though his roots were French, he considered himself an islander - a Seychellois. Born and bred under Seychelles tropical sunshine, these shores were his true home. To him, France was more of an idea, a mythical place, a distant land that belonged to his ancestors, to the ancient past.

"I have been quite satisfied with the productivity and performance of the Alouette since her launch. I am confident that this new enterprise we embarked on eighteen months ago will continue to flourish in the years to come." He paused, more for the drama of suspense than any other reason.

"Which brings me to my present dilemma. Now, I find this to be a very troubling issue…" Genevieve shifted in her chair. What could it be that was troubling her husband so? Albert too leaned forward, wondering what Christophe was focusing on that he did not already know.

"It seems both my sons have been seduced by the charms of the sea." he went on, glancing at Captain Francourt. "No doubt, the good captain's seafaring stories played some part in that. Mind you, neither Louis nor Henri has spoken to me about this, but a father is able to see things before they are shown." He sighed deeply. "It seems that it will be only Albert and myself manning the land of the du Barré estate, whilst my two sons ride the sea."

He sighed yet again. "So, it appears that all that being the case, I have no choice but to commission a second schooner."

At this news, it seemed that everyone around the table drew in a breath at the same moment. "After all, it would not be proper to have two skippers on a single boat now would it?" He turned and smiled broadly at Louis.

"Oh, Papa, merci" Louis said, looking adoringly at his father, and matching his broad smile. Christophe had just granted him his dearest wish, his own schooner.

"This is really splendid news," Genevieve declared, smiling at *her men*. She turned and looked at her younger son, reached out and squeezed his hand. Then she leaned forward and gave him a motherly kiss on the cheek.

As his wife displayed maternal affection, Christophe looked directly at Captain Francourt. "I will leave the details for you to sort out, Captain. I am sure you will find both Louis and Henri only too eager to assist you. It would make me very happy if the new boat could be ready for launching in two years time, on Louis's twenty-first birthday, the twenty-fifth of September 1914."

Hours later, Albert was returning to shore with Captain Francourt in the last pirogue from the Alouette. In the sky the full moon had long before replaced the sun, and the bright blue sky had been replaced by a dark, star-sparkled canvas. Exhausted from the long day, but filled with satisfaction from a job well done, Albert watched as his labourers used the long coconut tree trunks to push the pirogues up the beach, where they were stored for the night in the thatched sheds beneath the branches of the huge takamaka trees lining the sandy stretch of beach.

A colony of fruit bats squeaked and squealed as they flapped out of the branches where they had been feasting on the ripe seeds. They circled the skies above the trees, their black shapes ominous in the soft moonlight. One by one, they landed in trees further along the beach. Distant squeaking and flapping could be heard as they fought with other bats, desperate to establish their place in the feeding ground.

Across the still waters of the bay, a single light flickered from the bow of the Alouette. She was loaded to capacity, her hull packed full of sacks of copra, cinnamon, patchouli and salted fish. She would sail to Port Victoria at the following dawn. After unloading her cargo, she would travel on to Silhouette Island to pick up yet more cargo.

Albert stood at the edge of the beach, his body was tired but his soul fulfilled. He went about the ritual of packing his pipe, striking the match and lighting the rich tobacco. As he puffed on the stem of the pipe, drawing the smoke into his mouth and lungs, he was rewarded with the sensation that accompanied that first, sudden rush of nicotine.

He remained there for a short while, gazing out on the still waters reflecting the night sky as the sweet smell of the tobacco perfumed the air. He could feel God's goodness all around him as he tapped the bowl of his pipe and relit it. Then, the fullness of his satisfaction descended upon him like a benevolent spirit. He tucked his left hand in the pocket of his full-length khaki trousers, and took long pacing strides as he made his way across the valley and up the footpath that led to his cottage. A soft smile of anticipation illuminated his face as he wondered how Therese and the children were doing. He continued walking, feeling fully blessed.

Whilst Albert was getting ready to take the last pirogue ashore from the Alouette, at the cottage two dinners were laid on the dining room table.

Anna looked up and tried to find the words to express what she felt but, once again, she simply lowered her eyes, silent once more.

Yvette Letourdie sat across the dining table, her heart troubled as she looked at the pensive and clearly disheartened young girl. *What is weighing on this poor girl's soul?* Yvette asked herself, trying to decipher the message hidden in her sad, green eyes. Yvette's many years of midwifery had worked with her intuitive nature to give her a sensitivity almost unheard of, even amongst a very sensitive population. By being so engaged in the near-mystical rituals of birth, it was as if she had crossed a magical line, becoming part spirit-being as well as fully human. She felt the joy of a new birth as much as the new mother, and knew the sadness of every loss more deeply. It is not easy to bear such powerful feelings, but without them, how could she be there for every woman needing her?

Yvette wanted to ask Anna what was troubling her; what distress had gripped her so tightly that she could not even speak. But she knew that even the sound of her voice at the wrong time, no matter how comforting she tried to be, could chase away the emotions that were struggling to find voice back into Anna's skittish heart. So she waited, watching the young girl with sympathetic eyes, hoping and praying she found words to express the distress that was tormenting her.

Yvette was certain that the thing that was tormenting Anna could be found in some elemental connection – or disconnection – between the young girl and her mother that was nothing to do with the delivery bed scene she had witnessed. Although Anna had remained behind of all Therese's children, remained to do all the household chores, and to get help when needed, she was nevertheless a young girl, and as such was not allowed to know about adult things. But that fact apart, there was definitely some other problem there, something which Yvette could not put her finger on...

Anna had attended to lunch and to dinner. She had returned with tea when asked, but whenever possible, she had kept to herself, not even asking Yvette how her mother was doing. Not even when all the groans, and later the screams, had echoed around the cottage. What could have happened between the two to bring about such a breach? Yvette knew them both and had always known them to be close and loving. What could have happened to change that? Yvette waited as long as she could, and then she tried to address what she thought might be troubling Anna.

"My child," she said softly, "you do not let what happened here today, and the suffering you witnessed, trouble you. It is the way of nature for a woman to suffer during childbirth. That's what we earned in the Garden, when we sinned. Now, we women are born to know pain in childbirth. It's the way of the world."

Anna remained quiet. She stared down at the table, refusing to raise her eyes to the kind woman sitting opposite her.

Yvette watched Anna. As she did, she poked at the morsels before her, taking a small bite of the sautéd spinach and pumpkin fricassee. With her eyes searching for something to understand about the young woman's suffering, Yvette reviewed the events of the day, hoping that this might help her understand. *This girl has been wonderful today. It's true, she was not allowed to attend the birth itself, but she worked hard all day, attending to all the household duties. And how many times did she go to that river and back, fetching me water? More times than I could count.*

It was true, she had been quiet and tearful when she made the lunch. Yvette had thought she was just being thoughtful, as she was when she prepared her mother's herbal infusion. But she had been ready at an instant to get the kettle boiling whenever Yvette called for hot water, which she did over and over again through the long, arduous labour and delivery. Yvette smiled to herself, recalling the image of this ethereal young girl with her two long tresses of black hair dangling on her shoulders, manoeuvring those heavy pig swill buckets. Despite all her hard work, and her being kept away from the birthing room, when Yvette needed her most, to help resuscitate the baby, she had not delayed even a moment. Oh! How that scene must have shocked her!

"Anna," Yvette had called. "I need your help in here now!"

The young girl had run quickly to her mother's bedroom, coming face to face with the searing image before her — her mother, barely clinging to life, lying in a puddle of her own blood and afterbirth.

"Over here!" Yvette had said urgently, drawing Anna's attention to her lifeless little sister. Anna had rushed over and, along with Yvette, worked to clear the baby's airway and get the struggling creature to breathe the breath of life.

And yet, for the poignancy and power of that image, there was still one that Yvette held that was more powerful still. With the baby alive, barely, and her mother still clinging to life by a thread, Anna went about the task of cleaning her mother of the blood and gore of this difficult birth, and then she managed to pull the bloodied bed sheets out from under her and carry the blood-soaked bed linen to the washing tub behind the cottage. With tears streaming down her cheeks, she scrubbed those linens with all the strength left in her thin arms.

Over and over again, she scrubbed the cloth until she had managed to wash away every last trace of her mother's pain. She would never be able to erase the image of the horror her mother had endured completely from her mind, but she was determined to save the others in the family from the same fate. So now, gazing at this troubled, silent figure across the dining table, Yvette's heart nearly broke for her.

"Yes, my child, there is pain in childbirth, but that is not the whole story. There is joy as well." Yvette leaned closer. "I have helped many, many women. And many times, that pain...well, birth can be horrible. But every time...you hear me?...*every* time I put that baby in its mother's arms..." Yvette smiled as her emotions relived that very moment. "When I put that baby in its mother's arms, well, it is like God came into the room. The pain goes away, like a cloud going away when the sun comes out. This is my life. I know these things."

Although Anna did not react at first, she listened closely to what Yvette was saying and then nodded slightly. "I was privileged to help you today, and your dedication has left me with a great admiration for you," Anna whispered sincerely.

So thrilled to hear the young girl speak, Yvette reached out and took Anna's hands in hers and looked directly at her. "I brought you into this world, daughter. Something's bothering you powerfully bad. You got to tell me what it is. Please, you tell me what is making you so sad."

Anna tried to look away from the older woman's deep, dark eyes, but she couldn't. Before she was even aware that she was speaking, words were pouring from her mouth.

"How could she?" she demanded. "How could she put herself to that?"

She went on that her mother should not have had yet another baby at the age of forty-eight, and for believing that being a good Catholic wife meant continuing to have children for as long as God gives them to you. Sobbing now, she talked about how her mother wanted her to start working on her wedding trousseau next year, pending a marriage proposal.

She looked at Yvette with hollow eyes. "I don't want to marry," she said straight out. Marriage, she went on, felt like a life sentence being imposed on her. "How dare I not even be given a voice in the decision!" she added, her voice rising with outrage. "Look at mother, she married late. If I get married before I am twenty years old, how many childbirths will I have to go endure by the time I am forty-eight years old?" She started to cry. "I don't want it, I don't want it."

"What don't you want, girl? Yvette asked.

"I don't want a life foisted upon me! I want my life for myself!"

Yvette was startled by the young girl's passion. "But your parents, the Church..."

"I don't want my life decided by anyone else, not by my parents, not by this village, not by the Church!"

Yvette did not even know what to say or do. She had never heard such talk before in her life. Of course, she knew that girls were sometimes scared about their future. That was understandable. The unknown is always frightening. But that was not what she heard in young Anna's voice or words. She heard rebellion there. She also heard something else, something that she rarely heard in the voices of girls and women. She heard strength and determination. And it both frightened her and filled her with pride.

"I wish I was never born a woman!" Anna concluded.

Yvette sighed deeply. "Oh child, we can only be born what we are, nothing else."

Anna looked at her and her green eyes flashed with fire. "Then, if I was born what I am, what I am is someone who wants her own life!"

Yvette Letourdie stood up from the table and the fullness of her physical presence filled the room. Heavy-set at twenty stones, she stood as tall as any man in her ankle-length nurse's uniform and white head scarf. As Anna's words sank in, they moved her in ways she could not control.

"Daughter," she said simply, extending her arms to the slender girl sharing the table with her.

Anna stood unsteadily and then let herself be drawn into the embrace of Yvette's huge, black arms and against her enormous bosom. Yvette had no words for the sixteen-year-old, neither wisdom nor reassurance. Certainly nothing that she could speak with honesty.

She had brought hundreds of souls into the world but never before had she needed to address feelings such as Anna's. She knew what the culture taught. She knew what the Church taught. She knew what she was *supposed* to say. For every young Catholic girl had to walk this same path. There was no choice. Rebellion was the work of the Devil.

"Oh, daughter, daughter," she sighed as she hugged Anna ever tighter.

She knew that the path for a young girl was never easy, and only good fortune brings the perfect partner, someone with a good heart and conscience. She too had suffered from an arranged marriage.

She was sixteen, like Anna, when her parents married her to a man aged forty. Oh, how she suffered at his wicked hands! He drank the local, potent brew *baka* all the time, sending him into dark rages during which he beat her unmercifully. He was rough and uncaring when he took her to the marriage bed. During her first three years of marriage, she suffered two miscarriages. Her *salvation* was hardly that at all. His heavy drinking took its toll on his health and Thomas Letourdie died from cirrhosis of the liver, leaving Yvette widowed and penniless. Certainly, her own family would not take her back. What was she to do? In desperation, she turned to the midwife who had shown her such kindness during her miscarriages. Under her care and tutelage, she entered a new life, one that she embraced with passion and dignity. She never remarried.

"My poor daughter," she sighed, holding Anna tight. "My poor, poor daughter."

Albert returned to the cottage not long after eight o'clock. Anna had seen him coming up the path, his step confident and happy. She sighed to herself as she realized... *he knows nothing.*

Later that evening, after he'd spoken to his wife and seen his new baby, he returned happily to the dining room where Anna had put out a meal.

"We have named her Eliane," he proclaimed. Anna stared numbly at him.

"Your new sister," he said, seeing her confusion. "We've given her the name Eliane." Anna lowered her eyes. He knew nothing, and he wanted to know even less.

That night, as she stared out of her window at the night sky, she could not still the trembling in her limbs as she was revisited by the image of her mother, naked and spread-eagled in a bed covered in blood. *Dead! My mother is dead!* She recalled the horrible screams that had come from the room. Madame Letourdie's voice pierced her shock. "Your mother is not dead," she had said plainly. "But your sister will be if you do not help me."

Anna's face was damp with tears as her eyes searched the night beyond her bedroom window, searched for peace to appease her troubled heart, for some serenity that seemed to be eluding her. The distant barking of a dog echoed over the sleeping valley. The black shadows of fruit bats glided across the full moon, heading in the direction of fruit trees with ripe offerings. From the *kalorifer* in the valley, the sweet smell of cinnamon leaves being distilled perfumed the air.

It was all so perfect and complete, this full world that she had always gazed upon from her window. And yet…she could not escape the sensation that there was also something important and significant missing. She had a brand new baby sister – something *new* had entered the world, and yet she felt only that something was missing. Just what, she couldn't say.

Anna trembled again, like a leaf in an insistent breeze. She felt anxious, frightened. But where could she go for comfort? She had no place to run. No one to run to. She felt desperate to find that solace, to know what the absence was that left her with such a sense of longing that was unbearable. She suddenly felt a great need rising deep from within her, a desperate desire to know exactly what was missing out there. She closed her eyes, and with the sensation of sinking deeper and deeper into murky waters, she reached the depth within her soul where she finally felt at one with her body and mind

There was at first a great stillness, and then she was suddenly overwhelmed as the pain and suffering she had endured this day all churned and flared anew. But in that deep turmoil, she found the answer...it was the sea!

The sea herself, mother of all island life, was suffering, and Anna could feel her pain. This dreadful, unrelenting heat had rendered her weak, her powers were all gone, the winds that blew at the backs of her waves were gone.

The sounds of the surf pounding the sand had been silenced, the gentle soothing echoes of the winds in the trees had disappeared. There were no more salt sprays mingled with the cinnamon perfume from the kalorifer to create the scent she most deeply associated with Beau Vallon. It was all gone. This is what was eluding her! This dreadful heat wave had silenced the songs of the sea, and with it, the rhythms of the life of the island.

Anna had a soulful quality that allowed her to commune with nature, to feel its joy and hear its cries. This night, she heard it crying in pain and her heart ached. She needed the fullness of nature to be there for comfort. She needed its reassuring calm and its comforting presence. Where she longed to feel a fullness, she felt only absence. Where she longed for comfort, she found only emptiness. Tonight of all nights, this was intolerable - both for herself and for the world that she loved. Closing her eyes even tighter, she delved deeper still, entering that inner sanctuary yet again, determined to find some way to heal what was hurting. She was certain it could be found – it must be found!

Then a peace illuminated her face and her inner self breathed in the scent of Beau Vallon. The special perfume of this place brought a small smile to her lips. It seemed she could hear the soothing echoes of the breeze playing with the trees as it swirled all around her, appeasing her anguish. She prayed. *Show me...show me.*

She opened her eyes and she found herself gazing upon the small footpath, illuminated by the moonlight and disappearing between the trees and down the valley to the sea. She felt a sudden overwhelming desire to follow the path down to the beach, to feel the soft sand beneath her bare feet, and to dive into the warm tranquil waters with only the full moon watching her.

Anna did not remember leaving her house. She not remember running along the path, nor feel of the night air on her skin, nor the leaves and branches brushing against her. Her first awareness was of being on the beach, leaning against the thick coconut tree trunk, with the sand beneath her feet feeling exactly as she knew it would. Soft and powdery, cool and soothing.

At that moment, the beach felt magical. It was a place she had visited a thousand times in her life, but this time, it was different. The soft moonlight shone down on her as all around she felt the serene beauty of the bay, the valleys, the mountains, illuminating the world that she had dreamed of as clearly as the one right before her. As much as she feared a husband's embrace, she longed passionately for the embrace of nature.

Like a bride to her lover, she comfortably let her cotton dress slip from her shoulders and land in a heap in the sand. Naked, she walked slowly through the sand toward the water's edge. The holy nymph had come home...

The warm Indian Ocean embraced her slender young body. Anna fell into a gentle stroke, enjoying the water's sensuality and feeling its touch on every part of her as it caressed her senses. Slowly, she increased the pace of her rhythm, drawing in deep breaths as she glided across the line of the bay.

How often had she swum these waters, but never before had she felt this sense of freedom, excitement and contentment! It really was a liberating feeling to swim unclothed. As she swam, she knew that everything within her sight belonged entirely to her. The world, and everything in it, was hers and hers alone.

The bay, the white beach, the green valleys, and even the glowing orb of the moon itself. All hers. She was at one with nature.

Midway across the bay, she paused to gather her breath. She trod water and looked over at the Alouette, floating gracefully at her mooring. Further across, the spire of the church at Saint Roch gleamed in the moonlight.

Gazing upon the church, she thought what a shock it would be for the old priest to see her swimming naked in the moonlight across the bay. A sin, he would likely proclaim. *But is it a sin?* she wondered idly. *I have certainly done nothing wrong. Just a swim, nothing more.* With that, she began to swim anew.

As she crossed nearby the home of the du Barré family, *La Residence*, she could not help but admire its elegance and grandeur. If such a thing as an elegant castle existed in the Seychelles, then this beautiful house with its lovely garden would most certainly qualify. It was the largest house on the entire northern coast of Mahé island, and from the stories Therese told, it was even more magnificent inside. As she swam, she imagined herself in its rooms and hallways. She would be a princess in such a castle! She continued to feel the glow of her fantasy as her swim ended and she walked slowly out of the water.

As her skin dried in the warm night air, she walked across the sand to where she'd left her clothes. Lifting the cotton dress over her head, she let it slip over her body, covering her now so that she was *respectable* in the eyes of the old priest and the night. Then she sat and leaned back against a long piece of driftwood that had become half-buried in the sand. She let her long, black hair spread over the wood, so that it might dry in the night air.

Closing her eyes, she thought of Yvette Letourdie and all that had happened earlier. Now, after her cleansing swim, revisiting that difficult scene in her mind brought not the panic and horror but rather, an image of Yvette's caring and dedication. Rather than focusing on her mother, the blood, or the unconscious baby, she considered Yvette's efficient actions. Her every move had been accomplished with such precision and expertise, as if she were performing an everyday task rather than holding the balance between life and death in her very hands.

The picture of her unconscious mother, painted in her own blood and afterbirth, would remain with her for the rest of her life, but for now she thought about how Yvette had managed the dire events, calmly enlisting her help in resuscitating the baby. For those few moments, there was nothing else but saving the baby's life. Time seemed to stand still. The necessity of acting, and needing to act immediately, had made her oblivious to all other emotions. Like Yvette, she too for a time had held the balance of life and death in her own hands.

And then, Eliane's first cry! Alive! What relief, what satisfaction! Even more, it was the look she'd received from Yvette that had filled her with an emotion that even now she could not describe. She had *partnered* with Yvette to save a life. Oh, she knew that she had played only a small role, and that Yvette had played the major part, but nevertheless she *had* played a role.

Just then, with her eyes closed and her head rested against the driftwood and the warm night air blanketing her body, Anna had a revelation. Not just *a* revelation, *the* revelation. She had her answer. She had a direction and a path to the foreseeable future. She had a way to reclaim her hold on her life. Rather than a headlong tumble toward obligatory matrimony, she could live a life of meaning.

Two hours ago she recalled herself standing at her bedroom window, contemplating a bleak future. *I was lost. But now, nature has shown me the way...* nursing! She would become a nurse!

Her excitement was tempered by what she knew would be her parents' reaction. They would try to dissuade her, or simply dismiss the notion altogether, but she would fight for what she wanted. Oh, how she would fight for what she wanted! It was a good path. It was the right path. She smiled to herself, then closed her eyes and let her breathing settle into a gentle rhythm. Soon, she was fast asleep.

CHAPTER 3

Mermaids in the Moonlight

Louis du Barré could not have been more thrilled by his father's announcement at lunch. It was a humbling and gratifying opportunity that his father had created for him, one that he had often dreamed of but never considered a possibility. Louis had completed his formal education at seventeen, but before that and from that point forward, Christophe had taken him under his wing, schooling him in estate management and entrepreneurial skills – just as he had with Henri three years previously. Just like, he enjoyed recalling, his own father had done with him. "An inheritance can only prosper if the person holding it knows its full value in sweat," Francois had said by way of explanation as to why he expected Christophe to work so hard.

Christophe, and Francois before him – and indeed, every father and grandfather with an estate of any worth – sought to ensure the continuance and growth of their inheritance. There are times in life when such strategies become obvious. When, for example, a child's birth causes a father to look to the future. Such had been the case for Christophe and Genevieve, and their fathers had betrothed them when they were still very young children. Their betrothal was in the interests of merging two wealthy and powerful families - Silhouette Island and the Beau Vallon Estate. Christophe, who was now responsible for these two magnificent estates, bore the responsibility of making sure his own two sons appreciated and respected what would one day become theirs to nurture and grow.

And then there are the unforeseen occurrences. Christophe's intention had always been to maximise the full potential of the estates, which he had presumed would be the work of another generation, or even two. Like his own father, he had focused on maximising the yield of the land. But now, a mere year and a half into 'the schooner experiment,' he found himself pleasantly surprised by its success and potential.

The land was a great provider. That truth had been worked into his soul by blood and by sweat. Now he realized that the sea, too, could be a great provider of wealth. Like the land, if cultivated properly the sea could yield riches far beyond the imaginings of most men, and was almost infinite in its bounty.

So, his decision to commission a second schooner, while wholly satisfying to his younger son, was also a shrewd business decision. Whilst his sons feared that they were somehow betraying their father by their love of the sea, little did they know that they had inadvertently enlarged their father's vision of the possible.

For Louis, the afternoon and evening went by in the blink of an eye, his emotions in an upheaval the entire time. For years, his love of the sea had felt illicit and wrong, a betrayal of all that his father intended for him. To receive his father's blessing to pursue this great love…well, it was a heady and overwhelming haze in which he found himself.

Long after he had retired to his room that night, Louis remained unable to sleep. He stood at his bedroom window and stared out at the bay reflected in the full moon. As his eyes rested on the noble schooner the Alouette, he imagined a second, equally noble schooner alongside her. *His* schooner. He entered one reverie after another, imagining the wonderful things that the future held for him when he suddenly caught sight of something moving in the still, dark waters of the bay.

His heart began pounding in his chest. Was that a tail slapping against the waters? Was that the face of a beautiful girl? On this second count, there could be no doubt. She was there. No amount of rubbing his eyes changed that. Her long, black hair floated gracefully after her as she glided across the water.

"It is true," he sighed to himself. "The legends *are* true!"

Looking down at the beautiful creature swimming so languidly through the waters of the bay, he was now convinced that, in fact, mermaids *did* exist. While this revelation left him feeling somewhat tingly and weak-kneed, it did provide him in that instant with the name for his eventual schooner –' La Sirène' – the Mermaid. *La Sirène* he whispered into the darkness, testing the name, as if actually speaking it would make it more real. Then, gazing down at the waters again, he saw that the mermaid was gliding quickly from his view. He turned from the window and ran from his bedroom and out the front of the house. After all, how often does a man have the chance to see a real mermaid?

He half-walked, half-ran down the long driveway, jogged across the main road and found himself upon the soft sand of the beach. As he hurried his steps across the sand to the water's edge, his eyes searched frantically across the bay. "Where has she gone?" he cried out in the moonlight, for there was no sign of the mermaid. He took himself to the water's edge, but the sea was as still as a bowl of thick syrup. He hung his head and turned back toward the house. "It must have been my imagination," he sighed, trying to be as rational as his father had taught him.

"There is always a good reason for everything," Christophe had taught both his sons, particularly when they were small boys and found themselves frightened of all sorts of imaginary things such as the magic and sorcery they'd heard the superstitious workers gossip about.

As he walked toward the shadows cast by the trees at the end of the beach, Louis thought he saw something unusual near a long, half-buried bit of driftwood. As he walked closer towards the strange shape he wondered what sort of fisherman would leave his net on the beach. He came to a sudden stop. The object on the sand was no net…it was the mermaid!

There she was, lying on the sand before him, her pale skin as luminous as the full moon, her black hair floating over the driftwood and becoming lost in the tangle of moon shadow behind it. His heart was pounding in his chest as he realized that this mermaid did not have a tail, but was wearing a dress! As incredible as it would have been to find a mermaid on the beach, finding a girl who was *not* a mermaid lying on the sands was an even more incredible discovery. A ghost perhaps?

There were so many stories and sightings of ghosts and *dandosya* woven into the fabric of the Seychelles that it was not unusual to hear the workers tell their tales of ghosts that returned on the anniversaries of their deaths. Perhaps this was a girl who had drowned, and who returned to this beach every year? The old priest at Saint Roch would scowl to know the thoughts in Louis's mind just then, but then a young man's imagination can be inflamed by so many things that would not meet with the approval of an old priest. He gasped as he came closer still. *I know her!*

Though she looked somehow different lying here in the night, more mature, more serene, and certainly more beautiful, could it really be the same girl he knew? The delicate, timid young girl, with her hair plaited in two long tresses, running the length of the bay to get to Bel Ombre school? He was both fascinated and embarrassed to find himself standing there, staring at this beautiful creature.

He had certainly intruded upon her in an intimate way. A trespass! But was he in the wrong? Why was she here? Did she need his help? Was she merely sleeping? What girl would fall asleep on the beach, alone, at this late hour? He could make no sense of it. Should he wake her? He could not, after all, remain to admire her as she slept so peacefully. That felt as wrong as it certainly was. But to leave her sleeping, alone and vulnerable on the beach, certainly that was equally wrong.

Unable to resolve his moral dilemma, he simply sat down on the beach alongside her, and continued gazing upon her gentle, beautiful, sleeping countenance. If, as he dared to think, she was nothing but a dream then he told himself that he had no desire to awaken, so taken was he by the image before him.

The fear that he was, in fact, dreaming, made him reach out and touch her shoulder. Gently. As gently as the first time he touched a butterfly. Perhaps even more gently.

"Anna," he whispered. "Anna, Anna."

Her eyes flew open, her panic obvious and immediate. "Do not be afraid," he said quickly. "It is me. Louis. I did not mean to startle you." He looked around at the beach. "But I could not leave you here sleeping."

She sat up, clearly embarrassed and disoriented. Perhaps she too had been dreaming. She lowered her eyes. She couldn't bear to look at him. "How long have you been here?" she asked, colouring with the impetuousness of her question.

"Only a moment," Louis said, lying. Oh, what shame she felt! "I…I must have dozed off," she said, her voice so soft he could barely hear it even in the still night air. "I came for a swim…it was too warm to sleep…I couldn't sleep…I thought…I thought a swim would help me sleep."

He smiled, trying to reassure her. However, without her looking at him, his smile only served to reassure himself. "I could not sleep either," he said, with some laughter in his voice.

"You see, I thought I'd seen a mermaid from my window!"

She looked at him and saw him smiling. "A mermaid?"

He nodded. "Yes, a beautiful mermaid swimming in the bay." He was so anxious to make her smile. He felt sorry for her. It was clear that her reason for being out on the beach was not the one that she had given, but he was not interested in her explanations just then. He only wanted her to not be so obviously discomforted by his presence.

She looked at him, her eyes almost playful.

"Yes," he went on, encouraged by that look despite feeling very foolish himself. "A wonderful mermaid. But, alas," he sighed with a self-conscious air. "It was no mermaid at all."

She smiled then. "It was me?"

He nodded. "Yes. And apparently your swim served its purpose for you were most certainly asleep." A worried look crossed her face.

"But you do not have to explain yourself to me," he said quickly, desperate for her not to feel uncomfortable again. He understood intuitively that he had unwittingly stumbled upon her darkest secret. An action and a secret that could have serious repercussions for her reputation if made public. Somehow, that understanding gave him the courage to help her trust him. "Do not worry, Anna," he said, leaning closer to her. "Your secret is safe. I promise you by all that I hold dear that no one will ever know from me that you went swimming tonight."

Her eyes, dewy with fear and emotion, turned to him.

The moonlight was captured in them in such a way that, when she suddenly smiled in relief and happiness, he felt as though he had seen a thousand stars exploding.

"Really?"

He nodded. "Yes."

As he looked at her, he wondered if she realised just how beautiful she was. Could she possibly know the effect she was having on him?

"Thank you very much, Monsieur du Barré. I so appreciate your kindness," Anna said demurely.

Hearing himself referred to with such formality confused Louis so much that he turned around, expecting to see his father standing behind him. When he realized that she was speaking to him, he bowed his head. "I would be honoured, Anna, if you would call me Louis. Monsieur du Barré sounds too much as if you are talking to my father."

She batted her eyes and nodded. They were both smiling now, when suddenly a cool breeze whipped through the takamaka branches, soothing their faces and giving a voice to the night. As if caressed by an invisible hand, the trees and coconut palms swayed with the rhythm of the breeze, and the dry, rustling leaves which had been stuck to their branches for months, flew off and fell to the sand below. Louis and Anna sat and stared in silence. Nature seemed to be coming back to life all around them. The waters of the bay kicked up, awakened from their oily slumber. The stars twinkled anew in their heaven. The heat wave had broken.

Something had prompted Mother Nature to turn her sympathy toward that small corner of the Indian Ocean, and she gazed down on the islands of the Seychelles, where her favourite protégée lay scattered. For months, she had been displaying her anger toward them, and yet they were no closer to understanding the reason for their difficulty. They fully deserved her displeasure to be unrelenting, but something had happened today that had momentarily touched her heart.

She had observed attentively, as a sixteen-year-old virgin had offered her purity and beauty to nature, and had relished its comforting powers. Earlier, she watched her again, swimming the length of the bay, immersing herself totally, at one with herself and the sea.

This very young tortured soul, who had been in search of protection and peace, had turned to her for help twice in one day. She had more than proven her deepest respect and appreciation for nature. She was looking radiant and peaceful now, as the full moon bathed her sleeping face, caressing her in its soft, comforting light. It was clear that she had finally found what she had been seeking, and that nature had responded to her cry for help. Maybe there was still hope. Maybe all was not yet lost for the Seychelles.

Up there in the skies beyond yonder, in a chair made from puffs of clouds, Mother Nature sat pensively, her face echoing the delicate complexion and beauty of eternal youth, framed in a timeless body.

Her hair was long silvery curls which hung loosely on her shoulders, immersing itself in the fabric of the chair. Her dress was full and bouncy, with frills in all the shades of the rainbow as it covered the floor around the chair, merging into the clouds.

Today her mood was reflective as she once more cast her mind back to those difficult times. She could remember everything, and for her, a million years was but the blink of an eye. She remembered two hundred million years earlier, when the Seychelles broke away from the Super Continent – Gondwanaland. What an upheaval! The very rock of the land quaked. Poor, unfortunate Seychelles, looking so lost and disoriented as she drifted on her way, separated from the larger land mass.

Mother Nature's heart had ached for the Seychelles. She decided to help by carefully guiding them to this sheltered spot in the middle of the Indian Ocean, just four degrees south of the equator, where they would enjoy 365 days of summer each year. Then she went a step further, by protecting them from all natural disasters, such as cyclones and hurricanes. Her care for the Seychelles further endowed the islands with a unique and treasured flora and fauna.

There was an abundance of green forests, complete with freshwater streams, and serene white coastlines surrounded by crystal clear blue sea, teeming with life. Up above, an abundance of birds soared in their skies. Those millions of years ago, the only inhabitants were giant land tortoises.

Then, for the grand finale, Mother Nature decided that the Seychelles would have to bear their own personal stamp. They were so perfect, she wanted there to be no mistake that this perfection was no mere chance. She wanted it known that the Seychelles were her special creation. So, she added a little touch of magic by planting two *Trees of Knowledge*, at their centre.

Male and female, she created them. Trees to mate on nights of the full moon, with the female tree then bearing the *Fruit of Life*. When she had finished, she sat back, very pleased with herself.

Over the centuries, she watched as the rising sea claimed most of the land of the Seychelles, turning her into a group of small islands. The first footprints of men appeared on her pure sand only in the last century, travellers who sought fresh water and who happened upon her Eden. They took food and timber and rested in her comforts. They were seduced by her beauty, but always departed promptly until…they unwittingly stumbled on her unique garden, where the *Trees of Knowledge* grew. Then everything changed.

From the middle part of the globe, hordes of white men with greed in their hearts landed on her shores, whipping armies of black men in chains before them, and with this the desecration of the Seychelles began. The echo of human pain and suffering, the torturous rattling of chains, the crack of whips on bare bodies, forever tainted her soils and marred her perfection.

Her pure and treasured creation had been brutally violated and stained with the blood of the weak. Although the sounds of those chains had been silent for decades, her abuse had continued. These men had enjoyed the fruits of *her* labour, but none of them had paused to pay homage to *her*. Not one. Not until today…

Not until a girl named Anna had sought the comfort and beneficence of Mother Nature herself. This day, Mother Nature had stood in witness of a true declaration of love and respect, made by a pure and clean soul. Anna had touched her heart deeply, and helped to appease her anger. It was time to give them a second chance, she decided. And so, she repositioned the wind to blow once more over her protégée, to disperse the leaden weight of the horrible heat wave.

As much as she adored the fact that Anna came to her with a pure heart, Mother Nature smiled upon Anna and Louis on the beach together that night. "Let it all grow and flourish in your hearts, my young ones. Keep my legacy of natural beauty alive, and remember to always keep the eyes of your hearts wide open, and to see with the beauty of your souls."

On the beach, more than the sudden relief from the heat, the two young people experienced something else, something deeper, something almost magical. Something that neither of them had words to describe.

CHAPTER 4

Personal Drama

Perhaps of all the inhabitants of Beau Vallon, Madame Josephine was the only one Anna could have gone to. Certainly not the priest or nun at the church of Saint Roch. This was not a confession that Anna could have taken to them. She needed someone who knew what it meant to live outside the rules, not someone who would be insistent on finding a way to contort her to live within them. And Madame Josephine knew only too well what it meant to break the rules, and to live with the consequences.

After months of engaging in a secret and illicit love affair with Jacques Morel, the eighteen-year-old Josephine and the twenty-nine-year-old Jacques made a fateful decision. Knowing in their hearts that they were meant to live their lives together, Jacques left his eight-year marriage and his two children, and Josephine left her twin sister, Norine, and her widowed mother. These poor people were left alone on the island of La Digue to face the full force of the scandal.

The lovers escaped to Mahé in Jacques' fishing boat, and set up a home together at the end of Beau Vallon beach. While they had hoped they had escaped, scandal has a way of chasing after those who flee it, and Mahé was quickly alight with the news of the couple. Not that their very existence as a couple would not have been enough to cause scandal. Jacques was a white man of French descent, and Josephine was of African descent, with skin as dark as the night. These two were simply not supposed to mix. It was against all the rules. There was no doubt amongst the inhabitants of Mahé that Josephine had cast a spell on the Frenchman. She had seduced him using black magic *grigri*, and the web of lust she created had shattered the bonds of his marriage. What else could explain his decision to condemn his soul to an adulterous life, outside the faith of his church?

There had to be consequences for such behaviour, not just in the heavens above but here on earth as well. So the two remained bonded in love and devotion to one another, but near complete outcasts to everyone else. No one called to mind the words of Jesus: "Let he who is without sin cast the first stone..." There was no reason to. The sin of these two was so great, so damaging. For fifty years the couple remained in blissful union, but also in utter poverty, loneliness, shame, regret and pain. "Life and love, she ain't simple," Madame Josephine always said. "But the heart wants what the heart wants."

After listening to Anna, Madame Josephine nodded slowly as she continued shifting the rice grains spread out in the *lavann* on her lap. Clean grains went to one side, grains with bits of dirt were kept at the other. Her fat, agile fingers continued their work as she contemplated Anna's words. She wondered if Anna appreciated the consequences of what she was contemplating.

Most girls wouldn't, but Anna was different. She was always different. Josephine had known that from the first day they'd met. Despite the seriousness of this meeting, Josephine could not repress a smile, recalling the younger Anna, setting off for her first day of school. She'd worn a coloured *vakoa* straw hat, one held in place by a pink bow tied under her chin. Her long black hair, plaited into two tresses, bounced on her shoulders. As she passed Josephine's modest hut, the young girl had turned and smiled at her. "Bonjour, Madame," she said sweetly. Josephine had looked at the young girl, somewhat stunned to be addressed directly, and so charmingly! To her eyes, Anna had that day seemed to radiate an excitement and glow that was so genuine and yet, her expression had a kind of daring, a recklessness that was at once invigorating and challenging. *These past six years have changed nothing*, Josephine thought to herself.

The older, black woman looked the younger, white girl directly in the eyes. "Have you spoken with your parents about your decision?"

A shadow came over Anna's face. The shift in expression was all the answer that Josephine needed. Poor Anna, sitting so quietly and patiently on the coconut trunk stool in Josephine's kitchen, hoping for an answer to her dilemma. *At least her decision is not as dramatic as my own. She is only shifting from her path by a bit. She is not abandoning it altogether.* It occurred to Josephine that if she could help Anna find her way without leaving the path, she might be able to redeem herself a little in the process. Clearly, Anna's parents did not fully grasp or understand her feelings and yearnings, to be different, to make a difference. Josephine knew that Anna's passion and fighting spirit, what some would call *stubbornness* and others would call *unholiness*, could cause disaster if not handled properly.

Josephine threw the rice grains up in the air, so that the bits of dirt would be blown away. Then she gracefully caught all the clean grains back in the lavann as they came down. And then, as if by magic, an idea came to her with great clarity. The nuns and the church could help, if indirectly. Smiling, she looked at the troubled girl. "Anna, I have an idea."

Even as Anna sat in Josephine's outdoor kitchen, her mind in turmoil, Madame Genevieve du Barré knelt on the hard bench in the church of Saint Roch, her soul equally troubled. As she was each time her menstrual cycle arrived, she was nearly overcome by guilt, shame, and unadulterated fear. The reason for her feelings were simple. She took a potion that ensured that she would not become pregnant again. A very un-Catholic thing to do, completely forbidden, and for which the Church would condemn and ostracise her. Her reputation and that of her family would be totally ruined if this knowledge was to come to light.

When she was a very young girl of just twelve, she overheard a conversation between one of the housemaids and the cook. She tried not to listen but when she heard her departed mother's name mentioned, she crept closer.

That day, she learned that her mother had not died from pneumonia, as her father had told her, but from childbirth. She had died giving birth to her. Genevieve remembered vividly the images of that day. With tears streaming down her face, she had ran up the little hill to where her mother's tomb rested peacefully under the shade of a *flamboyant* tree. Kneeling by the tomb, she had hugged the sun-bleached wooden cross and sobbed her heart out, begging her mother's forgiveness for causing her death. Afterwards, she sat for hours next to the tomb, soothed by the gentle fragrance from the blossoms of the tree, and with the tranquil view of the bay of Silhouette island spread out below, and the island of Mahé, tall and imposing in the distance across the water.

Her life changed that day, the sweet innocence of childhood replaced by the cruel reality of life. She had kept that revelation to herself, never being able to share it with anyone, not even Christophe. From that moment on, she was nearly consumed by guilt and fear, guilt that she was the very instrument of her mother's passing, and fear of her own eventual fate. It was with relief and gratitude that she found herself well and healthy after giving birth to Henri, her dear eldest son. But her pregnancy had been harrowing to her. She often recalled her bliss when she had been preparing to marry Christophe, and the joy of the wedding day itself. Everything had been perfect. He was her perfect husband and lover. Swamped in her newfound happiness, she kept her fears of childbirth locked away until she found herself pregnant with her first child. Oh, how that pregnancy tormented her soul! From gripping fear and a certainty that her young life was to end, to the unutterable joy that she would be a mother and produce an heir to the du Barré's fortune.

On the day of Henri's birth, between the contractions, she had held on to Christophe, telling him how much she loved him and would always love him. "Come, come," the doctor had said to Christophe, ushering the young man out of the room. "This is no place for you…"

When Henri was placed in her arms, Genevieve prayed a prayer of grateful thanks. Henri was the sweetest little boy Genevieve could imagine. As she watched him smile, she realised how unfair it would be for him to spend his childhood on his own, as she had done hers. "Maybe history was not meant to repeat itself," she had told herself. "I did not have any problems giving birth to Henri."

But her second labour was nothing like the first. It was longer, harder and more agonising, with extremely heavy blood loss. She managed to remain conscious until she heard Louis' first cry. "A beautiful, healthy baby boy…" and then everything went black. She remained unconscious for nearly forty-eight hours. When she finally opened her eyes, she was looking directly at the agonized expression of her beloved. It was too much to bear!

Even after the initial shock faded and he realised that she had come back to him, even after his features changed to utter relief, joy and love, it was still too much. Even when he held her in his arms and kissed her and told her just how much he loved her. "I have been so frightened!" he confessed.

Realizing how troubled his soul had been, she made a silent decision, one for which she prayed for forgiveness even before she'd taken any action. *Dear God, one day I will stand before you and you will judge me for the sin I am about to commit. I will do it for the ones I love. I will not see them suffer anymore. Please forgive me.*

Nineteen years earlier, right after the birth of Louis, Genevieve called her chambermaid, Agnes, into her private bedroom. "I want you to go to Madame Seraphine, and buy some of her potion which prevents pregnancy." Her voice was calm. Her decision made. "Don't pretend that you don't know her. I have heard you talking about her before" she told the pale and frightened Agnes directly. "You are not to utter a single word to anyone about this, ever. In exchange, I promise you your job for as long as you want, and I will give you twenty cents extra every month for your trouble."

And for nineteen years, those thick and coarse pieces of *bwa gadyak* tree bark, which Madame Seraphine boiled for six hours on the night of each full moon while she chanted in a bizarre and mysterious dialect as she squatted by her old *marmit lafont*, had never failed. But success is not forgiveness. Genevieve's conscience and her Catholic upbringing festered and gnawed at her. Her repentance and financial contributions to the church and the poor were her attempts at expiation. How she looked forward to the arrival of her menopause and an end to her monthly nightmare.

On the altar the lights from the candles on the two sides of the small crucifix flickered, almost going out. A fresh breeze from the bay had just streamed through the wooden lattice windows on the side of the church, soothing the afternoon stillness, and Genevieve's face. The incense from the morning mass circulated once more, perfuming the air. "I should go home now," Genevieve decided, crossing herself. The cooing of the pigeons in the bell tower seemed to agree with her. She was in no fit state to come face to face with the old priest. It was best to leave now, before he returned from his pastoral visits.

Her mind wondered momentarily, and she could see all the hard work and devotion of Père Valer. It amazed her. He performed two masses per day, with endless confessions before each. But it was his devotion to the sick and infirm that stood out. Old Père Valer would climb any rocky slopes, trek for hours along narrow footpaths, and even do a tricky balancing act on a coconut trunk crossing over a gushing stream, if his parishioners were bedridden and needed his services. Even in the dead of night, he would travel for hours by the light of a flaming torch to reach a sick parishioner in need of last rites. And still he found time to perform burial services as required, and baptise new babies every Sunday. *Your strength and devotion is admirable*, Genevieve sighed. *Despite everything, your enthusiasm never fades.*

She was aware of the financial difficulties of the church. Keeping the village school going and paying wages to the teachers was one such difficulty. The Catholic Church believed in free education, and offered it to all children without distinction. Even if it often proved difficult to convince the parents of poor families, who saw going to school as a waste of time, as opposed to their offspring getting employment on the plantations to bring in an extra income. Unfortunately therefore, most children from poor families only attended classes when they were being prepared for their First Holy Communion and Confirmation.

Genevieve made a decision as she left the church, the weight of her sin still heavy on her conscience. *I will double my donation.* It was a way she could seek forgiveness and it would also be satisfying to see the joy and happiness on old Père Valer's face when she told him that extra funds were available. *All in a good cause*, she decided, as she made her way back to La Residence.

On this bright and sunny August afternoon, in the most idyllic spot on earth, it was hard to imagine anything but beauty, peace and tranquillity.

Yet, beneath the strict Catholic appearance projected by the inhabitants of the Seychelles, some hard and disturbing secrets, contrary to the teachings of the Church, lingered silently in the darkness.

On the south western coast of Mahé, another personal drama was unfolding that day, this one in the small village of Baie Lazare. Only tenuously related to events happening at Beau Vallon, this drama carried with it the promise of catastrophic repercussions to come.

"Non!" Monsieur Gustave Benezet cried out, bringing his fist crashing down on the dining table with a loud bang. "Non!"

His son, Robert, stared at his father, his face drained of all colour. He had only just returned home from skippering a schooner trip to the neighbouring island of Île du Nord. Before leaving the island, Monsieur

Victor Payet, the island's owner, had summoned him to his grand plantation house and there informed him that his monthly schooner service would no longer be required.

"I...I do not understand, sir," the younger Benezet had said.

"I have made other arrangements to transport my crops to Port Victoria."

Robert did not know what to think. What 'other arrangements' could he have made? The one thing he was certain of was that his father would be furious. It had been bad enough when they had lost the business with Silhouette Island after the Alouette was launched. "It was inevitable," Gustave had muttered then. "They are now owned by one family. It makes more sense for them to have their own schooner."

But this? This would be a bitter blow not only to his purse but to his pride. Victor Payet had no family connections with Christophe du Barré.

"This is purely the greed of Christophe du Barré rearing its ugly head," Gustave bellowed. "He is trying to undercut us and steal our livelihood."

The man shook with rage, his green eyes aflame with hate and his thick red moustache, which normally curved upwards at the ends, was now jutting out in a straight line. In truth, Robert had never seen his father so enraged. And that was saying a lot.

Unlike her hot-headed husband, Madame Gertrude Benezet was a strategist. She had come up with a plan. So when she appeared, carrying a tray with a big pot of freshly-brewed coffee, she knew what she wanted to say, and how she wanted to say it. Let her husband rant and rave, she knew cooler heads would have to prevail if her family's livelihood was to be saved. Pouring a large cup of strong black coffee, she added four teaspoons of sugar and gently placed it in front of Gustave.

"Did you have a written agreement with Monsieur Payet?" she asked her husband casually.

"Of course not!" he snapped, as if a written contract was at all relevant. "You keep out of this, woman. It is none of your business." He glared at her as he downed a huge gulp of the hot coffee. "My father and his father before him have been doing business with Île du Nord. We have always had a gentlemen's agreement." He directed his words to Robert, making a point of keeping Gertrude out of the conversation.

"Maybe times are changing, Papa," Robert replied in a quiet voice, wishing fervently that Rolland, his elder brother, was here. Gustave ignored the comment. "I will have to make a decision and very quickly."

With that, he stormed from the house, leaving a speechless Robert and Gertrude staring after him. He headed in the direction of the beach, where he could watch his favourite schooner Dauphin, moored in the tranquil water of Baie Lazare. He swore under his breath. *I will get you for this one day, du Barré.*

In the end, it had been easier than Anna had ever believed possible. Exactly two months after the birth of Eliane, she was free. *Free.*

She wanted to laugh and cry at the same time. Joy, relief, thankfulness, humility…she could not find a single word to describe the energy coursing through her. Whatever it was, it was good. Very, very good. She could hardly believe how easy it had been. Now, in only a matter of months, three to be exact, she would finish school. By January 1913, she would be embarking on her career as a nurse. She wanted to race all the way to the little hut at the end of the beach, to hug Madame Josephine and thank her for all her help. But, of course, that was out of the question. Theirs was a clandestine friendship. They could never be seen together, ever. *It will have to wait until tomorrow. I will see her on the way to school.*

Josephine's plan had been foolproof. Ironically, it was Therese herself who was the instrument to make it succeed, as she had been the one to encourage Anna to become a member of the church choir. Anna had been indifferent to her mother's suggestion but Josephine, recalling Anna mentioning the suggestion to her in passing, saw how it could be used to turn things to Anna's advantage. She insisted that Anna join the choir as her mother had suggested. "And you have to promise me that you will do your best there. It is very important, my child." Anna did not understand, but she did not have to. "This is exactly what you need," Josephine continued. "If I am correct everything will work like magic."

Anna had followed her advice. As it happened, she did not have to try very hard at all. Singing came naturally to her. When she took her place at the choir stand on that first Sunday, she caught the eye of a nice young man, sitting tall and poised in the first row of benches at the front of the church, where the elite of the parish has their reserved seats. She smiled quickly at Louis du Barré, then she blushed slightly. *He is a true gentleman*, she thought, knowing that he had kept his promise to her.

During that service, she had sung from the heart. Her clear soft voice rose with the rhythm of the old organ, filling the church.

Every member of the congregation, particularly the small group of nuns sitting just behind the front benches, had turned and looked at the newcomer in the choir who had the voice of an angel. After mass, Sister William, the nun in charge of her school, approached her. "You sounded wonderful in the choir today, Anna," she remarked. "Thank you, Sister," Anna replied modestly, giving a quick curtsey. Sister William was accompanied by several other nuns, one of whom was Sister Patrick, the Matron of Victoria Hospital. As soon as she introduced Anna to Sister Patrick, Anna's eyes lit up.

As Josephine counselled, each Sunday Anna had made a point of speaking to Sister Patrick, inquiring about nursing, showing her eagerness to learn more and more, until the Sunday when, with her eyes downcast, she confessed that she wanted nothing more than to become a nurse, but that she feared her parents might think it was not an appropriate step.

"I can see your dilemma, my child," Sister Patrick said. "I will pray for an answer. Don't worry too much about it. God will show us the way. He always does".

She spoke to the other nuns and they all agreed that despite the accepted custom of white girls not going into work, they should on this occasion intervene on Anna's behalf and personally talk to her parents.

So it was that one Sunday afternoon, Therese, who had just concluded her forty days of bed rest after the delivery, had the unexpected pleasure and honour of having no less than four nuns visiting her small cottage. Over a cup of tea, Sister Patrick explained to Therese and Albert why nursing was almost like a vocation. She emphasised its religious and humanitarian aspects, as well as the added asset it would be for a young girl who would one day become a wife and mother. "The medical knowledge a young girl acquires will be invaluable in caring for her own children."

Whatever reservations Therese had crumbled before Sister Patrick's status, personality and powers of persuasion. "Well…"Therese hazarded, "if that is what is best…"

Perhaps she would have not agreed had it not been for the special circumstances of the discussion; the veneration of the visit, the nuns' presence in her house, combined with all the good religious reasons brought forward, particularly the idea that nursing was almost a vocation. But, all these things were in place. Therese could not imagine responding in any other way. After all, if these nuns felt so strongly about it… "If my husband," she said, glancing at Albert, "has no objection…"

Albert simply nodded. It would have seemed unchristian to do anything else.

Anna was free.

CHAPTER 5

A Little White Sand Crab

It was mid-October, the mango season, and the Seychelles were once again basking in tropical beauty. Temperatures remained between 23 and 26 degrees, accompanied by a cool and fresh breeze from the sea. On the slopes of the hills, and in the plains of the valleys, the red blossoms of the flamboyant trees were piercing the green canopy, adding colour to this abundance of green, competing with the white masses of the albizia trees which were also showing off their beauty.

The white seagulls glided in the skies along the coastlines. Thousands of other tropical birds kept to the valleys and the hills. Every tree was laden with green, yellow and red fruits of all sizes. The air was rich with the sticky, ripe aroma of mangoes. There was the occasional rainfall, sweet and plentiful, cleansing the fruits for the evening bats to gorge on their soft flesh. Life was once more as it was meant be, the terrifying heat wave of the earlier part of the year was but a distant memory, a horrifying and terrible nightmare. God was in His Heaven. All was well on Earth. Mother Nature smiled.

Then, on one of those serene mid-October afternoons, something nice happened.

What can that be about? Madame Florence Savy wondered as she walked toward the sound of her dog barking.

"Good afternoon, Madame Savy," the postman said, standing nervously in the courtyard as the dog continued to bark.

She clapped her hands to quieten the dog and then walked toward the postman who handed her a pristine white envelope. She smiled and thanked him as she glanced at the envelope. It was addressed to Monsieur Lionet Savy.

She held the envelope with some curiosity and interest. She could not remember the last time they had received a letter.

For the next three hours, she paced the veranda, growing more concerned about the possible contents of the letter while she awaited Lionet's return home. *What could it be?* she asked herself a thousand times, weighing the envelope in her hand. Finally, Lionet came cycling along the driveway, returning home from work. Rushing to meet him, she cried out, "Please hurry, you have received an important letter."

Lionet's eyes widened at the news. He stood his bicycle against the side of the veranda, and rushed into the house. He quickly tore open the envelope and unfolded the sheet of white paper. As Florence looked over his shoulder at the letter he grasped in his trembling hands, she gasped. On the top right hand corner a delicate drawing of a beautiful red rose stood out proudly against the white background. "Heaven be praised," she uttered, "Who is he?"

As it turned out, 'He' was Monsieur Claude Maillet of Anse Royale village. Lionet was an acquaintance of Claude's younger brother, Monsieur Bertrand Maillet. Like Lionet, Bertrand also worked at the Queen's Building in Victoria. The Maillet family of Anse Royale were Mahe's best vanilla cultivator and processor. Their plantation, in the seaside valley of Anse Royale, was run by Monsieur Andre Maillet himself, whilst his elder son, Claude, managed the processing side of the family business. And Claude Maillet was at the very desirable, marriageable age of thirty years…

Florence's heart leapt in her breast as her eyes scanned the letter. Their only child, Mademoiselle Ghislaine Savy, was twenty, a perfect age to marry. She whispered the Creole proverb under her breath…*sak kitouz i trouv son brenzel.*

"Read it aloud, Lionet!" she urged him.

And, so he did. *Je trempe ma plume dans l'encre pour vous demander…*

Florence fanned herself. "Oh Lionet, I beg of you, tell me that you approve of this match!"

Rather than say anything, Lionet smiled a deeply satisfied smile, which told his wife all she needed to know. When he did finally speak, his voice seemed to come from a distant past, from a day many years before, when her own father, Monsieur Francis Mancienne, had given his blessing and approval to Lionet's *let demann*.

"He comes from a good family and I am sure Ghislaine will be well looked after," he said softly.

"Merci, Lionet, merci," Florence said, wrapping her arms around her husband and hugging him. When she released him, her eyes glistened with tears of joy, mixed with a sort of sadness and anticipation.

Ghislaine Savy and her grandmother, Mère Monia, sat upright and impatient as they stared across the dining table at the expressions on the two faces looking back at them. Lionet looked flushed, his wide grin seemingly painted on his face. To look at him, it would have been possible to assume he had just received an important promotion from the British Government. But Florence's expression was much more difficult to read, particularly in the context of Lionet's obvious satisfaction. Despite her radiant smile, her eyes were puffy and red, signs of having recently had a little cry.

We have received a letter today," Florence said, measuring her words. "A wedding proposal for you," Florence said softly, looking at Ghislaine. The young woman drew a quick, audible intake of air.

"The gentleman concerned comes from a good Catholic family of Anse Royale, Monsieur Claude Maillet," she went on, glancing at a smiling Monia, who was very well acquainted with the Maillet family.

"Your father has given his consent, and we would like to answer this letter and invite him to visit us next weekend."

For her part, it seemed to Ghislaine that she had forgotten how to breathe. So she was shocked to hear her own voice say, "Oui, Maman, I would like that very much." Then she turned to her father and she smiled. "Merci, Papa, merci."

That night, Ghislaine's eyes were wide as she lay in bed listening to the house whispering its nightly sounds. The wavering orange light from Mère Monia's oil lamp cast a dim glow on the wooden ceiling, and because the bedroom partitions did not reach the ceiling, the glow could be seen from all the rooms. So many thoughts and images went through her mind. She recalled the night when the oil lamp went out. She was a young girl and was awakened by Mère Monia calling from the adjoining bedroom. "I am suffocating, I cannot breathe!"

Ghislaine had jumped from her bed in an instant. With her heart pounding, she ran to her grandmother's side. As it turned out, there was nothing wrong with Mère Monia. She was simply deathly afraid of the darkness.

"It felt like I was falling into a black hole and the further I fell, the more I could not breathe," she confessed to Ghislaine later, after she was calm again.

This night, as Ghislaine lay awake thinking, she could hear her grandmother's soft snoring. She smiled, comforted. Mère Monia's snoring was one of the house's nightly sounds, one which Ghislaine had grown accustomed to over the years. As if on cue, Monia broke wind loudly.

There had been a time when Monia's flatulence embarrassed and maddened her, but tonight she simply began to laugh. And she could not stop laughing as the sounds continued. *How could it be that this small, plump little old lady could produce so much wind?*

But no amount of her grandmother's noise could draw her thoughts fully from the wonder of that long, unbelievable night. Sleep was not to be had. Her mind and emotions were too alive. *Monsieur Claude Maillet.*

She whispered his name softly, playing with it with her mouth, as she would a tasty morsel. She wondered about him. Would he be handsome? Would he have a beard or a moustache?

She so wanted to be able to picture his face. She had been trying to imagine his face throughout the evening, since her mother had told her the good news.

It all seemed so wonderful. Four long years of patience and prayers…and now finally, an end in sight. The previous year had felt so bleak to her. In December, when she had turned twenty, she felt overcome by an apprehension and sadness, combined with a sense of unease that maybe nobody would ever ask for her hand in marriage. It only made her feel worse to know that her mother and grandmother were thinking the same thing, but would never say anything to her.

In the soft nightlight of the room, she looked over at the two solid *bois noir* wooden trunks in the corner of her bedroom, next to her matching wardrobe. She could almost smell the mothballs scattered at the bottom. These trunks were filled with a precious treasure – her trousseau. They represented a true labour of love, the painstaking and meticulous handiwork of the past four years since she left school.

They were all made from good quality cotton and beautifully finished with embroidery, cross-stitching and crochet. For her marital bedroom, Ghislaine had three sets of bed sheets with matching pillowcases and a beautiful patchwork bedspread. To show off her superb needlework capabilities, she had made two sets of coffee table cloths with matching side table cloths, as well as identical armchair headrest covers to decorate her sitting-room.

Whilst for those fortunate guests who would be invited to dinner with the newlywed couple, the two sets of superb dining room tablecloths with matching serviettes was a showpiece made with true determination. She wanted her new husband to be proud not only of her cooking abilities, but of the warmth and hospitality of their new lives. She could visualise her eighteenth birthday present from Mère Monia, the lovely antique silver candelabra, taking centre stage on her dining table.

Ghislaine had made four delicately embroidered nightdresses, and two matching gowns. One, a special white one, was the one she would wear on her wedding night. Even before she finished it, it was, and remained, her favourite. She wrapped some perfumed soap inside it, to keep it smelling nice, and occasionally she would sprinkle it with a few drops of Eau-de-Cologne. She considered that nightdress her special companion. They would share a special journey together, the first time that she would spend a night sleeping in a bed with a man. That thought had always troubled her, there seemed to be such a grey area about the whole thing.

Would she feel ashamed to be wearing just a nightdress and sharing a bed with a man? But he would be her husband, so why should she feel shy or ashamed to be next to him? It would surely take a lot of getting used to, being a married lady. A married lady! That thought sounded so nice. Then she shuddered, thinking of the part of this whole episode which she truly dreaded. Though customary, she found it appalling that early in the morning following her wedding night, *lev lasanm* would occur.

Her own mother and her new mother-in-law would come to them and ask permission to inspect her bedclothes and bed linen, to confirm that she had been a virgin on her wedding night. Just how are they supposed to know that I was a virgin by just looking at the bed linen? She shivered.

Surely by sharing a bed with a man means that a young girl is no longer a virgin? The bedclothes and linen are of no importance! Or are they?

Ghislaine remembered a wedding she attended a few years back, and a conversation she overheard between two ladies who had had a number of drinks too many. "She is looking radiant," one had said watching the bride dancing with her new husband. "Oh yes," the other had replied, "but we know the real test will come tonight! Tonight, in bed! She will have to become his wife! We know what happens if he does not find it there! Oh yes, we know, don't we." They had giggled, like it was some closely guarded and mischievous secret.

She remembered how puzzled she had been by that revelation. What had they meant? And what was supposed to happen in bed? What was that 'red evidence' they kept referring to? And what did they mean by the bride's reputation and that of her family being sullied if they do not find that red evidence? What red evidence?

It was on that night that she learned all about *lev lasanm,* as those two guests, oblivious that they had a listener, kept on rambling about the customs and traditions. She had almost felt sorry for the young bride who was clearly enjoying the dancing, unaware of the night of uncertainty in front of her. She obviously had no clue about it.

Ghislaine shook her head, clearing her mind of the image. No, she would think only of wonderful, happy things. She conjured up an image of herself walking slowly up the aisle on the arm of her father, her long white veil trailing behind. She could see Mère Monia wearing her special blue dress, the one she had repeatedly told her she was saving for her big day.

The small tears which she felt sliding down her cheeks were soft and light, and seemed to be telling her to believe in it now. *Soon the waiting will be over. You will have your own husband and your own home.* It was no longer just a dream, or a heartfelt wish, but a reality. Soon she would become *Madame Ghislaine Maillet.*

It was early November. Anna sighed as she gazed at the bay sleeping peacefully under the soft glow of the moonlight. *The calm before the storm.*

She knew that by the next full moon the scene before her would be completely different. December at Beau Vallon is the start of the ferocious North-East monsoon.

As she looked upon her beloved bay, she rested in the embrace of an enormous branch of driftwood which had washed ashore during the storms of the previous year's monsoon, and was now partially covered with sand, making it a very comfortable back rest. As the bay's water lapped gently on the beach, she closed her eyes and relished the peacefulness as all around her the sounds of the night whispered soothing melodies.

Her thoughts drifted back over the many events of the last four months since her birthday, especially the latest happy affair, the wedding proposal which Ghislaine had received. She remembered vividly the happiness and pride illuminating Mère Monia's face when she had told them the good news. "Ghislaine is very lucky to be marrying into such a good family," she claimed with a beaming smile of satisfaction, typical of a very proud and dignified grandmother about to marry off her first granddaughter.

Of course, her reaction had been quite different a few weeks before, when Albert had informed her that he had given his permission for Anna to become a nurse. Then, her face had turned stony, followed by a long silence during which her expression grew increasingly sad and reproachful. Finally, she sighed, her head shaking in disbelief…

Next to the driftwood, a tiny white sand crab had been at work for quite a while now, digging himself a home. A tedious task, becoming more strenuous as the hole got deeper, because his tiny claws could carry very little sand from the bottom at any one time. But he looked determined as he darted down the hole, which was about the same size as his body, only to surface a few seconds later with another small pinch of sand. This was carefully piled up into a white heap next to the opening of the hole, creating something resembling an open door, next to the entrance of his new home. Opening her eyes, Anna became aware of the work going on near her. As she watched her tiny companion at work, she made a mental note to walk on the other side of the driftwood when she got up.

Still, her thoughts remained on her grandmother's disapproval and she spoke softly to her little companion. "Never mind. Maybe one day she will be proud of me as well."

She watched as the little crab stopped his work and stared at her, as if he clearly understood what she had just said, and was prepared to stop building his new home to listen to what she needed to tell him. "At least Ghislaine's news has brought her happiness and joy," she said aloud. Even in the quietude of the beach, her voice was not convincing. Deep inside, her heart was saying something different. She wished that Mère Monia could have been happy for her too, she wished that she had received her grandmother's blessing to follow her path. *It was just too much to expect...*

Anna knew that in their society, girls from her background did not go out to work. It was just not done. Only girls from black families went into service or took up jobs on the plantation. White girls like her were meant to stay at home awaiting a marriage proposal, or enter the convent as nuns.

Those who did neither always ended up as sad spinsters. They had to rely on male family members to support them, if they did not find work as a lady's maid or a governess. However, Anna could not feel sad for herself for long. She was too consumed with joy for her cousin. She pictured Ghislaine's smiling face and thought about the changes this wedding proposal had brought for her cousin. Within a month of receiving the beautiful red rose letter, and Claude's subsequent Sunday visits to Lionet's house, Ghislaine seemed to completely blossom into a very proud, happy and confident young lady, ready to embark on this long awaited journey.

"It was love at first sight," Ghislaine had told her excitedly as they sat sipping tea under the shade of the big *zanmalak* tree in Tonton Lionet's garden a few weeks after Claude's first visit. "I am so very happy, Anna. Deliriously happy."

She did not even mention Anna's news. Anna could not help but feel that her cousin considered her prospect of becoming a nurse like something sad and ugly that would simply cease to be if not talked about aloud; it was going to leave a bad stain on the family name as young ladies like them were not meant to go to work. Anna sensed that Ghislaine wanted to avoid the subject entirely for fear it might reflect badly on her own reputation. Of course, Anna did not say anything about these feelings. She kept her disappointment and sorrow to herself, smiling instead as she kissed her cousin's cheek, wishing her a future full of happiness.

"My wedding day has been set for Saturday the twenty-third of July next year," Ghislaine blurted excitedly. "Of course, I will get engaged first, which will be on New Year's day."

Anna was thrilled with the path she had chosen. So why was this feeling of worthlessness engulfing her again, just as it had that afternoon when she had realised that Ghislaine, the person she had been so close to all her life, was abandoning her. In her heart, she had hoped that Ghislaine would understand her desire for something different. She had hoped she would take her side, as they were of the same generation, with only a few years difference in their age. But alas, it was not to be, and it left Anna feeling rejected and very lonely.

It was at these times, when her emotions were in turmoil that Anna turned to nature for strength. Sitting alone on the empty beach, poor, lonely Anna opened her heart to nature, seeking the friendship and closeness of its power and grace, seeking its wisdom in analysing and understanding her emotions, until the answers could find their own way to her. She could not remember when she first found herself expressing her thoughts, feelings and opinions aloud to nature, to sand crabs, to trees, to the stars and the moon. She could not remember when nature did not embrace her.

Why do the ones I love and care for loathe me, just because I want something different? Am I really so different from others, just because my desires are different?

Her eyes drifted from the heavens to the direction of the Saint Roch church at the end of the bay, as if she was giving God yet another opportunity to speak to her feelings. With no response coming from the direction of the church, she looked back to nature and, slowly…slowly, they started to fill her heart…inch by inch. Nature answered her need. Nature answered her questions.

"Look deep within your soul, find your source of inner strength, it is your path to ascend above the sadness and the disappointment," the stars encouraged her. "Believe in yourself, believe in the guidance of your heart," the bay whispered to her. "Forgive and love those who cause you pain, it is your only way forward," the swaying tree branches counselled.

As she received her answers, she felt overwhelmed. She began to tremble as she hugged herself in the still night air, goose pimples erupting all over her skin. And still the answers came…vivid, clear, and genuine. "Love yourself…Love yourself…Love yourself."

The voices of nature shouted out to her, filling her soul to overflowing. She was overwhelmed and humbled in the presence of this overpowering force, this genuine, infinite love. It occurred to her that maybe God and Nature were one and the same. She looked again to the church and tears trickled down her cheeks.

Thank you she whispered, understanding that she had found her own way to God.

Earlier that same day at the atelier of La Residence, Louis was feeling frustrated. The metal chisel in his hand seemed to have taken on a life of its own. Louis' hands grew tired and weak, yet he was determined to succeed in this fourth attempt. As he chipped away at the block of wood on his work bench, his frustration exploded into anger. Suddenly, the chisel slipped. He saw what was happening as if it was happening to someone else. The sharp chisel dug deeply into the flesh of his left hand. Blood gushed crimson over the woodchips scattered on the work bench. "Damn!" he cried out as he hurled the blood-stained block of wood out of the atelier window. Grasping his wounded hand, he stormed off for La Residence.

"What in God's name is wrong with me?" Louis wondered as he stared at the white bandage on his left hand. He had avoided everyone's gaze at dinner, saying only that it had been a 'stupid and careless mistake.' But he knew better. Henri's comment that morning still echoed in his ears. "Have you lost your touch, mon frère, or is something clouding your imagination?"

He had smiled, but the truth was he felt lost, dulled in a strange way. Rather than competent, he felt unsure of himself. How long had he felt that way? He could no longer be sure when it began, this force seeping into his being, tightening around his chest, making him question why he had never noticed this weakness in his knees before. And now, even worse, completely destroying his appetite, so that a mere two spoonfuls of his favourite dish sated him completely.

Tonight, standing at his bedroom window, he gazed at the bay of Beau Vallon below yet another full moon. The stars lit the vast heavens like clusters of fiery diamonds. Louis drew a deep breath. *Damn it!* He knew he needed to do something, and to do it now. So, he decided to be true to himself. Fighting the feeling was only making it worse. He knew that he would have to face it. But how and where would he start?

Four months earlier, on another fateful full moon night, Louis had walked Anna home, and watched her disappear through the back door of her home. No sooner was she out of his sight than the questions started. *Why had she been out in the middle of the night on her own? What had driven her to such an action? Was he doing the right thing by keeping her secret? Should he try to find out what had prompted that action? Was it any of his business to try and find out why?*

At first, only questions, but soon enough they transformed themselves into deep concerns, and as he replayed the incident in his mind, those questions grew to become powerful feelings of anxiety and apprehension.

But why? He had felt only happiness when he heard her voice and saw her face over those past few Sundays.

What had triggered this fear? He had tried to sort out his feelings rationally, to piece together all the relevant events leading up to this moment. He remembered watching her every Sunday after mass, engrossed in conversation with a group of nuns, and he remembered seeing that same group of nuns going up the hill to her parent's home. But it had been the memory of his mother's comments on more than one occasion in the more distant past that had ignited his fear. "Therese is such a strict Catholic. I would not be at all surprised if one of her children becomes a nun or a priest."

Then *that* was at the heart of it! *Is she going to become a nun? Is life in the convent the right answer to whatever had been troubling her?* Even so, why did all that have to do with his fear and sadness?

There was no obvious answer, only that she was so different. Incomparable with other girls. For years, he had only looked at her as the daughter of their overseer, but now it was this *difference* which he had found out, which held his attention and was creating all these confusing emotions within him.

She'd been so at ease, sitting on the beach next to him in the middle of the night, in her plain cotton dress, with her hair hanging loose, and still smelling of the sea. There had been none of the coyness of other girls. He had detected only strength, certainty, and genuineness in her composure and yet so proper, sincere and correct. They had talked mostly about nature. Her voice and manner betrayed her passion for this natural world and, to his surprise, he had found his own feelings and love for nature echoing around him, like she was reading *him*, revealing his innermost thoughts.

Louis walked along the small footpath, traversing the green carpet of *patatran* creepers. He took a deep breath as his feet felt the powdery softness of the sand. Since *that* night, he had made it something of a habit to enjoy a walk along the beach on the night of the full moon. His path was always the same – straight in the direction of the driftwood.

"Please be careful, do not step on his home," Anna whispered with a welcoming smile as she pointed to the little crab hole next to where she sat.

He returned her smile. "Good evening," he said softly as he settled down into the sand. As soon as he saw her...as soon as he was in her presence, he felt as if a weight had been lifted from him. He felt relieved and happy, even as he kept his bandaged hand out of view.

Dawn. Christmas Eve. The first cock had crowed at exactly four in the morning, breaking the silence over the hills and valleys of Beau Vallon.

The North-West monsoon was already well settled in, having arrived just over three weeks earlier. Long, white rows of water danced upon the crest of each wave striking the shore. The sea was rough and choppy, with very high underwater currents, causing heavy displacement of sand and murky-looking water.

The wind blew strong and forcefully, in long heavy gushes, breaking down branches, and in some cases, whole trees, and ferrying salt sprays from the crashing waves from the beach to the green trees in the hills. Behind it, hundreds of bird nests littered the ground, exposing small lifeless bodies, and minute eggs of various sizes and colours. What was disaster for one creature was celebration for another. It was feasting times for the brown geckos darting between the fallen branches, in search of the defenceless eggs.

The North-West monsoon also heralded the start of the rainy season, a time of torrential tropical downpours and violent winds. In tandem, these two elements sent all the inhabitants of the northern coast of Mahé scurrying for shelter, praying for a temporary respite, and hoping for a roof and home still, once the storm ceased.

Every resident knew that the next sixty days would be trying and, at times, almost unbearable. Even so, the end of the year carried a feeling of thrill and excitement, mixed with anxiety and apprehension, at the sight of all the destruction it littered around their daily lives. The calm periods in between those storms were always pleasantly sweet and reassuringly comforting.

On this crisp and cool December morning, there was a sense of real anticipation in the air. In the backyard outside Albert's cottage, an enormous slab of rock rested on a small knee-high wall, where it had been mounted the day before. A pair of sharp, long and gleaming knives rested in the centre of the rock slab. The dim, early morning sun glimmered off the blades, an air of menacing finality abounded. Alongside the man-made altar, a large, black cauldron rested rigidly upright on tripods of rocks, brimming with rainwater from the previous night's downpour.

Anna yawned and hugged herself against the cool as she made her way to the outside kitchen. The yard was still very wet. Still, she smiled to discover that her stack of cinnamon firewood tucked on the side of the kitchen floor had been spared and was still dry. As she waited for the kettle to boil, she relished the brisk morning air, soothed by the repetitive echoes of waves crashing forcefully on the beach down in the bay.

This comforting melody, which had heralded the beginning of the monsoon was now at its peak, and reverberated throughout the hills of Beau Vallon.

She could *smell* Christmas in the air, that unique smell which only Beau Vallon could produce. She loved Christmas, but this particular Christmas was special, for the New Year held a brighter promise, one which made her heart skip when she imagined herself in the nurse's uniform she would wear when she began at Victoria Hospital. *Nurse Savy*. She smiled, whispering her own name into the water vapour cloud that formed before her lips. *Nurse Savy*. Meanwhile, the cinnamon branches were burning bright red under the black kettle on the stone tripod, crackling as the smears of oil trapped under the thick bark of the wood ignited with the heat, releasing their aromatic scent into the morning air.

Therese surveyed the eager faces of her family as they gathered around the dining table, patiently awaiting their coffee mugs. She uttered a silent prayer for the rain to stay away as she painstakingly meted out the dried *cassava galet*.

This was the longest and most exhausting day of the year. It was also the most festive. "Heaven help us if it rains like yesterday," she sighed to her family. If it poured like the day before, their task would be made even more monumental.

"It will be a literal blood bath," Albert agreed, as he visualised the bright red rivulets streaming down from his man-made altar. Not for the last time, Therese prayed again for the rain to stay away.

In one strong, quick slash, the sharp knife severed the jugular vein. The high-pitched squeals halted immediately, replaced by low grunting sounds which faded to silence in a few, short agonising minutes. It had only taken one quick thrust to the thoracic cavity, followed by the sudden gush, spurting out with force, drenching Albert's hands, arms and torso as he withdrew the knife and positioned a container to collect the stream of steaming blood.

Under the black cauldron, coconut shells and cinnamon branches burned, creating a thick haze of aromatic heat around the big pot, whilst the bubbles from the water boiled and bubbled, releasing steam vapours in a straight column that dispersed in a cloud of rapidly cooling moisture.

Albert wiped the perspiration from his brow as he dipped the container again and again into the boiling cauldron, and splashed the lifeless carcass with a river of scorching hot water. When the skin was fully soaked, he skilfully scraped off all of the visible hair, firmly holding his knife as it relentlessly worked its way up and down, in between the splashes of the boiling water, until the skin was rendered to a smooth and pinkish-white texture.

Meanwhile, in a big galvanised oval *bake* lined with an assortment of old bed linen, five-month-old Eliane made happy noises as her three siblings, Joseph, Didier and Maryse, paused as they played hide-and-seek around the *bake* so they could clap and sing to her. Eight-year-old Chantal watched her younger siblings with a broad smile on her face. Those five members of the family were clearly enjoying themselves under the cottage's veranda, lost in their games and blind to the commotion and hard work taking place in the backyard.

It was Christmas night. Chantal had told them why that was so special. She told them about the baby Jesus and how he was born outside in a cow's stable, because there was no room inside the inn for them, and his mother, *La Sainte Vierge Marie*, had to lay him in a manger filled with straw, because there was no cot and mattress in the stable.

"Didn't it hurt, sleeping on straw?" a pensive-looking Maryse asked.

"No, he was fine, his mother had put some cloths on top of the straw," she reassured her sister. "Look, it was just like in Eliane's bake. The straw was at the bottom and the cloths on top." She lifted Eliane onto her lap and showed them the inside of the bake. They peered inside, imagining straw at the bottom covered by bed linen, until they were satisfied that baby Jesus had not been hurt while he slept in the manger. As the story went on, Chantal and her young chorus sang and chanted every single Christmas hymn they could remember, deliriously happy that Christmas was here once again.

Unlike the younger children, for whom the day was all games and songs, for Anna, Antoine and Maxime, their day had been extremely exhausting – and it was far from over. Their arms ached from carrying the sloshing weight of bucket after bucket from the river, over half a mile away, from collecting and carrying the heavy bundles of firewood, and from the work of keeping the water in the cauldron at boiling point. All that in addition to their everyday chores – cleaning, fetching and tidying after their meticulous father. With all that, the enthusiastic, if somewhat off-key singing of Christmas hymns coming from the veranda did little to bring them joy. Their exhausted and aching bodies told them that the thing to be happy about on Christmas was that it only came once a year.

"More firewood!"

Again, they dutifully stacked cinnamon firewood under the cauldron, bringing the water to boiling point, this time for the special purpose of cooking the black pudding. All the young leaves which they had collected early that morning from the sweet-potato patch had been finely minced together with handfuls of parsley and thyme, mixed into the container of blood, and seasoned with salt and black pepper.

The mixture was then poured down the long tubes of intestines which they had cleaned to squeaky perfection, turning them inside out in the flowing stream of the river, then scrubbing and scraping using fresh limes and hard rock salt, whilst paying special attention to getting them thoroughly clean without breaking the skin.

Once filled, the tubes were tied into big loops and hung from one main vakoa rope. Cooking black pudding demands skill; the outer skin must first harden, without tearing and spilling its fluid content.

Albert held the end of the rope, lowered the strings of black pudding into the boiling water for a few short seconds and then immediately removed them. They cooled for a few seconds and the procedure was repeated again and again, until the outer skin was cooked hard enough to stay in the boiling water. The whole process took well over two hours.

By mid-morning, it was the thick square pieces of pork skin and fat that had taken possession of the now empty black cauldron. Antoine had fashioned a young *bwa dir* tree into a 70-inch stirring pole so that he could keep the pieces of skin from sticking together, stirring and churning for hours, until all the fat was released and the skin turned into a light, golden-brown crackling, with a crispy texture and a succulent flavour.

Albert and his three elder children breathed a collective sigh of relief as Saint Roch's midday bells struck twelve. Their hard work was done – and the rain had mercifully held off the entire time. An array of large bamboo baskets lined with green banana leaves were placed on the stone altar. The severed head of the pig was in the first basket, looking curiously peaceful. It was destined as the customary Christmas present to Albert's oldest and favourite worker, Msye Julien, whose small thatched hut was not far from their cottage. He was their closest neighbour, although the last eighteen months had seen him spending most of his time aboard the Alouette as the *gardyen*.

The second basket held an abundance of appetising-looking crackling. The aroma from the bundles of steaming black pudding loops rose from the next basket. Two tall and pot-bellied earthenware jars next to the altar held the freshly-salted pork portions which would see the family through the bad-weather days, when fresh fish supplies were scarce. The fourth basket boasted a few prime choice cuts, some of which would be delivered to Lionet's house later that day, and Therese's special Christmas dinner joint, which would become a delicious pot roast later that afternoon. All was on course for the most festive night of the year.

All ten members of the Savy family were in their Sunday clothes. Even baby Eliane, cooing in her bake next to the dining table, was in her pink dress. There was an air of excitement buzzing in the room, and everyone was happy as they took their seats around the old dining table.

Handmade embroidery decorated the white, sun-bleached tablecloth that covered the table, covering the scratches and stains of time. A vase of freshly cut flowers from the cottage garden occupied the centre of the table, flanked by two candelabras. Everything looked and smelled clean, even the wooden floor sparkled from all of Therese's determined efforts with her *mangliye* polish and coconut husk brush earlier that afternoon.

The age-old tradition handed down from their French ancestors of setting an extra place was dutifully observed, as it had been by generations of Savy families. The empty seat signified remembrance of family members no longer of this world, as well as a warm welcome reserved for any unexpected stranger who might happen upon this festive Christmas night.

"Let us say grace," Albert announced. Each member of the family lifted their hands to those next to them. With hands held, Albert thanked the Lord for the bounty of their table and for the new life cooing in pink in her bake on the floor at their feet.

Therese was beaming with pride and joy as she looked at her family. She felt the fullness of her maternal love and responsibility fulfilled as she looked upon the Christmas dinner she had lovingly prepared for this special night. Her thoughts turned briefly to the trauma of Eliane's birth, and she shuddered at the horrible consequences averted. With fervent gratitude, she uttered a silent prayer, thanking God once more for the gift of her life, and that of her daughter, for allowing them both to be here on this Christmas night surrounded by their family.

Much later that same evening, at the far end of the bay of Beau Vallon, worshippers all sat quietly and patiently as they listened to the vast silence that followed those last echoes of the bell's peal. As the seconds turned slowly into minutes, each believer breathed in that profound silence mixed with the heavy scent of burning wax from the hundreds of candles alight in the small church. Saint Roch was bursting at the seams, the congregation overflowing onto the veranda and even the lawn. It was that kind of a night. All manner of headgear, elaborate and simple according to status and means, adorned the head of each member of the congregation, while the orange glow of the candles reflected a peaceful expectation in all the faces, despite their colour or origin.

'*Les anges dans nos campagnes.*' The faraway voices of the choir broke the silence and grew stronger as they circled the outside of the church in procession. They entered through the arch doorway of the church at exactly midnight, just as they reached that verse in the hymn, '*Ils annoncent la naisance du liberateur d'Israel,*' and simultaneously the sea of humanity with hearts full of glee joined abundantly in the chorus of '*Gloria, Gloria, Gloria in excelsis deo.*'

A ten-year-old altar boy led the procession. The single flame he carried, symbolic of the light and love that the birth of Jesus brought into the world. A few paces behind him, flanked by two more altar boys carrying the smoking thurible of burning incense, Père Valer cradled the statuette of the baby Jesus in his arm. In the left hand corner of the church, before the steps leading to the altar, a manger scene decorated with green coconut leaves, ferns and foliage awaited the arrival of baby Jesus.

Each congregant witnessed this magnificent procession, and it evoked in him or her the serenity and virtue of this special night, this powerful night that saw the beginning of everything they believed in and abided by. There were many tears rolling down the faces of the singing congregation, as their eyes and voices followed Père Valer, as he gently laid baby Jesus in the wooden manger and then headed to the altar to start the biggest Mass of the year.

As the congregation held its breath and awaited Père Valer's ascension to the altar, one of those notorious midnight mass calamities occurred. As the hymn ended and the church descended into total silence, one of the many *not so proper* Catholic members of the congregation, who only came to mass on Christmas night and who had been celebrating Christmas with his mug of *baka* since daybreak, suddenly lost his balance and banged his forehead on the wooden bench in front of him. The booming sound amplified around the church, as everyone's attention turned in his direction and he clambered to his feet, emitting two loud and consecutive farts, stinking his fellow churchgoers in the pungency of decaying baka as he shouted, *Alleluia, Alleluia!*

He was promptly escorted out of the church by two *proper* Catholic members of the congregation, who held their breath as they hurried him through the sea of red faces, each trying their utmost to contain the laughter in their throats.

"*Joyeux Noel*, Monsieur du Barré," Anna said softly, offering her hand to Louis as the members of the du Barré family greeted their overseer and his family on the veranda of Saint Roch.

No one else there could have guessed that a special friendship existed between those two; no one but they could have noted that their hands had lingered for that extra moment, just as nobody noticed Louis cradling his hand, the hand she had touched, and occasionally pressing it to his cheek as they made their way home. Why should they have noticed? They were engrossed in the serene joy of the early hours of Christmas day, of walking along the length of the strikingly beautiful beach at low tide, their hearts filled with the profound emotion of having participated in the birthday celebrations of their Saviour.

The sky was full of stars, with a new moon softly illuminating the mountains and valleys. Some still hummed the melodies of the Christmas hymns as the waves broke against the sand, mingling their echoes and ferrying it up the hills. Their candles and lanterns flickered in the wind blowing in from the island of Silhouette, sleeping peacefully across the bay.

It was a beautiful and intense picture, one that gave rise to such remarkable emotions as to make each person feel strangely mystified. The image, the scent, the sounds, the faith, the experience...all too delicate, sensitive and touching, the fear of losing it being almost unbearable.

The moment was so fraught, so magnificent, so transient...the stream of flickering lights and bodies strolling along the deserted beach in the pre-dawn light...it was beyond mere words. There was a presence there, a presence that was almost as real as touch, bonding everyone, filling their hearts to overflowing and creating a closeness which was, at once, other-worldly, and yet the most natural thing in the world. This was Christmas for the residents of Beau Vallon, black and white, servants and masters alike. Tonight, their prayers had been answered. God had spared them from torrential rains and heavy winds, on this the holiest day of celebration.

In a few hours, the first light of dawn would creep slowly up from behind *Krev Ker* mountain, everyone would awaken to a day of joy and celebration. A small cup of strong, freshly-ground black coffee sweetened with wild honey would kick-start it, followed later in the morning by the smell of garlic and onions frying dominating the breeze, as the appetising aroma of pork being prepared for lunch surfaced from every single outdoor kitchen. There would be joy and anticipation in all the dwellings scattered under the canopies of coconut palm, as the traditional white cucumber salad with watercress and red onions took its prominent place on the dining table.

By mid afternoon, the big earthenware jars of homemade brew, prepared two months before, would have long lost their foaming heads, whilst the adults of the households would be light-headed and intoxicated from its potent alcoholic powers. Christmas day also meant visits from neighbours, and therefore more homemade brew being consumed, as well as the traditional Christmas fruit, the pineapple. The juicy and succulent part of the fruit would be served with black coffee, while its coarse skin was reserved for an intriguing use. This would end up chopped into chucky bits and placed in the potent residue at the bottom of those earthenware jars, followed by lots of honey and boiling water. After all, New Year also needed to be celebrated in style!

Much later, when the light from the bonfire replaced the fading rays of sunset, the songs of marten birds, high up in the branches of the trees, slowly heralded the night, triggering an exodus of villagers, young and old alike to the bonfire. Before long, the sound of the birds faded as well. The silence was brief, taken up by the beat of the drums echoing throughout the village, stirring and reinvigorating the African blood, already intoxicated from their potent homemade brew, into active motion.

Bare feet stamped the bare soil around the bonfire, perspiration flowed freely in the humidity of the night, and the bouncy skirts of the wide-hipped and very well-endowed ebony women were raised waist high in rhythm to the beat of the drums.

Bare thighs were exposed in suggestive forms to their men, as they in turn circled them in response, hands on hips, emitting high-pitched shrills, and groans of a sexual nature, as well as great joy, old pains, and the remembrance of their dying culture, all the way into the early hours of another new day.

Christmas came and went in a haze of glorious sunsets, heavy winds and torrential downpours, which did not manage to dampen Ghislaine's soaring soul as the anticipation of her approaching engagement approached. It rained all day and all night on the last day of December 1912, but somewhere, high up in the hills of Saint-Louis, a jubilant and passionate heart, in love for the first time, prayed it all away.

As the echoes of the six o'clock bells from Saint Roch rang out for the first time in 1913, the bright and glorious sunlight was already at work, illuminating the island of Mahé in its warm and radiant blessing. An early sunrise, evoking life beyond the emerald canopies of wet trees, penetrating through obstacles and swaying branches, headed for that yearning land. The soil of life was heavy with excess moisture. As dear Earth basked in the bright, warm rays, allowing them to penetrate deep within her open fissures, she sighed with fulfilment, exhaling back into the air the pure and deep fragrance of life's first *etensel*.

Distant rivers rushed, conjuring images of white cascading veils, as they rolled over the boulders of Saint Louis' mountain. Chirping *troutwel* darted back and forth to the ground, accompanied by an array of other small birds, welcoming the abundance of food exposed by the heavy rain and the drying effects of the sunshine.

Along the long winding driveway, approaching this grand old wooden house, the earth felt soft and spongy, with designs of minute empty streams in zigzag patterns, almost as though it had been made by a giant broom. Bordering the driveway, the white flowers of the *lys* plants hung their heavy heads towards the earth. Soon their weight would lessen, as the morning sun would lift their drooping necks once more on this, a brand new day of the New Year.

Standing in the centre of the big yard, the very old zanmalak tree with age-old bumps and nodules dominated the entrance to this picture. The house was old, worn by the passage of time and the perilous proximity of a climate so close to the equator. It had been built on dozens of stone pillars, strategically positioned to hold its main framework, while at the same time allowing a free flow of air underneath its floorboards to ventilate the house. It boasted a long and wide veranda, with sun-bleached wooden rails surrounding its whole frontage, as well as tall wooden lattice windows and a pair of heavy wooden doors.

Anna stood before the house and felt a serene tranquillity. There were memories here, Anna thought, as the majesty and nostalgia seemed to reach out and touch her. There was an intimacy here that seemed to embrace her, an atmosphere that she could almost touch with her bare hands. She had to blink her eyes, to know whether or not she was dreaming.

As she crossed the yard underneath the zanmalak tree, the cascading pink cloak of the *lantigonn* creepers in bloom which covered the massive boulder by the side of the house, seemed to take her breath away. The white-topped bushes of *boul de nez* looked so insignificant next to it. Anna smiled contentedly. *An absolute celebration of colour!* All around her, the vivid, tropical blooms lapped up the morning sun, perfuming the air with their delicate fragrance. She was simply entranced. But just then, the spell was broken as Samson darted merrily from behind the house, barking to Anna, and Ghislaine appeared through the open door with a broad smile. She rushed down the steps and embraced Anna in a big hug.

By late morning, the two cooks in the outdoor kitchen drew a deep breath of relief. They had created a lavish banquet of the scale that had never graced this house before. That did not stop Lionet from fretting and pacing up and down the veranda, checking his pocket watch, and pressing it to his ear to ensure that it was ticking properly. For the umpteenth time he surveyed the wooden posts of the veranda which had been beautifully decorated earlier by Florence, using green ferns and white flowers from her front garden.

At the same time he mentally went over the list of preparations again and again, reassuring himself that he had not forgotten anything. Meanwhile, around him on the veranda, an array of comfortable wooden armchairs with pretty headrest covers displaying the ladies' skills of crochet and cross-stitching, awaited the arrival of their distinguished guests.

Inside, in the coolness of the large sitting-room, tranquillity reigned. Not a speck of dust was visible on the highly polished wooden floor, not a chair nor table was out of place, not an ashtray or piece of silver was unpolished. The faint scent of floor polish mingled with that emanating from the roses in the tall vases, perfuming the room. Across the hall in Ghislaine's bedroom, the painstaking process of getting dressed was almost accomplished. Anna had outdone herself, mostly in keeping Ghislaine calm.

"Let me," she said easily, gently taking a string of pearls from Ghislaine's trembling hands and fastening it around her neck. Then she smiled at their shared reflection in the mirror. "Now, you are truly ready."

Tears welled in Ghislaine's eyes as she wrapped her arms around Anna and gave her a long, sisterly hug. They both knew that soon their lives and their relationship would take very different paths.

It was three in the afternoon. The moment Ghislaine felt she had been waiting for her entire life had finally arrived. Across the sitting room, Claude Maillet sat upright in his navy suit and tie, waiting for the signal from his father, seated next to him on the sofa. On the wooden coffee table in the middle of the sitting-room, a large plate full of white rose petals was centre stage, sitting delicately on the crochet cover, bearing the treasure of this very special day, the gold engagement ring with a bright white stone.

It was quiet enough to hear one's heartbeat, which Ghislaine was quite certain she could hear echoing in her breast. She clasped her hands on her lap, tighter and tighter, trying to keep them from trembling. She was vaguely conscious of her father sitting next to her, but she did not dare turn and look at him. Lionet nodded to Andre Maillet, whose stiff moustache looked as though it had been starched for just such an occasion as this. Andre Maillet placed his hand on his son's shoulder. In a voice as stiff as his father's moustache, Claude looked straight at Lionet.

"Monsieur Savy, I am here to seek your permission to become engaged to your daughter."

"I grant you my permission, Monsieur Maillet," Lionet answered.

Claude arose, walked to the coffee table, and picked up the ring from the plate of petals. He crossed slowly to the other sofa, knelt down on one knee in front of Ghislaine and placed the ring on the fourth finger of her moist left hand. Then, raising her hand to his lips, he gently kissed it, the smell of cold sweat and Eau-de-Cologne slowly infiltrating his nostrils. So, it was done.

Later that afternoon, the newly-engaged couple, much more relaxed and displaying broad, happy smiles, swirled across the sitting-room to the rhythm of a Creole waltz. They were trying to have a nice time and to enjoy the traditional first dance without disobeying protocol by holding one another too close.

Ghislaine, with her head held proudly high, and her long black hair delicately coiffed in a large chignon, looked every inch the most resplendent bride-to-be. The two glasses of wine she had consumed over lunch, when being toasted by her father and prospective father-in-law, brightened her naturally rosy complexion and illuminated her sparkling eyes, making her quite a picture in the arms of her tall, dark and tanned fiancé.

The parents and future in-laws were filled with pride and joy as they looked at their offspring. But, it was Mère Monia's gaze that was the most striking, in fact overpowering, as the afternoon light cast its glow on her kind, soft face, illuminating a unique form of complete happiness. As the waltz gathered momentum and Ghislaine smiled at Claude with tenderness and love, Monia felt the fluttering of her 85-year-old heart.

It seemed like only yesterday that she too was a young bride, and the memories of tender moments, untouched by time, floated in her vision once again. Just like the clear manifestation of wild, passionate nights, reaching out and touching her soul with their vividness and intensity. She could feel her husband's arms holding her tightly, capturing and immersing her in his manly scent, as her heart accelerated to the rhythm of his own. She looked deep into his beautiful ebony eyes and smiled at him once more, just as she had done then. For this brief, fleeting moment, she was once more that young woman, that sensual, alluring and beautiful young woman.

CHAPTER 6

The Little Mermaid

The pier jutted out from Port Victoria, clearly visible from the old and weather-worn boat building yard at *Le Chantier*. There, the rows of wooden sheds, filled with the various export commodities, formed the hub of the Seychelles' economy. It was a concrete reminder of how reliant these islands were on the overseas markets, and how precarious and volatile those markets could be. Their few export products, insignificant in quantities, were always swamped by the vastness of those bigger and greedier countries around them. Only the quality of the Seychelles' merchandise tilted the scales in her favour, giving her a small but not insignificant edge.

On this gloriously sunny and calm May morning, the azure waters of the port were blindingly transparent, with even the white coral core of Mahé Island exposed. Lying in a perfect horizontal curve, just four miles out in front of the port, a collection of small green islands stood as a faithful and protective guard along the entire frontage of the port. These islands created the inner haven of sanctuary, affording safety from the heaviest winds and most violent waves.

Towering over them all, the ever-observant gaze of the spectacular and majestic mountain of *Trois Frères* floated in silence. Standing 3,000 feet above sea level, this densely luxurious emerald mass magically drew man's gaze to its mesmerising beauty. Massive cascading slopes of grey granite emerged at random, co-existing peacefully among the deep, sensual green ravines of this exotic jewel, which was governed at its summit by the three gracious mounts evoking its name, safeguarding dutifully this tiny defenceless little town and port at its feet.

At least, that was one perspective on this natural environment. It was not the one being pondered by Police Constable Lafortune as he strode purposefully along the sun-baked clay of Port Victoria's roads, making clear with every step his undisputed authority, protection and presence among the oxcarts, rickshaws and pedestrians in his territory.

He was not a man who could go unnoticed. He was large-framed, with broad muscular shoulders and an Olympian pair of ebony legs which were further enhanced by the smart, heavily-starched, calf-length khaki uniform which creaked from his steely, British-trained march.

Beneath the thick felt police hat, sweat collected and then flowed down his scalp and onto his clean shaven and beautifully-sculptured African slave descendant's face. His physical presence was not sufficient in his eyes to establish the control he sought to establish. His hard and imperious stare surveyed his territory. He could feel the weight of his truncheon, which had known the backs of numerous trouble-makers, held securely in his hand, ready to command obedience and respect, as he would make them bow to His Majesty's insignia he carried proudly on his chest.

Earlier that morning, an impressive-looking British India Steamship, now peacefully anchored, had announced her arrival to the islanders with three sharp blasts of her siren. She was breathing out those last remaining puffs of smoke from her chimneys, momentarily clouding the skies over Port Victoria's horizontal green guards of honour as an army of small barges and pirogues ferried to and forth, bulging with cargo, illustrating the monthly buzzing and exciting activity which accompanied each visit of the steamer.

From his vantage position at the boat building yard, Henri observed the activities of the port with satisfaction, happy in the knowledge that all of the du Barré's crops had been duly delivered to the agents the week before. He could see them now, looking very official in their long white trousers and long-sleeved white shirts, complemented by that unmistakeable hard-rimmed white hat. They would be shuffling through piles of papers, while simultaneously screaming orders to the shirtless black labourers glistening with sweat. They were merciless in their actions, endeavouring to get all the incoming cargo off the steamer and all of Seychelles' products safely loaded. It was a few days of non-stop hustle and bustle, of endless barefoot and grunting processions by scores of muscle-bound bare backs heaped with the weight of the tightly-packed gunny bags, trotting from the wooden sheds to the barges on one side of the pier.

They offloaded their heavy burdens, releasing a huge sigh of relief as they stretched their backs, before crossing over to the other side of the pier where the incoming bales and wooden casts of merchandise from the steamer stood in piles. The trot back to those wooden sheds was always harder, the weight more intense, and the very same length of pier seemed twice its original length. It was a sad, yet an indispensable sight, crucial for the survival of the Seychelles' fragile economy, but hard to watch as humans were turned into beasts of burden.

Families living in the vicinity of Port Victoria and even some coming from villages far out of town, or just anybody going about their daily business, would have heard about the arrival of the steamer. Over the next few days they would make a point of visiting near the pier and observe this monthly treat, which always looked so tall and massive among the schooners and pirogues around her.

There would be happiness in the knowledge that the stores of the Indian and Chinese shopkeepers had been replenished and, for now, life could go on undisturbed. The worry of having enough supplies was the most difficult burden of living on an isolated island.

In addition to the supplies, the steamer brought the added pleasure of news from the outside world, letters and parcels from relatives who had long left those shores. However, by far the most exciting aspect of the steamer's arrival was catching a glimpse of the glamorous passengers disembarking for a few days onshore while the steamer was in port. Always so very well dressed and exotic in their own way, and of different nationalities. Indian ladies in vividly colourful saris with elaborate embroidery and massive golden jewels dangling from their ears and nose, and bangles on their wrist and ankles. Their male counterparts looked stern and unapproachable, with thick beards and moustaches that curled upwards, their heads covered by massive bejewelled turbans. European travellers, on the other hand, were more demure, but heavily covered from the sun with wide-brimmed hats, parasols and dresses that reached down to their ankles.

Those few days when the steamer was in port were also profitable but extremely arduous for the rickshaw drivers, as those visitors would hire them for the whole day to visit the island. For the children in the villages along the coast it was hugely exciting to see the visitors waving at them.

Overall, the monthly arrival of the 'B.I.' as the islanders had fondly named their visitor, was a time of heightened happiness to be savoured in the life of the island.

Henri looked across the yard as Louis surveyed the selection of wood to be used in the next phase of La Sirène. His love for his brother had only grown over the months they had worked on this new project. They had debated, argued and laughed over big and small issues, both coming to the conclusion that they were perfectionists. Papa and the Captain had observed them with amusement and growing admiration as they approached their shared goal – a better schooner.

It gave Henri great joy to see Louis happy again. He had even heard Louis singing in the atelier as he shaped the mermaid sculpture which was to grace the bow of the new schooner. Yes, it was good to see him happy again. It had weighed on Henri at the time when Louis was clearly struggling, and it had pained him deeply to realize that Louis did not feel able to fully confide in him.

He had never imagined something could come between the two of them and yet, with each sunset, it became quite clear that such a barrier did exist. He watched his brother in the atelier, evening after evening, *knowing* he was struggling, but found himself unable to do anything. He knew that his brother's unease was the cause of the accident with the chisel. Louis referred to it as 'a stupid accident,' but Henri knew better.

But then, as if by the magic of the full moon on the night of the accident, Louis returned to his usual smiling self. Henri was overjoyed. Although he could not understand exactly what had happened to return his brother, he hoped that the day would come when Louis would share with him the inner turmoil he had endured. Some day...

A couple of days after the arrival of the B.I., an exhausted Anna cut a path from the hospital through the Botanical Garden. Two weeks of night duty shifts were over and she was looking forward to two days off. Though achingly tired, she always felt rejuvenated by the garden, where the bright May sunshine played with the fan-shaped leaves of the *latanyen* and *coco de mer* palm trees and the sweet music of the *katiti*s wafted through the sweet air. Rather than follow the path the other nurses took, which joined the main road of Mont Fleurie at the bottom of the garden, Anna turned inland, to its middle.

She sought that peaceful oasis where the small stream flowing down settled into a rounded pool, among the small moss-covered rocks and silent grey granite boulders, where the wild orchids and bougainvillea bushes stood alongside the giant palm trees and boulders. It was more than the beauty of nature that quickened her heart, that day. It was her anticipation that he would be there, waiting for her.

Even though she knew he would be there as always, sitting patiently on his favourite rock by the small pool, her heart still skipped a beat when she came around the path and saw him. Here, in their shared oasis, their private Eden, they were free from the eyes of all Mahé.

Their first meeting had been accidental. Anna had been walking along the path with another nurse and as they joined the main road of Mont Fleurie, she spotted Louis walking from Victoria, going in the opposite direction. She smiled to herself. She was not surprised at all the following day to see him cheerfully strutting along the path. That was the day that they found their hideaway. It had been their sanctuary ever since. During the past four months, their meetings had become more frequent, sometimes as often as twice a week. They always coincided with Anna's hospital schedule, and Louis' demands as skipper of the Alouette.

Their *friendship*, *relationship*, *bond*, call it what you will, had been formed on that fateful night a year earlier and had blossomed into the highlight of their lives. Intuitively, Anna felt completely safe with Louis. She spoke with him as a dear, trusted friend. The fact that they were opposite sexes and were not, by tradition and Catholic teaching, to be together without chaperone, did not inhibit them at all.

Of everyone, he was the one to hear her love of her new-found profession. He understood her enthusiasm and encouraged her. He thought she was a wonderful and fulfilled *person*, not a member of the inferior sex.

This respect touched her deeply. Just as she shared her love of nursing with him, he shared his own dreams with her; his love for the sea and what it represented to him, his passion for sculpting, his love of music, particularly the piano. His openness allowed her to see those passions through his eyes. She began to understand the kind of feeling a man gets, slightly different from a woman's, but equally profound.

The only shadow on the happy innocence of their friendship was the sadness at having to conceal it. It should not have felt like a bad secret to be ashamed of, but something to rejoice over, which is what it felt like in their hearts. But that was one of the sad aspects of their society…it denied as many opportunities as it created.

On this balmy first day of July 1913, Louis removed the cloth from his masterful creation. He smiled as he gazed into her upturned face. So real, so lifelike. He ran his hand along the contours of her neck, her outstretched arms. He stroked her long hair as it flowed into, and became, the scales on her back, and finished off in the fan-shaped, upturned tail. Each time he saw her, he saw her anew. Each time, exactly as his vision of her had been on that full moonlit night. This had been a labour of love which he began in earnest soon after the wound in his hand had healed. As the block of wood took shape, he shared this happiness with Anna. During their meetings, he explained the progress and helped her understand his feelings as the wood was transformed into this beautiful creation.

As he explained all this to her, he watched the emotions show on her face, knowing that she was only too familiar with the scene he was describing. She could close her eyes as he spoke and see not only the mermaid take shape in the atelier, but an image of herself that full-mooned night when she was on the beach. Louis glanced at his hand, remembering the day he injured himself. More than the pain of the chisel cutting into his flesh, he remembered the utter joy and relief he experienced that night when Anna had shared with him her excitement about being a nurse in the coming year.

"Then you are not to be a nun?" he asked, barely able to form the words.

She looked at him curiously, as if to ask him where he'd ever got such a notion. But she didn't say anything. She simply smiled and shook her head. And with that, a weight that had felt like a beached ship was lifted from his heart. He could not, of course, outwardly display his relief and joy. Somehow, he managed to simply nod and say, "I'm sure you will be a very good nurse." Her smiled broadened.

It was only their second meeting, but already it felt as though they had known each other forever.

In addition to his masterpiece sculpture, Louis had created a miniature replica. As he picked up the smaller, perfect image, he kissed it affectionately then placed it gently in his pocket.

"Tante Florence is expecting me at the seamstress's for the final fitting of the bridesmaid dress," Anna said happily as she greeted Louis at their botanical oasis.

Louis smiled. "We will not stay for very long," he replied with a curious, mischievous smile. He stood and reached into his pocket, bringing out a small packet wrapped in brown paper. "I was hoping to see you today to wish you a happy birthday and to ask you to accept this small present as a token of our friendship," he said, handing her the packet.

Her hands shook slightly as she accepted the packet and carefully unwrapped it. "Oh, Louis," she sighed. "Qu'est-ce qu'elle est belle." She brought the small sculpture to her lips and kissed the mermaid's head. Then she stared at it, mesmerized. All those weeks as he explained the progress on the sculpture, whilst she had tried to imagine the reality of what he described to her…she was not prepared for how powerfully the reality struck her. It was so…so…*lifelike*. She expected the small creature to begin to move in her hands. Tears, unbidden, began to slide down her cheeks. She raised her eyes and looked into his. "You made her for me?" He smiled. "I wanted you to be the first person to see her." At the time, Louis did not know that his father and mother and brother, unable to contain their curiosity, had gone into the atelier the previous day to gaze upon his masterpieces, and had come away overwhelmed by the power of what he'd done.

"You have created something so beautiful…"

"No," he said. "*We* have created this. She is our joint creation."

They did not speak. They did not have to. They knew all they needed to know. He moved closer to her. He gently grasped her upper arms and brought his lips to her face, kissing her lingeringly on both wet cheeks, tasting the saltiness of her tears of happiness.

"Bonne anniversaire, Anna," he whispered against her cheeks, so that she could feel his lips move as he spoke.

There was an air of regal reverence about her that held your gaze and made you dream. Years of monsoon winds and salt sprays from Anse Royale's bay reflected in the freckles on her tall, arched wooden doors and lattice windows. The granite stones of her walls were still defiant, immune against time and the elements, insulating her interiors from the heat of this July afternoon.

The tiny church of Saint Joseph, patron saint of this small village, was adorned today in sprays of white blossoms and green ferns, decorating her arched doorway and veranda posts. Inside, in the peacefulness and coolness, massive flower arrangements strategically positioned around the altar were doing proud to Anse Royale's oldest family, her very own benefactor.

Halfway across the village, Ghislaine knelt on one knee, her head bowed, her long white wedding dress covering the floor. She clutched the bouquet of white, tropical flowers in her hand, as her godmother and grandmother stood proudly on the veranda of this old house and laid a wrinkled old hand on her veiled head. Monia's eyes were closed. In the brief benediction she placed upon Ghislaine, she sought to grant all the happiness and blessings of her own marriage on her first grandchild, on this the beginning of her long anticipated and embraced journey. She sought the soul of her beloved Maurice in heaven, praying that he might intercede today so that Ghislaine and Claude would know the fulfilment and happiness that they once shared. Then she bent down and kissed the crown of her granddaughter's head.

Ghislaine trembled with such feeling as the majesty of '*Oui devant Dieu, devant les hommes*' played. She gazed into Claude's eyes and felt so overwhelmed with love and devotion that she was at that altar exchanging vows and rings. It was as if her entire life and all that she hoped and prayed for was being fulfilled, and the joy of it left her nearly breathless.

As Père Jean Leonard blessed the couple in the holy sacrament of marriage, Mère Monia and Florence shed tears that betrayed a powerful emotion.

"… husband and wife…"

It was time. They were ready, ready to face the world, ready to face this very joyous congregation. Overwhelming happiness and love radiated from Ghislaine's face as Anna approached her cousin and handed her the beautiful white bouquet. She tidied the long white veil and the trail of Ghislaine's dress, so that she would look her best on the arm of her new husband. As the bells of Saint Joseph rang out long, joyous peels of blessing, the young couple walked slowly down the aisle. Madame Ghislaine Maillet was fully welcomed to her new parish.

For Ghislaine, the rites and traditions were fully uplifting, and she did not find them restrictive at all. She was grateful that family and Church had defined the contours of her life. So it had always been, and so it was now as tradition dictated that she walk in procession with her husband, arms linked, shaded by the customary lace parasol, followed by the bridesmaids carrying the train of her trailing white veils. Families and friends smiled, wiped tears and chatted as the new couple were serenaded to the music of guitars and violins behind them.

The throngs of well-wishers, plantation workers and bystanders lined the road from the church to the Maillet's family home. They viewed the couple with smiling faces as they threw confetti, clapped and cheered and called out their good wishes.

"Long life!"

"Much joy!"

Under the shade of the *sal ver* occupying the lawn in front of Andre Maillet's home, the wedding guests enjoyed the true hospitality of the south. They feasted on a sumptuous buffet, with all the traditional trimmings. Claude and Ghislaine led the first waltz, '*Mes Chers Amis.*' The first dance – a joyous tradition but a perilous task indeed, given the length of Ghislaine's veil. Yet on that day there could be no shadow, no negative, no problem. Smiling happily, they enjoyed this first dance, this first duty as a newly-married couple, cheered on by everyone.

As much as they were thrilled to cheer the newlyweds, the guests were impatient to take to the dance floor themselves. This was a magnificent celebration and they were determined to enjoy every moment of it – dancing, eating and drinking until the cocks crowed at the first light of dawn. Then, far from flagging, the taste of strong, bitterly sweet, early morning coffee would revive them as they listened for the anticipated sounds of the fire crackers which would confirm the satisfactory consummation of the marriage. The loud bangs would echo throughout the village, bearing witness to the loss of her virginity.

God was in His Heaven. All was well with the world.

Several weeks later, on a bright and sunny August afternoon, the Alouette hoisted her sails in preparation. The southeast monsoon was blowing in from Pointe Larue, flowing over Port Victoria and the group of islands guarding her entrance. Everyone was happy and excited on board as they went about their duties. Both old and hardened, and young and jubilant 'sea salts' worked in earnest as the wind whistled through the masts and the rigging. Young and old, they all yearned for the immortal magic of a sea journey. As Alouette glided gracefully out of Port Victoria, her white sails ballooning with the southeast winds, Henri stood alongside Louis at the helm.

It should be a very pleasant trip, four to five hours at the most, he thought as he watched his younger brother. He felt his heart swell with pride, and happiness. To be alongside one another on their boat. He shifted his gaze and looked to the other faces gathered on the deck. Captain Francourt, dressed in his pristine white ensemble, had his pipe lit as usual and was surveying the horizon, whilst watching Louis' every move and manoeuvre out of the corner of his eyes.

He never misses a single detail, Henri thought, knowing that as soon as they anchored at Île du Nord, the captain would be going over all his observations with Louis. For both Henri and Louis, just having the captain with them made them feel safe and secure. It was almost a fatherly presence, or maybe even something a bit more?

Henri looked at young Antoine Savy's expression as they sailed past Sainte Anne's island, leaving the inner sanctuary of the port. He remembered perfectly the feeling of sailing out the first time. He could see young

Antoine making a detailed mental map of all her contours, beaches and curves for future references, in between adoring backward glances at the mesmerising picture of *Trois Frères*, now slowly receding in the distance. There was something mystifying about the picture of that mountain towering over this small port, that could reach out and touch your very soul.

A combination of an awesome spectacle of natural beauty and glorified presence, the mountain exuded an overwhelming sense of affection and protection, guarding the little port and everyone in its shadow. This powerful picture would undoubtedly remain as a monument for posterity, but for a young heart on his maiden trip, it was the most magnificent of gifts. The same image stayed with Henri to this day, even after his countless trips out of the port. At the far end of the deck, Julien's cotton-white mop of tight African curls stood out against his tarry black, bare muscular torso. Henri smiled as he looked upon his old mentor.

As he was growing up, Julien was an enigmatic figure. Physically powerful, physically present, but also fervently private. He was, in truth, something of a recluse. His tiny one-room hut perched on the hillside seemed settled in an air of mystery. For years, up to the launch of the Alouette, Julien had been the foreman of the six-pirogue fleet and all the fishermen employed by the estate. Rowing the products from Beau Vallon to Port Victoria every week was their primary task; that and transporting the family around the island to visit friends. Between those duties, Julien kept the fishing side of the du Barré business booming.

He was hardworking, meticulous and possessed a wisdom of the sea that was the envy of others. These qualities, along with his physical strength, earned him the respect of the men working under his command. Or so it appeared. It was by accident that Henri had one day overheard the conversation of a group of disgruntled fishermen. It turned out that Julien and Marie had been lovers, but Marie had found him one day in bed with a labourer named Constance. She had never looked at him again, and both had remained single ever since.

He certainly had the respect of Christophe. Henri recalled the time he had been taken along on his first full-moon fishing trip, together with Albert and Julien. It was clear to him, even as a boy, that both his father and Albert held Julien in very high esteem. Henri watched as the moon bathed their pirogue in its soft light, the three men enjoying their pursuits with great contentment and amiability, without any apparent distinction of race or status.

He was astonished to see his father and Albert in very different lights that night. They clearly deferred to Julien on the boat. If he said something, they listened and obeyed without question. It was Julien who taught him how to bait his first hook. When he felt a tug on his line, it was Julien who crouched behind him and held his hands, showing him how to pull his catch in, how to hold the line, when to let go slightly, and when to start pulling it in with force. He still remembered the power of those strong arms around him and the musky odour of Julien's sweat, remembered working in concert with him until his first catch slid gracefully over the side of the pirogue and he roared with joy and pride. He also learned in passing that night that Julien had taught both his father and Albert the art of fishing.

In the years that followed, it was Julien who instilled in him a knowledge of the sea and its inhabitants. Julien taught him that there was an art to rowing a pirogue in good and bad weather. He taught him to read the skies and to anticipate imminent changes in the weather, and how to read a passing cloud to know if it would bring a downpour or not.

From Julien, he learned to respect the sea for the abundance it gave, by taking what was needed and no more, as well as how to be gracious in victory to its inhabitants. One night, after a relentless three-hour struggle, he landed a *vyey* almost as big as the pirogue they were in. As Henri stared down at his massive prize, helpless and exhausted, and then at his hands, bruised and bleeding from the pressure of the *lalwa* fishing ropes, Julien had patted his back and said, "Remember, down there he was the master. You have won the fight, but now you owe him a swift end." Then he handed him the wooden bludgeon.

Julien taught him to read the stars and the cycles of the moon. He taught him to anticipate the reaction of the sea, the wind and even the fish. Although Henri was not always the best student, Julien was always the patient teacher, allowing Henri to be amazed at these wonders of nature, but also to appreciate nature's darker side. Some would look at Julien and see only *an old black man* who could not read a contract or write his name. Henri knew better. He knew Julien to be a sage of the natural world, a teacher and a guide.

When the Alouette was launched, Julien insisted that he wanted to be the full-time watchman. Within a month of being on board, Julien's jet black hair turned to white.

It was as if his hair was a marker that he had arrived at the final leg of his journey, that after a lifetime of absence he had found his real home and his true age had come forth, showing for the very first time.

He felt close to her, almost as though he could reach out and touch her face, but then Louis heard that sound again, that sound that was bringing him back to reality, shattering the beauty of his dream, awakening him. As he strolled out onto the veranda, Louis could see his morning coffee on the small table next to the flickering candle, the maid who had woken him now long gone. The images of his dreams were still vivid and he could sense Anna's presence around him. *Bonjour, ma chérie,* he murmured softly with a tender smile.

The sounds of waves crashing on the beach echoed around the pitch darkness of this pre-dawn, whilst on the horizon a thin silver line, visibly drawn, separated the sky from the ocean. Louis sat in the old canvas armchair, holding his coffee cup, ready to welcome this new day.

Outside the old plantation house, the dripping dew on the vegetations and trees waited patiently too.

Nature at its best, Louis thought, as the areas around that silver line slowly took a light shade of grey, pushing away the dense blackness of the sky away. It was followed by a light blue shade that appeared next to the silver line, pushing the grey further upwards, as Louis continued sipping his coffee. It was easy to imagine someone with a box of beautiful colours, gently releasing one colour at a time.

By the time there was enough light from the imminent sunrise for the naked eye to see the outline of trees, it was a light shade of orange crowning the silver line. The yellow and blue had moved further upwards, trying to reach the grey. It took a whole thirty minutes for this miracle of nature to fully manifest itself, erasing the line completely and painting the horizon in a kaleidoscope of colours. Louis' longing was intense. He felt as though he carried a heavy weight in his chest. Whenever he stood in nature, he wished she was there with him to share it. Without it, nature's magnificence was somewhat diminished. Only by placing her in nature, was the beauty of it fulfilled.

As Louis strode down to the beach, scores of black labourers, their muscles rippling in the bright morning sun, moved to offload the schooner with their three black pirogues. The captain stood out at the head of the first pirogue next to Henri, his white uniform a sharp contrast to everything and everyone around him. The oarsmen expertly manoeuvred the pirogue over the incoming waves, arriving at the secure area on the far side of the breakers and the awaiting Alouette.

On the beach, the *rezier* was readying the second pirogue for launching. The oarsmen, knee deep in foaming surf, were holding on tightly whilst they counted down the waves. Then, all at once they roared, *An nou ale!* as they heaved their pirogue into the eighth wave, well known to be the smallest of the full set of incoming waves.

Louis smiled, understanding clearly why oarsmen were held in such high esteem. They were the lifeblood of the isolated island. Whether off-loading vessels or getting a sick resident to the main island quickly, the inhabitants relied on the skill of these oarsmen. There were many stories of those who had defied time, distance and the elements and had rowed to the point of exhaustion to get patients at death's door to the doctor.

These stories had been retold many times, as well as others, gruesome in character, of prices paid in human limbs and lives for this sort of isolation. Life on these small islands was most of the time good and beautiful, but tenuous. Most of these islands were only agricultural outposts. They had no indigenous residents, only, among a few others, French descendant owners and their families. Each island had administrators and overseers along with one or two 'proverbial relics' of its own, the old timers who decided decades earlier that the main island of Mahé was just too big for their liking.

The remaining temporary residents of these islands were labourers, descendants of freed African slaves who worked the coconut, cinnamon and vanilla plantations, and were employed on twelve-month contracts at a time. Mostly men, they worked the year to save money only to see most of it spent in a frenzied burst of socialising, alcohol and freedom once they reached Mahé after a whole year of absenteeism. Then they could be seen heading sluggishly back to the island's representative in Victoria to put their thumb mark on yet another twelve-month contract, vowing to themselves that it was all going to be different 'next time.'

The arrival of the Alouette the previous evening had been greeted with exhilarated cries of *Selo, Selo* as soon as her sails were spotted. Everyone ran excitedly to the beach to welcome the schooner. In each face gathered eagerly in this early morning light, Louis could see the anticipation bubbling, for the schooner held fresh merchandise from the main island, as well as those special boxes full of personal treats from their relatives.

For the labourers, the twelve-month contract meant a year far from their loved ones, which was unquestionably the hardest part of working on an isolated island. The arrival of the schooner was the highlight of each month. The boxes of treats were a small consolation, a way of communicating in their world of illiteracy, and soothing the hurt of isolation, celibacy and alcohol prohibition.

Enforced as a cardinal rule by the administrators and overseers, alcohol was strictly prohibited among the labourers. On occasions, when caught tapping the coconut trees for *toddy*, or using their sugar quotas to make home brew instead of morning coffee, some labourers had spent the night in the island's one-room prison and had their wages cut. Of course, these cases always raised the question of whether it was really their loved ones, or the alcohol that they missed the most.

By the time the sun was once more poised to submerge itself into the azure ocean, the sails of the Alouette had long since disappeared from the view of the Île du Nord residents for yet another month. All the products of hard sweat and labour were securely stored in her hull, as well as those precious wooden boxes destined for relatives on Mahé, whose contents had been painstakingly and lovingly fished, salted and dried as treats for loved ones.

Meanwhile, on deck, a few starry-eyed dreamers with pockets full of a whole year's graft, were already seeing themselves as the envy of their friends on Mahé, without a single thought spared for all those mates they had just left behind, especially those sad-looking faces that had just got off the schooner that morning to begin their twelve-month incarceration.

CHAPTER 7

General Gordon's Connection

Earlier that day, back on the main island, Anna was about to finish work. She most loved this time of day, that last hour when all her patients had eaten their lunch and the work on the ward was done for nurses on the morning shift. Freed of exacting chores, she had some time when she could get to know her patients better. Often, this was very difficult, especially with the older patients as they were reluctant to discuss and confide in a very young nurse, particularly a *white* one. These talks demanded a great deal of tact. Anna found that she could be most successful when she engaged her patients while she created the illusion that she was involved in some other task, like fluffing up their pillows, or adjusting the bed sheets.

She gained a great deal from those conversations. In the elderly, and in Seychellois society generally, it was presumed that 'wisdom only comes with age' and the younger generation were expected to go to their elders for advice, never the other way around. A corollary was that the young were expected to show utmost respect and politeness to the elders. This understanding conspired to make it inconceivable to an elderly patient that a young girl could have knowledge of sickness and remedies. God forbid that she should give them advice! However, Anna had been able to navigate those difficult conversations by employing diplomacy and sensitivity.

Being hospitalised was a frightening experience. Whatever pain or illness the patients suffered was compounded by being in a strange setting far from their families. Of course, the stern looking figure of the doctor, in his long white coat, always seemed to have the God-given ability to make you tremble when they head towards your bed.

Most difficulty was for the elder male patients who had to bear the indignity of being attended to in their private moments by young ladies. A bed bath was considered an utter violation of dignity.

However for all that, it was the soft, continuous moans which were most unnerving. Tucked into a corner at the far end of the ward, hidden behind a rickety *baravan*, a person bearing only the mere resemblance of a human being, long past caring for this world, still drew breath, emitted soft and ominous moans, through pursed, dried lips, as heaven itself neared. The presence of this patient, making it clear just how close that final transition was, was emphasized by the attendance of the old priest in his brown cassock, leaning close to the poor patient, blessing the soul as it hovered between this world and the next. All this leaving others on the ward fearful and wondering. *Am I next?*

However, there were also a few patients who held a different feeling toward the hospital. Those who had, of necessity, been in and out of the hospital more than once, tended to have a higher regard and respect for its institutional methods and habits, and a higher regard for the many people working there for the betterment of everyone. So naturally, all the new patients got to hear their views, whether they liked it or not.

During the last minutes of her shift, Anna tried to make things more hopeful and positive for her patients, to lessen the fear that was so obvious in the expressions on their faces. "Don't you look much better today!" she greeted each patient. "Did you know that a patient who came to us feeling much sicker than you went home today, feeling better. Why, he was laughing with the nurses as he left…" Such comments went a long way toward easing the concerns of patients. Of course there was always a sombre and tense mood when there had been a death on the ward. Diplomacy was imperative then, even if the nurses were hurting just as much.

She reminded them that God listened to their prayers, even as she was mindful that they also believed in the magical powers of *grigri* and their *gardkor*, the small cloth pouches hidden inside the hems or stitching of their bed clothes. She knew these contained pieces of dried tree bark, human hair and nails, as well as many other magic concoctions from their favourite *bonnonm dibwa*, and were decorated with a small silver medallion of Saint Christopher, held in place by a safety pin.

She accepted that the black population of the Seychelles had equally strong beliefs in their African roots, cultures and customs, as in the Catholicism they practised. So, in the hospital as elsewhere, the two opposing worlds of witchcraft and Catholicism cohabited in a sometimes uneasy peace. The *gardkor* afforded its wearers mental and physical protection from the malevolence of the black magic practitioners who were a feared force in the secret world of the Seychellois society. Nurses and patients held those pouches in closely guarded secrecy.

The wrath of Matron, the Irish Catholic nun running Victoria hospital, was not to be tempted. She was a Catholic nun first and a Matron second. In her hospital, Catholicism reigned, instilling fear and her own brand of strict righteousness in nurses and patients alike. To Matron, nursing was a second vocation. There was a sense of sanctity, a religious awe, in caring for the patients in her wards. She made certain she cared for their souls as well as their bodies.

The old priest offered daily confession, prayers and communion for those who were bedridden. Patients able to walk were expected to attend the daily six a.m. mass at the small chapel. During Lent, meals reflected the same sombreness of this pre-Easter interval, just as they did outside the hospital's walls.

No meat was served on any Friday. Good Friday was a fasting day for all but the most extreme cases. Matron expected her nurses and patients alike to conform to her rules with absolute dedication. This dedication was best exemplified by the nurses' dress code. Even a slightly under-starched apron or cap could result in a reprimand and possibly an extra hour of work in the sluice room, cleaning bedpans.

During the years of training until becoming a Staff Nurse, which for most was a very long time due to their low level of basic education, nurses were not allowed to get married and have children. Worst still, pregnancy out of wedlock carried the ultimate penalty – immediate dismissal. There was no question that there were draconian rules and harsh expectations, but for the nurses the most difficult thing was educating their patients as to the cause of their various maladies, so as to prevent a worsening of their condition or relapse. This task became more delicate when the cause of their illness was the direct result of a patient's lifestyle. Tact and sensitivity was required when clarifying the nature of the disease in a way that did not belittle the patient, their culture or their way of life.

The simple truth was that the extreme poverty of most of the population conspired with the lack of education and unsanitary living conditions to create the opportunity for a variety of tropical diseases, germs and bacteria to thrive. Sanitation facilities among the hut dwellers on the numerous plantations were almost non-existent. Whole families would unceremoniously relieve themselves behind bushes close to their dwellings.

Others, living further down the hills, collected their drinking water from streams and rivers that had run through soiled grounds or pigsties, somewhere along their downhill route. Naked and barefoot children played happily in the yard among the chickens, pigs, dogs, and all their droppings.

It was therefore with great trepidation that Anna approached Angeline Victoire. Anna had been on duty when she had been admitted to the hospital, gravely ill. For the first days, Anna had little hope of seeing her get better. Although nurses are trained to be professional no matter who they treat, in this case it was very difficult because she knew

Angeline quite well. Her husband worked the cinnamon plantation on the du Barré estate, and they lived in one of the huts reserved for the estate workers. He was a known bully, and notorious for getting drunk on payday and getting into fights.

Anna knew the black Creole people of Seychelles to be a very proud race despite their poverty and illiteracy. As a group, they upheld a level of domestic harmony along with following the teachings of the Catholic Church. Indeed, it was the total blind faith in their religion which kept them going during the most challenging times. Their presence in the house of the Lord each Sunday, where they worshipped among the white, prosperous and rich, albeit at the back of the church, was an endorsement of their values as human beings. Their poverty and illiteracy notwithstanding, they were accepted and recognised as Christians. It was their one source of true identity and pride. Anna knew all this. She also knew that if Angeline was to improve, she would have to change some of her practices. Communicating that truth was going to be hurtful, no matter how gently she tried to deliver the message.

Angeline was emaciated and fragile, propped up against her pillows. Weeks of intense diarrhoea, pain and fever resulting from multiple liver abscesses and infection had taken a toll on this fifty-five-year-old woman. She was now in her fourth hospitalisation in just under two years, all due to the same recurring amoebic dysentery condition. This time, her condition had been worse. She was now in the secondary stages of the disease, and the amoebas which had caused damage to the mucous membranes of her intestines had entered her veins and travelled to her liver.

Even if the past few weeks of treatment had resolved the infection and the abscesses, the damage to her mucous membranes put her at a greater risk of suffering from severe infection from the normally harmless bacteria in her intestines. In short, she was now in a very precarious position.

"I'm sorry," Anna concluded as she explained all this to Angeline.

The proud Creole's face was a mask of doubt, pain and suspicion as she stared back at Anna. Anna felt the full brunt of the woman's emotions, but she remained calm. *This is real life,* she told herself. *This is a real person, not a case from a medical book.* She wished she did not have to be the bearer of bad tidings, but there was no other option. Angeline's life was now at risk. She either had to alter her habits or the next illness would very likely be a fatal one. And still Angeline continued to stare at her. The poor old woman. During her weeks of illness and pain, during which she had barely had the strength to pray for a divine cure, she had never considered the nonsense this little wisp of a girl was telling her.

"Contaminated water supply? Cooked food contaminated by flies that had been on human excrement?" Who was this mere girl to suggest to her that her drinking water should be boiled? Or that all cooked food remain covered? Or to even consider building a pit latrine?

Her initial pain and disbelief was quickly turning to anger. She wanted to shout at this impudent girl. "I am a clean person! I am a good Catholic wife, a good mother...!" She wanted to shout it all at her. She was a good person, even if she was poor. How dare this person suggest otherwise! But her words and her strength failed her.

Anna's gift and curse was her ability to read all this in the woman's face. Anna desperately wanted to reassure her that she had done nothing wrong, that she *was* a good person. Instead, she simply sat on the bed and took Angeline's thin, wrinkled hand in her own. Her words had injured the older woman badly. Her gesture was a healing one.

Angeline had always done everything as she had been taught. She believed without reservation the teachings that had been drilled and beaten into her by her own mother and by the Church, and she had conducted her life accordingly. She married the first labourer who asked her parents for her hand in marriage.

She was a virgin on her wedding night. She had borne him eight children, as well as having three miscarriages. She had endured beatings on the nights when he had come home drunk, which was always accompanied by a violent session of rape, mounting her like the farm animals, her anus bleeding from his unrelenting assault all through the night. She had withstood it all because *that was the way it was supposed to be*. She believed herself to be the epitome of a good mother and Christian wife. A woman who believed in the holy sacrament of marriage, even if God had blessed her with a difficult husband. Who was this girl to tell her otherwise?

From the first light of dawn to dusk she worked the vegetable plantation and tended to the chicken and pigs they kept on a *mwatye* basis with the du Barré estate. Then by the light of the oil lamp in the evening, she would iron the heaps of clothes from the washer woman who ran the laundry of the plantation house. A valuable contribution to the household, as her husband drank most of his wages away in *baka*. Should she not grin and bear it, as the good Catholic wife she was? Night after night he woke her because he wanted a woman, and she allowed him to exercise his rights, no matter how tired, or pregnant.

She knew that a good wife should always say 'yes' to her husband. It was the teaching. And to accept with good grace and humility the children that God blessed her with. "How dare she judge me?" Angeline thought, staring at Anna.

"Maybe you could try and make the smaller changes first," Anna suggested softly. "I know it will not be easy, but you are a strong person, and you can stop the infection from coming back again. Try it for a while, for the sake of your children. You know how they miss you when you stay in hospital."

Anna saw a glimmer of pride when she mentioned her children. It was then that she knew she had made a connection, no matter how small. Even as she was doubled over in pain, even as her body expelled the bloody, watery faeces, even when she feared that death was upon her, Angeline prayed for her children. She also remembered that throughout her illness and confinement, this young girl at her side, gently stroking her hand, had been with her.

She had cared for her, as a mother cares for her child. There was compassion, not pride, in her green eyes. No malice. No animosity. Just genuine compassion.

Angeline nodded. "Thank you," she whispered, so softly Anna had to strain to hear her. "Thank you."

From her desk across the ward, Sister Patricia Kent observed Anna with her patient. Even beyond earshot, she could read Anna's expression and body language. She knew exactly what was happening and for a brief moment it took her all the way back to 1874, when she was seventeen, the same age as Anna. She had only recently begun her training at the Florence Nightingale Nursing School in St. Thomas' Hospital in London. She knew that the only difference between the two of them at this stage in their lives was geographical.

Whilst she had had all the advantages of being trained in London's post-Florence Nightingale's revolutionary era in nursing, as well as the auspiciousness of being in the original school of nursing set up in 1860 by *The Lady of the Lamp* herself, Anna had started off in a different world altogether. But somehow she was coping remarkably well. Despite the differences in their circumstances, she recognized the mirror image of herself in Anna. There was the same confidence and passion, the same thirst for knowledge, the same determination and deep sense of humanity.

From that very first day in January, when she surveyed another meagre group of new recruits, Anna had stood out. She had felt drawn to her then just as she did now. She recognized the impatience in Anna's green eyes. The desire for adventure. The aura of human kindness surrounding her. Over the past months, Anna had proved herself to be an exceptional student. It was an adventure in itself, teaching one as eager as Anna.

Back in 1874, Sister Patricia Kent had had her own vision of the great things she would accomplish as a nurse. It had been those dreams that had drawn her to nursing in the first place. Now, as she concluded her fourth decade in nursing, she could rejoice in an array of positive and gratifying memories, as well as mourning silently for the sad and tragic ones.

However, nothing in her career had prepared her for the frustrating predicament in which she had found herself over the past three years while working at Victoria Hospital. Her years as a nursing sister and later as matron of the Royal Herbert Military Hospital in Woolwich, England, had been fulfilling, whilst the climax of both her personal and professional life had materialised during her participation in the great 1884 to 1885 Wolseley expedition to relieve General Charles Gordon and his troops in the besieged city of Khartoum.

During those painfully tedious months in the torturous heat of the desert, she had witnessed fierce battles, atrocious killing and she had nursed horrific wounds inflicted on courageous young men. All her beliefs, perceptions and compassion were tested, as the desolation of that appalling climate, with its maddening insects carrying their loathsome diseases, had made the memory of a cold and grey England seem almost like paradise.

Then, on one baking hot afternoon, he had walked into her life, carrying one of his injured colleagues. It was love at first sight. Lieutenant David Longhurst's cornflower blue eyes had pierced that protective armour behind which she had hidden all her adult life. The days and weeks that followed saw this inhospitable place transformed before her eyes into a realm of hidden beauty as her heart and soul soared with the magic of true love. Even as Patricia watched Anna reassuring and comforting her patient, her mind's eyes were far away, very far away…and she was next to him in the desert…

It was during an enchanting and passionate night under the moonlit skies, on the shores of the Great River Nile, that she gave herself fully to him, shedding her virgin blood, and for the first time in her life, she had felt complete. The remainder of the expedition rolled by in a dreamy haze as their love flourished, until that fateful day in January 1885 when they finally reached Khartoum, and realised that their efforts had all been in vain. Two days earlier, the city had fallen to the enemy and General Gordon had been killed.

The followers of the holy Mahdi's army who had held the city under siege for months, were still in their exhilarated state of ecstasy, elated in Allah's victory against the infidels. One of their volleys on General Wolseley's approaching fleet caught Lieutenant David Longhurst in the chest. She was with him when the last sparkle left his eyes. She hugged him helplessly as his soul soared to that firmament over the great Nile. And with it, went her own heart.

Twenty-five years later, as 1910 dawned, she awakened on the anniversary of his death with the realisation that she still desired to make her mark on history. She could feel her beloved David urging her on. She could see his broad smile and those blue eyes telling her to reach for the stars. A few weeks later, on a bitter, icy March morning, she had stood silently in a fresh snowfall, shivering inside a heavy, grey woollen coat, with a thick scarf shielding her head and neck from the biting winds of the river Thames, watching the hectic activities taking place on the vast West India Dock, the busiest dock in the Port of London. The British India Steamer was puffing out grey smoke against the sunless sky. She turned one last time to look at East London, her true home. The very same dock where she had disembarked alone and miserable twenty-five years earlier was now poised once more to take her away.

But now, as she went forward, it was with a different sense of *adventure*. This time, she knew, she was embarking on her final journey. This time, as she stepped onto the gangway, she knew she was bidding adieu to England.

During their months together, David had shared with her his feelings toward his hero, General Charles Gordon. In the twenty-five years of her grieving, as she had nursed countless soldiers at the Royal Herbert Military Hospital, she had devoted time to her pet project, researching the life and exploits of General Charles Gordon. Her research kept David's passion alive in her heart. Like David, as she learned more about this great British hero, she had come to revere him as well. What had begun as an homage to David resulted in deep affection for her subject.

It was one of his adventures that called to her - the General's quest to find the original Garden of Eden ended in 1882, when he visited the islands of Seychelles.

"Thus far, I think any requirement is fulfilled for deciding that the site of the district of Eden is near Seychelles. I could even put it at Praslin, a small isle twenty miles north of Mahé." As evidence, he cited the islands of the Seychelles as not being volcanic like the other islands in the Indian Ocean, but formed from an ancient type of granite, and being the only mid-ocean granitic islands in the world. To him, that fact alone suggested that they were not originally of the Indian Ocean area but might have drifted to their present position from very far away, during the great continental shift.

The second piece of evidence was the presence of the unique and exceptional palm tree, the *Coco de Mer*, also known as *The Tree of Knowledge*. The double nut in the form of the female pelvis, as well as its counterpart with its peculiar catkins protruding from the male palms, conjured the images of Adam and Eve's nudity. As Praslin was the only place on earth where those trees were found, it was further proof to Gordon's mind that it was the one and the only *Garden of Eden*.

When Patricia discovered this revelation, she'd been amazed. How it must have felt to have finally realized his quest! For a man of the General's stature, that revelation must have been enormous to prompt him to risk his reputation for such an assertion. At the same time, she couldn't help but wonder what the Seychelles looked like. How special were they? Did they still look and feel like that first garden? She felt a yearning in her heart to one day set foot in such a place, to discover for herself just what the General had felt like.

On that January morning in 1910, the Seychelles had been alluring but, in truth, her own subsequent research about the islands had proved decisive.

A tiny and relatively insignificant British Colony in the middle of a vast ocean, with a small population of no more than 22,000 and a British Governor at its head, had caused her to conjure images of tiny and remote agricultural villages scattered around rural England, where everything was produced locally and everyone knew everyone and their relatives before them; where respect still ruled, where it was possible to feel a sense of calm and tranquillity wherever you went.

She shuddered as she reflected on just how quickly London had been losing all of these qualities over the past few decades. She dared to imagine finding such a way of life once more. She imagined the natives of the Seychelles to be similar to those she had seen during the expedition in the Middle East. She could almost smell the harvest, almost feel the warm rays of sunshine on her upturned face. Yes, she was certain. She had found the perfect destination for her next, and last, adventure.

Her skills, experiences and knowledge would revolutionise their health care system and write her name in their history books.

In the early hours of 30 May 1910 her long journey came to an end. Sailing towards the island of Mahé at the break of dawn had been beyond her wildest imagination, a vision that would remain forever in her memory. She could *feel* the peace and serenity welcoming her, wrapping her in its beauty. As the first light of dawn erased the darkness and revealed that emerald jewel in all its glory, her heart had swelled. How could she help but feel anything other than pure love and belonging? She felt she had finally come home.

On that morning when she had landed on Mahé and felt the bewitching beauty of the island welcome her, she could not have imagined the dark years that lay ahead. It would have been inconceivable then, surrounded by the extraordinary beauty of nature, to imagine anything but peace and serenity in the hearts of everyone privileged to live in such a place. But she would have done well to remember, even Eden was not perfect.

Shortly after her arrival, she was informed by the office of the British Governor, His Excellency Sir Terence Hastings, that despite her over-qualification for the position, he was unable to appoint her as Matron of Victoria Hospital. The situation was awkward. Having been the matron of the prestigious Royal Herbert Military Hospital and finding herself in a lesser position, in a small and much less impressive hospital, was discomfiting. However, she remained focused on her original goals and decided to accept the post of Deputy Matron.

Unfortunately, she had not bargained on working under an Irish Catholic nun, nor had she anticipated the frustrations and helplessness she was going to have to endure because of her faith and nationality.

Nothing in her experiences had prepared her for this clash of principles. From day one, when she had presented herself at the hospital with her written authorisation from the Governor's Office, she was aware that 'battle lines' had been drawn. Before she had introduced herself, the old nun seemed she knew everything she needed to know about her, who she was and where she came from. Patricia felt the burden of the nun's unspoken condemnation of her Protestantism, and felt the weight of all the miseries endured by the Irish under British rule.

It had not taken long for her to realize that her fate was going to be worse than that she had endured in the desert. It was going to be her ultimate test.

The Catholic Church in the Seychelles was a powerful force, governing institutions like schools and hospitals with an army of nuns and brothers.

It had succeeded where the Anglican Church had failed, and was backed by all the French Catholic plantation owners. Even though the Seychelles had formally changed from a French Colony to a British Colony in 1814 as part of The Treaty of Paris, the French descendants of the islands continued to feel they were being put upon by British rule. In ways both subtle and overt, they sought to restrain the spread of 'Anglophilia.'

To this end, they were greatly strengthened by the army of freed African slaves – the Creoles – who spoke only a broken French patois and had all been baptised into the Catholic faith. Representing over ninety per cent of the entire population, the Creoles added powerfully to the influence of the Church. Indeed, the Anglican Church remained on the island only to represent the faith of the occupying British Rulers.

Three years. Such frustration! But Patricia had endured, feeling the sting of being a Protestant in a close-knit Catholic environment. What was most difficult was the resistance to the obvious need for the modernisation of medical treatment and the draconian laws and practices in the workplace, which were nearly unbearable to a professional of her calibre. But her passion for her work kept her going. She did enjoy the support and friendship of the other British residents of the Seychelles, and she had a wonderful relationship with a number of French descendants as well.

What gave her the greatest strength was the kindness and hospitality of ordinary Creole people who, despite the difficulty in communication, made clear their fundamental goodness. The beauty and peacefulness of the islands surpassed all her expectations and made her new life worthwhile and pleasantly comfortable. And, she had a brilliant young nurse to work with!

Anna smiled as she made her way towards Patricia's desk. She had got through to Angeline. She had done what she was able to do. Now it was up to the older woman to take the advice to heart, and Anna thought she would.

Patricia watched as Anna walked toward her. The dedication and enthusiasm of this girl had amazed her. From a Catholic home, in a world still decades behind time, and with the full knowledge that she would be expected to quit nursing once she received a marriage proposal, it was remarkable that she was able to approach her responsibilities with such sincerity. Her heart ached for Anna, knowing what it meant to her to be a nurse. What a shame that her future was already mapped out and she would be expected to leave nursing.

But then again, perhaps Anna's circumstances were more complex than she could imagine. After all, how had Anna become a nurse to begin with? Good white families did not allow their daughters to work, yet here she was. Perhaps, she thought, there was more to Anna than met the eye.

CHAPTER 8

The Mauritian Visitors

Christophe du Barré smiled at his reflection and shook his head. *Fifty-five years! Where did the time go?* His smile faded as the image of his twin, Monique, came to him. How he missed her! The first of September had always been their day, but twenty years had already passed since they'd celebrated a birthday together. In February 1891 their father, Monsieur Francois du Barré, had died suddenly. Despite the sadness and shock, Christophe had a new wife and child to think about. His mother and sister had one another. Two years later, Madame Marie-Antoinette du Barré told her son that she and Monique would be returning to her family home in France. "You have a child, an heir. It is right that we go back."

Mademoiselle Marie-Antoinette Baralle had arrived in the Seychelles in 1855, from a small wine-producing family in Bordeaux, as part of an arranged marriage. In 1856 she was married to Francois du Barré. On the first of September 1858 she gave birth to twins, Christophe and Monique. Christophe grew up into a strong boy, while Monique suffered terribly from asthma and chest problems. She was weak, underdeveloped and on constant medication. From an early age, Christophe assumed the role of big brother, caring for the frail Monique.

He used to carry her on his back, keeping up with their father as he surveyed the plantations, checking on the labourers collecting cinnamon leaves or de-husking coconuts. Monique, always with an eye for detail, often pointed out when she thought something was not being done properly. Marie-Antoinette had been convinced that leaving the Seychelles for a less humid climate was exactly what Monique needed for her health. As Christophe now had an heir, she decided the time was right for her return to France.

On a bright and sunny May morning in 1893, Christophe stood holding three-year-old Henri in his arms while Genevieve stood at his side on the pier of Port Victoria. They waved together to the two ladies in the pirogue, heading for the awaiting steamer bound for Europe.

He had not heard Genevieve come into the bedroom. Her reflection appeared behind his in the mirror. Her eyes were knowing as she kissed the nape of his neck, where his black curls lay.

"Je t'aime, mon chéri."

He turned and took her into his arms, hugging her tightly.

"I know that she is happy in France, but I miss her," he sighed.

Shortly after their arrival in Bordeaux, Monique wrote page upon page to Christophe about the journey and the wonderful country to which they had returned. *Vast, endless open fields of vineyards.*

Just as Marie-Antoinette thought, less than a year after their return to France, Monique had made a complete recovery. Over the years that followed, her letters had made real the country he had never seen, and he came to know and love France through his sister's words. He experienced the beauty and hardships of winter, as well as the hopes and freshness of spring along with her. Some five years after leaving the Seychelles, Monique had written about the small town of Agen, near Bordeaux. There had been something about the way she had described the land, with a passion and intensity that told him that Agen was special. So it came as no surprise when in her next letter she wrote that she had bought a small farm there, where she intended to cultivate prunes. *I have named it 'Beau Vallon.'*

He smiled, reading the letter. He knew she would be successful. Despite the physical weakness of her early years, they had both shared the same passion for the land and its yield. What he had not expected was, four years later, to read that she was now a married woman. He read the letter over and over, feeling the happiness and love radiating from its pages. As his eyes moistened with tears of joy, he prayed that Monsieur Philippe Burkhardt would love and care for her as she deserved, giving her the extra happiness for all those long years of suffering she had endured. He was extremely happy for her, to have finally found love and companionship at the age of forty-four years. Although, it still felt strange for him to think of his fragile little sister as a married woman, as 'Madame Monique Burkhardt.'

Genevieve reminded Christophe that their guests would be making their way to the dining room for breakfast. He nodded. With a final glance at the two of them in the mirror, he acknowledged how much he had been blessed. He had the deep love of a beautiful woman for twenty-five years, two strong and loving sons, and a happy and prosperous life in a world full of opportunities and prospects. All that and only fifty-five years of age!

Monsieur Fernand de Ravel, enjoying his first cigar after a hearty breakfast, was obviously pleased. "We shall make the announcement tonight, at the ball."

Christophe smiled. His suggestion had been well received by the visiting *Mauritian Confrere*. Henri looked at his father and future father-in-law, his face beaming. Monsieur George de Ravel, who was sitting beside Henri at the dining table, arose and embraced Henri in the cordial and sincere manner befitting a future brother-in-law.

"My congratulations, Henri."

"We shall inform the ladies of this wonderful news when they get back from church," said Christophe. "Come gentlemen, we have a lot to organise and to celebrate on this glorious day." He draped his arm on the shoulder of his first-born as they made their way out of the dining room.

Their families had a long history together. In the latter part of 1790, the great-grandfathers of Christophe and Fernand found themselves on the same ship, leaving France as they went off in search of their fortunes in the colonies of *La Mère Patrie*. The arduous voyage saw the beginning of a great friendship between the two young adventurers.

Upon their arrival on Île de France, de Ravel had been immediately impressed by this volcanic island with its great plains of sugar cane, a lucrative crop which the Dutch settlers had introduced decades ago before they decided to move to the greener pastures of the Cape of Good Hope. Du Barré meanwhile had opted to venture further afield to the Seychelles, where the hilly terrain of those enchanted islands had captured his imagination. They both witnessed a great deal of history from the places they occupied – de Ravel on the Île de France and du Barré in the Seychelles.

The Franco-British war being raged in the seas of the Indian Ocean was one such important part of history. The naval forces of both France and England were determined to gain total domination of this important trade route to India. Although the islands of the Indian Ocean had all been colonised by the French, due to their lack of defences its inhabitants were still vulnerable and at the mercy of the British war ships. One such example was the decision of Monsieur Jean-Baptiste Queau de Quincy, Civil Commandant of Seychelles, in offering the island's capitulation to the British in 1794.

Then, days after they played host to the Squadron of Commodore Newcome's fleet, they hoisted back the French tricolore once the British ships had disappeared from the horizon. It was the perfect form of defence. These faked capitulations continued until 1814 when France and England divided the islands of the Indian Ocean among themselves in the Treaty of Paris. It was a devastating blow to all the French settlers of the Seychelles and Île de France to have to live under a new British master. To make matters worse, the new British Rulers inflicted further shame by renaming the beautiful Île de France as 'Mauritius.' The settlers were livid.

Then 1835 saw the abolition of slavery, and the end of an era of free labour. It was a very difficult time for all the French plantation owners. The Seychelles were to play a major role in the black market slave trading thereafter, its 115 islands scattered over a large area ideal for concealing new slaves destined for the Mauritian sugar cane plantations – and right under the noses of their new British Rulers.

It was proof of what the spirit of French collaboration could achieve – for they still did not think of themselves as English!

The du Barré and de Ravel families maintained the friendship and bond forged by those two original 'colon' through the decades that followed, and although they learned in time to collaborate with their British rulers, they continually strived to preserve their French identity.

Fernand de Ravel had become interested in business prospects in the Seychelles two years previously, when he received an order from Christophe du Barré to supply sails, riggings and accessories for a schooner he was building. In that same letter Christophe had renewed his standing invitation for them to visit the Seychelles. But, it had been only four months before that his interest had truly been piqued by the order for the second schooner being commissioned by du Barré. This time, he wasted no time in accepting the invitation to visit the Seychelles.

The four weeks of that visit exceeded their expectations. The Seychelles had not set out to impress, but her charms and beauty had still conquered the hearts of her Mauritian visitors. They had always regarded her with the fondness of a smaller sister, tiny in size compared with Mauritius. They presumed her to have little economic significance, but to the pleasant surprise of the four members of the de Ravel family, they discovered that she could boast a very selective and well-established 'Plantocracy.'

The finest tables, comparable with their peers in Mauritius and France, were evident at all the grand Plantation Houses on Mahé that had welcomed them to the Seychelles. They had feasted on fresh turtle meat, delighted at the degustation of exotic wild fowl and marvelled at the delicacy of rare, migratory sea bird eggs, all accompanied by the finest wines imported from France. They were presented as du Barré's honoured guests to the British Colonial Establishment of the Seychelles and the elite of the island at the grandiose official ball, commemorating the grand opening of the British Governor's newly-built residence, on the most prestigious date in the island's calendar.

But despite it all, it was the courtesy, warmth and genuineness of the welcome they received from the du Barré family that had impressed them most, making them feel like long-lost relatives who had returned home after a lifetime's absence.

Genevieve and Marguerite de Ravel got on right from the very start, but it was the kind nature and genuineness of Danielle de Ravel that deeply touched Genevieve's heart, as she watched the demure sixteen-year old marvel at the natural beauty of the Seychelles. There was an aura of calmness, accompanied by a deep sense of well-being, that was always vivid in Danielle's eyes and face, a special kind of warmth.

Genevieve had not been blind to the way Henri became momentarily lost in this very special aura she exuded. Silhouette Island played host to their long weekend breaks, as the two families got better acquainted and Fernand marvelled at the potential business opportunities this island represented. The Alouette had sailed them all around Mahé, Praslin and La Digue, watching the dolphins at play and enjoying a fine red wine while watching the sun set over the horizon. It had been pure enjoyment and sheer luxury, and the betrothal of Henri and Danielle had crowned it all. It was the perfect ending to a memorable holiday, and the beginning of a new chapter in the lives of those two families.

"I really cannot believe that the Mauritians have hunted and eaten all those poor dodos," Louis told Anna, his tone a mixture of mirth and seriousness. "The species is now extinct. Not a single dodo left in the whole of Mauritius!"

They were in their favourite spot in the botanical garden, under the giant latanyen leaves, enjoying the tranquillity of the small stream flowing past them. Anna was seated on her favourite rock on the edge of the small pool, letting her fingers tickle the cool water while she half-heartedly listened to Louis rambling on about the Mauritian visitors who had departed from the Seychelles a few days previously. She learned of the link between the du Barré and de Ravel families, and of Henri's betrothal to Danielle. She heard his words, but even more, in the tone of his voice, she also heard his longing for faraway places. This sudden passion made her shudder. It was more and more difficult to mask the feelings that had been floating to the surface over the past few weeks.

"We are all going to Mauritius in March 1915 for the official engagement. It will be Henri's twenty-fifth birthday," Louis added. "The wedding will be held here in the Seychelles in July 1918, to coincide with Danielle's twenty-first. Maman is extremely happy. She has already started making plans!"

The memory of Therese's remarks, when Albert had told his family about Henri's news, resurfaced in Anna's mind once more. *What a suitable couple! Both rich and from similar upper-class families!* Anna felt as though she were sinking. *Oh Lord, please help me,* she prayed silently, her heart drowning in fear. Those aching and troubling feelings of the past few weeks swirled in her heart then, mixing painfully with her mother's remarks. *You are not of the same class, you are nothing!* It had settled like a veil on her heart, and with each passing day it had grown heavier.

As the weeks went by, Louis' social commitments to the visitors meant not being able to meet with her. The veil had become denser, harder to endure and fraught with questions she had never asked herself before, and which she was unable to answer. She had become unsure of herself, unsure of the feelings filling her heart. At first, she had felt a sense of loss, although she was not sure exactly what it was that was missing. Then, she felt fear and pain mixed with low self-esteem, which had culminated in bitter anger. She was angry about her status in life, angry at having been born poor, and angry at the injustice of it all. These emotions worried her most of all, for each time they left her feeling drained and eroded. Only her work in the hospital gave her any sort of relief and a sense of purpose.

Now, looking at Louis as he sat contentedly in their own little oasis, it was difficult for her to understand why their friendship was causing her so much pain. They had much in common, much they had shared with each other over those past months.

Feelings and appreciation for everything around them, their mutual love for nature and for the Seychelles…so what had changed? She was certain that *something* had changed. Had *she* changed? Had these past weeks changed everything and she was the only one to have noticed? She concentrated her gaze on the dried bodanmyen leaves floating down the stream towards them. She felt his eyes watching her, but dared not look up at him, for she was suddenly overcome by a feeling of vulnerability.

She felt naked beneath his gaze and she had no doubt that her eyes would betray those feelings if she dared look up. It was a sad and frightening feeling that engulfed her then, sad that she had to conceal her emotions from him, and frightening because it felt like she had lost the one person who really understood and appreciated her.

It was a great relief when he started talking again, this time about his excitement with the progress being made on La Sirène, and all the brand new rigging and fittings that Fernand de Ravel had brought from Mauritius for the new schooner.

"Anna, are you all right?" he asked, concerned when he noticed just how distant she seemed to be. She nodded. "Yes," she said, trying her best to steady her voice and hide her deeper feelings. "I am fine."

"You don't seem fine," he ventured.

She shrugged, determined to hide her feelings. "I am just concerned about a patient who was admitted with chicken-pox a few days ago," she replied, her eyes still focused on the dried leaf floating in the current of the stream. "The doctor transferred him to the isolation room today. He is very sick. I have never seen chicken-pox have such a destructive effect on anyone before." She was amazed that she had managed to keep her voice steady.

After they parted, she wanted nothing so much as to simply *get home*. It was only as she turned the last bend in the road and the bay of Beau Vallon came into view, that she realised just how much ground she had covered.

The journey from the hospital to Beau Vallon at a steady pace normally took well over one hour, but judging by the sweat pouring down her face and the dampness of her dress sticking to her body, she was certain that she had done it in less than thirty minutes. She only vaguely remembered leaving the botanical garden, rushing her goodbye to Louis and avoiding his gaze when he suggested that they meet again in three days time. She said yes, just to get away quickly. Saying no would have meant looking at him and explaining why not. She remembered nothing of the hurried walk to Beau Vallon. Her mind had been consumed with the memory of the night of the big ball at La Residence.

Her father had supervised the last-minute details to what he described as the biggest party the du Barré family had ever given. She could not sleep for the sounds of the lovely music floating uphill to their cottage. She got out of bed and stood at her open window, watching the slither of moon casting a dim glow over the valley below. It was an enchanting night, a perfect night.

She wondered, half-dreaming, what it would be like to be a guest at such a ball, how nice it would be to be dressed up and dancing to that lovely music, swirling across the dance floor in his arms. *Oh God.* She realized that not she but many other young ladies would be floating around the dance floor tonight in his arms.

To try to stop the pain she felt, she threw all her neatly-folded garments from her wooden chest until she found her little mermaid sculpture lying there, at the bottom. She kissed her on the head in a desperate attempt to stay close to him, but even the little mermaid had been unable to stop her tears from flowing. As the night wore on and her sobs racked her body, the thought of those rich young ladies in his arms became too much to bear. The pain was so intense…those images, sounds and emotions lured her in the darkness of the night to the garden in front of La Residence.

She found herself taking shelter behind one of the big bougainvillea bushes bordering the lawn and there, in the obscurity of the night, she looked on as the rich and powerful enjoyed themselves.

The ladies were dressed in exquisite ball gowns in every colour of the rainbow. They were enhanced by beautiful embroidery details and cascading waves of frilled lace that reached the floor, whilst the thick petticoats under the skirts gave the illusion of tiny, feminine waists. Pearls and precious stones dazzled around their bare shoulders and ears, complementing their hair which was set in high and elaborate fashion.

Anna recognised some of the black servants, all dressed in their white, long-sleeved cotton drill ensemble, standing out in this sea of ball gowns and suits, and carrying enormous silver platters of food and drinks. They enticed the guests to more refreshments as they left the dance floor and ventured onto the veranda for some fresh air from the bay.

From her vantage position, the laughter and jokes coming from the veranda were clearly audible, and the scent of tobacco from the cigars and pipes of those elegantly-dressed gentlemen drifted in the night air. Small lace and ivory fans could be seen cooling the semi-exposed and bulging cleavages of those beautifully-dressed ladies partaking of refreshments on the veranda. A scene which was clearly being enjoyed by their male counterparts.

Anna's heart skipped when she saw Louis step out of the lounge and stride across the veranda, stopping right outside the house on the wide concrete steps. She was too scared to breathe. She was almost too frightened to look at him, but look at him she did as he stood there, his hands tucked in the pockets of the elegant dark suit, the frills of his immaculate white shirt dazzling against his tanned neck.

He was admiring the effects of the flaming torches decorating the driveway, occasionally looking up at the new moon and stars in the sky. *What is his thinking?* she wondered. She could see him perfectly in the torches' light, his handsome features illuminated against the dark night. He turned and flashed one of his broad smiles, thanking the servant with the silver platter who had just handed him a drink. She watched as he brought the glass to his lips, his eyes gazing out towards the bay embedded in the night.

The girl's approach was magical. She didn't step so much as glide through those double-doors, floating on an undeviating line. She was the picture of perfection, a real-life princess. Her full and bouncy skirt swayed, a pair of big, puffy, short sleeves that sat on her upper arms gave the rest of her body a slim and delicate contour, whilst her bare neck and very low cut décolletage glittered with sparkling jewellery, drawing attention to her cleavage, enhanced by the blond curls dangling on her shoulders. Her dazzling smile illuminated her pretty face. She curtsied to Louis, who smiled back, and offered her his arm. Gently, she laid a dainty white lace gloved hand on his arm and slowly, they glided back together across the veranda and through those wide double-doors.

Anna did not feel the bougainvillea thorns against her skin, nor her plain cotton dress tearing, nor remember running at full speed all the way to the end of the bay. She was gasping for breath when she finally stopped, straining for more oxygen when she reached the spot where the hill met the ocean, where the massive boulders tumbled straight into the sea. She hugged one of the smaller boulders, trying to find solace as her emotions and feelings broke free. The pain felt unbearable.

The image of Louis smiling at that pretty girl and offering her his arm replayed over and over in her mind, stabbing at her like a knife.

She was lost in her distress when suddenly, she froze. She grasped at her dress, stuffing her hands deep into both pockets. Then she dropped to her knees and clawed at the sand, frantically searching around the boulder. She was gone! The little mermaid was gone! She had lost the most precious gift she had ever had, in fact the only gift she had ever had, that beautiful and treasured piece of creation, that symbol of their friendship and Louis' labour of love which he had created with his own hands just for her...and she had lost it.

In that moment it all became too much for her to bear any longer and she screamed, a tortured cry of pain, distress and torment, then sank into oblivion.

CHAPTER 9

A Dark Cloud

The contingency plan was hurriedly put in place. It was not foolproof by any means, but it was the best they could come up with given the circumstances. The predicament was dire, the risks immense. Behind the closed door, the document was passed from hand to hand. The four white-clad figures, two men and two women, had added their signatures next to their names, each of them conscious of the enormity of the decision they had just taken and of the horrendous hardships that lay ahead.

It was at 2 p.m. precisely on Monday 15 September 1913, that Victoria Hospital was officially sealed by the order of the Governor of the Seychelles, His Excellency Sir Terence Hastings, under the terms of the written declaration posted on her door. Armed police were posted outside the entrance. She was now held under the British Colony's Quarantine Laws. Mankind's most dreaded scourge, *La Variole*, had been confirmed within her walls. It was a horrifying and highly contagious disease, capable of spreading like wildfire in a community, killing its victims without mercy, or leaving those who survived with permanent disfigurement and blindness. For the British Administrators, this was the first real test of their authority and capability in a dilemma of this magnitude. It was a test they had to pass if they were ever to gain the respect that had long been denied them by the French settlers and the Catholic Church.

At the conference table in the dining room of the Official Residence of the British Governor, the hurriedly-convened meeting was about to start. Already, the collection of men of very different designations sitting patiently around the table could feel the tensions and uncertainty.

Sir Terence Hastings knew all of them personally, because even nationality and patriotism were not allowed to hamper the benefits of a good social circle. After all, every gentleman, no matter the creed, understands that his true strength comes from knowing his opponents intimately. It was a globally accepted theory, one which was observed to perfection in the Seychelles.

Freshly-brewed coffee was served repeatedly. Stiff moustaches and beards were stroked continuously. Cigar and pipe smoke clouded the room, while the Laws and Conditions to be imposed on the islands and its inhabitants during this smallpox epidemic were debated, taking close consideration of the guidelines given in that white document from the four medical professionals.

When they finally left the meeting, the twelve members of the representatives of the British Government, the Medical Profession, the Catholic Church, the Anglican Church, the Judiciary System, the Chamber of Commerce, and the Law and Order Establishment, were too-smugly certain that they had had their own way and they would be able to turn this calamity to their advantage in future. They were now ready to go out and implement the resolutions they had agreed to, with the common aim being the safety and well-being of the Seychelles, of course.

For generations, the ringing of church bells signalled every aspect of significance in the daily life of the small villages all over the island, from alerting villagers to the time of day, to summoning the faithful to masses, weddings and funerals, to being a constant reminder of God's presence in everyday life. The church bells were sounds of comfort and attention to the islanders. Rarely, as now, did the ringing of the church bells signal alarm. A forest fire out of control? A ship losing its way in a storm and headed for the reefs? This day there was no sign of smoke anywhere and the sky was bright and blue. Why would the bells be ringing so desperately?

Whatever the reason, the response was uniform – mothers with babies astride their hips rushing barefoot, shirtless labourers carrying their machetes from the coconut and cinnamon plantations, fishermen in dripping wet trousers, children scurrying between the adults, some naked, being chased by various dogs, the white-haired and white-bearded elders with their walking sticks – all came as one in response to the call of the bells. At the top of the steps in front of the entrance of the church of Saint Roch, a solemn figure in a brown cassock stood his ground, dignified yet defiant. God's messenger knew he was never alone, particularly in moments like this one. The white document he was clutching in his hands was not his usual Holy Bible. He gripped the document like a missive from God, one with a message not to be confused.

The villagers making their way to the sound of the bell came to a stop on the lawn in front of the steps. They stood motionless, expectant, filled with apprehension as the bells continued to ring, on and on and on.

Then the bells stopped, the last echo of their pure sound lost to the silent gathering. Before he spoke, the old priest uttered a silent prayer. *Please guide me, oh my Lord, guide me and show me how to protect them in this ordeal we are about to face.* He raised his eyes to heaven and then blessed the gathering with the sign of the cross.

Louis studied the silver antique pocket watch he had received for his seventeenth birthday from his parents. Three o'clock exactly. He snapped shut the cover and sighed. He had been waiting for over one hour. She had never before missed one of their rendezvous, and the questions raged.

What could have happened? Why did he feel this sense of foreboding? Why was the tranquillity of this garden suddenly lost to him? Was she unwell? Had someone learned of their meetings and caused problems for her with her parents?

His fears and suspicions began to unravel. In a desperate attempt to try and find an answer and to stop himself from further panic, Louis decided to focus all his thoughts on their meeting here last Friday. Perhaps the cause of her absence could be found there…suddenly, he hit himself in the thigh. *How could I have been so stupid, so blind!* He cursed himself, as he realised that there *had* been something wrong, something very different about her whole composure and attitude on that day, and he had been too preoccupied in his own world to notice. She had been extremely quiet and reserved and had hardly uttered a single word and yes, he remembered now that she had avoided his gaze completely.

It was all coming back, her nervous response about being concerned for a patient and then her abrupt departure, and all the while she had been unable to look at him, but why, why?

He felt a cold shiver as he remembered those strange marks on her legs. At the time they had looked look like two long nail or claw scratches…maybe they were something else, something more sinister. Could they have been the marks of the cane? *Good Lord no, not that!* He jumped up and ran toward the hospital, only to stop as he realised he was not allowed to inquire about her. Their friendship was a secret. So he turned, his mind in turmoil and started the walk back to Beau Vallon. He found himself breathless and panting, caught up in the middle of the large crowd standing silently outside the Saint Roch church. The priest's words had not sounded real.

"Victoria Hospital is under quarantine because of an outbreak of smallpox."

Everyone in the crowd quivered with fear and immediately created space between themselves and their neighbours, murmuring under their breath. Not Louis. All he could think about was Anna. She was out there in the hospital, in the middle of it all. He remembered his walk from the botanical garden towards Beau Vallon, while he had desperately tried to figure out what could have happened to her.

Why did she not turn up for their rendezvous? Then the sounds of the church bells non-stop ringing had greeted him as he had come over the top of Saint Louis' hill. There had been an urgency in their tone, one that could not be ignored, one that was calling out to him personally. He had felt a cold shiver run down his spine, and for the second time today started running...this time towards the summons of the bells.

Now, as he watched the crowd disperse slowly in silence, he wondered what would happen to them all. How bad would things get? How long would it last? Would Anna survive this ordeal? This last thought filled him with horrible pain and anguish. The statue of Saint Roch and his dog in the small alcove at the entrance of the church seemed to call to him then, urging him to seek the guidance and strength he needed within these old walls in front of him. He desperately needed the sanctuary of the church now, right now. He could not wait until eight o'clock to attend the four-hour candle vigil that Père Valer had said he would be holding every single night until the dreadful scourge had vanished from the soils of the Seychelles. He needed God's help now, right this very minute.

From the first floor balcony of Victoria Hospital, Anna stood quietly, her hands gripping the cold metal of the balcony railings, staring towards the harbour at Port Victoria far away in the distance. The first light of the impending sunrise was coming up from behind those small islands dotting the front of the port, lifting the darkness.

In the past, that scene had always been so calming and reassuring. But now, it all seemed like only the illusion of a peaceful dream, a dream so distant. She gratefully breathed in the sea breeze that caressed and soothed her face. Yes, there was still hope, it told her. She closed her eyes and drew in several more deep, slow breaths. For a brief moment the fresh, salted air seemed to cleanse her lungs and her soul, and dispel the lingering scent of putrefaction, despair and death that seemed to lay on her like a blanket.

"Quite beautiful, isn't it?"

Anna turned to see Patricia Kent joining her at the railing.

"Yes, it is comforting," Anna answered.

They stood alongside one another, gazing toward the sunrise as it performed its magic right in front of their eyes. In their hearts, they both uttered the same prayer. One Catholic, one Protestant, they asked God for an end to the suffering; they asked for a miracle in ten days time, on Christmas Day.

It had been three months of pain and misery, death and suffering, as the stream of admissions had grown day by day. Scores of faces in total despair, knowing only fear and the certainty of what awaited them. They were brought in by the police, who found them in hiding after neighbours and even family members had reported them, being terrified for their own safety. Mothers and fathers, knowing they would never see their children again. Scared of being buried alive. Yes, even that was rumoured on the island, as the epidemic reached into every grove, house and garden. The rumours and fear found their greatest strength in ignorance. There was so little real information, just a world turned upside down.

The Government had instituted changes which upended traditional practices governing deaths, wakes and funerals…all in an effort to prevent any further spread of the virus. Superstitious by nature, many people read ulterior motives in these new rules and regulations. How could they not be allowed to see their loved ones? How could they not be allowed to say proper goodbyes? How could they not be allowed to ensure that their bodies and souls were carefully prepared for burial and the hereafter, beyond the grasp of the sorcerers and witchdoctors who resided all around the island?

They were convinced by the rumour that the Government was trying to rid the island of anyone who fell sick by burying them immediately, while they were still alive. As the stories flourished, they were embellished with gruesome details, such as the screams of live patients trying to claw their way out of coffins as they were being lowered into the grave. All lies, of course, but rumour has a way of embedding itself more than the truth, especially in the minds of the Creole people.

In the hospital, even the strongest disinfectants were not able to hold off the stench of the disease. Big painful blisters covered the patient's entire bodies, producing a foul-smelling scab which took weeks to drop off, and in some cases causing gangrene of the skin. The tropical heat made matters worse, causing more hardship for the patients suffering from high temperatures, and for the nursing staff trying to keep them comfortable. The smell of decaying flesh had a way of adhering to everything, lingering, adding the terror of rotting away while still alive to the existing fear of being buried alive.

It was a horrendous experience for any nurse, having to helplessly watch fellow human beings going through this nightmare. But, whilst they tried their utmost to be as efficient as they could, there was also a great fear accompanying their daily toil. Any mistake whilst tending their patients would result in them becoming infected, as the smallpox virus is highly contagious. It was a harrowing and terrifying prospect.

The rattling of the oxcart wheels on the coarse sun-baked clay brought Anna out of her momentary reverie. The cart turned the corner of the hospital and crossed to the front of the building, coming into view. It paused for a few seconds, before starting its slow descent down the long driveway which led to the main road of Mont Fleurie, at the bottom of the hill. The two wooden coffins lay side by side in the back of the cart, on a bed of white coral lime, bare of flowers, forbidding in the early morning light.

Two barefoot porters dressed in grey calico walked a few paces behind the oxcart, whilst two others walked on opposite sides of the oxen, guiding and steadying its pace.

A few steps in front of this small funeral procession, an old priest dressed in a brown cassock and brown leather strap sandals and carrying a wooden cross on his chest, escorted these two souls on their final journey. Anna made the sign of the cross as she watched the two casualties from her night duty shift. One had succumbed to the virility of the smallpox, her face disfigured almost beyond recognition, whilst the other had been a victim of skin gangrene that had spread without control, covering large areas of his body.

She recalled the despair in their eyes when they sensed the end was nearing, and the sadness and determination she felt as she had carefully written down their last messages to their loved ones. She had tried to make those last moments as comfortable as possible, replacing in a small way the presence of those who could not be there with them. She prayed silently as she watched them go. *Dear Lord, please grant them eternal peace.*

Later that day, around the conference table at Sir Terence Hastings' residence, there was unease as the meeting was started. At the onset of the epidemic, they had all had visions of themselves being hailed as the heroes who made the right decisions from the start and who managed to contain this deadly scourge. But now, three months down the line, circumstances were dictating a different story altogether.

The motion that '*all ships should be cleared by a Medical Officer before being allowed entry into Port Victoria, and if any signs of disease were detected, then the ship and all its passengers should be quarantined away from the main island of Mahé*' was carried unanimously, and apparently without irony. The outside world had already quarantined itself against the Seychelles.

No country or islands of the Indian Ocean wanted anything to do with the Seychelles, and no ships had called into Port Victoria since the outbreak of the epidemic had been officially declared. Seychelles' neighbours, and indeed the world, had shown her the true face of isolation in her dire moment of need. She was on her own, faced with a deadly scourge that one of her neighbours had inflicted on her, and now three months down the line she was also staring at another daunting prospect. Famine.

How he longed to hear another voice call out, "Good day, Constable" but the market square was empty and the streets deserted. The hustle and bustle that made the square and his task so robust and enjoyable was long gone. Instead, he walked the empty roads and pathways, hearing only the echo of his own boots.

Ten days before Christmas and the place was eerily quiet. There were no oxcarts filled with baskets of supplies juggling for space in between the rickshaws and ordinary pedestrians going in all directions.

No petty thieves and drunken trouble makers, no ladies performing a 'cat fight' whilst tearing at each other's hair and screaming accusations about who had been having an affair with whose husband. All was silent and empty. Even those grey-haired old-timers squatting along the roadside with their miniscule metal weighing scales, selling pipe tobacco in green banana leaves, had long gone. It was just like a very bad nightmare, one from which Police Constable Lafortune wished he could wake up.

His instructions from the Sergeant had been clear. Constant patrol and surveillance of all the stores and sheds by the Port. Any unauthorised person found in the vicinity, without good reason, was to be arrested. Furthermore, from that point on, any and all oxcarts carrying supplies from any store needed written authority duly signed and stamped by officials of the Queen's Building. Any unauthorised supplies leaving the Port were to be confiscated at once and escorted to the police station. With immediate effect, all food and commodities in the Seychelles were being strictly rationed, and it was the duty of the police to see that this new law was properly enforced.

He had never felt so alone. The enormity of the Seychelles' predicament and his duty as a Police Officer stared him squarely in the face. It demanded his strongest stance in this dilemma, and he felt a strange and ominous chill slowly infiltrating his being as he contemplated the nature of his position.

Walking from the market square towards the port he could feel her presence. She had always been there, part of the background, part of his patch, but he had never stopped and really looked at her properly. The wooden pier of Port Victoria was deserted, even the old 'sea salts,' its permanent fixture, were nowhere to be seen.

His heart felt heavy, the heat of the bright afternoon sunshine did nothing to clear the cold feeling that had consumed him. He stood for a long moment at the end of the pier, staring helplessly at the empty port. He felt her aura before he even turned around. In the depth of his subconscious her images started to form, and he turned and started back at her. He was awestruck. For the next few seconds it felt as though there were only the two of them on this island, in this whole world. He was rooted to the spot, her vast presence enveloping him in its bewitching aura, connecting to a part of himself he did not realise he possessed.

The mountain of Trois Frères stared at the solitary figure on this empty pier. She could feel his helplessness. History had taught her to be stronger in times of difficulty, to stand taller when times are hard and demanding, just as he would have to learn to do now. It filled his heart and soul to overflowing. It was a feeling of pure love, genuine peace and yet a strong and confident force.

It was commanding him to stand firm, deliver his role with dedication and to believe in the future. Believe that God will always love and protect the Seychelles. Cold perspiration was running down his face as he raised his shaking hand and made the sign of the cross. Acknowledging this celestial order, the tiny white cross, standing reverently proud on the first mount of Trois Frères looked down peacefully on him. He recalled the old nun who had taught him catechism prior to his First Holy Communion. It was then that he learned all about the bravery and determination of the men who had built the massive cross on Mahé's highest mountain. They had made it big enough so that it could be seen with the naked eye some three thousand feet down on the shores. It thus became the Seychelles' eternal monument for all posterity, a laborious endorsement of Christian faith, erected by those very first Catholic crusaders, those original *colon* who had brought the true faith to these shores.

She was looking so beautifully resplendent now, glistening against the clear blue sky directly behind her, dominating this whole spectacle at her feet in a divine fortitude and sincere form of perpetual protection. He could feel that cold chill easing slowly, his being returning to normal, as this added sense of warmth took hold of his heart, and he knew then, deep down in his soul, that all was going to come back to normal again. *Very soon*, the feeling was telling him. *Very soon, my son, stand firm.*

About noon on Christmas Eve Louis left the boat building yard, heading home to Beau Vallon. As he joined the main road, he saw an oxcart loaded with gunny bags of *laso*, coming from the direction of the kilns at Cascade, or from further afield in the east of Mahé at Anse aux Pins. He felt a cold tug at his heart as he watched the cart, as he knew its destination. The mortuary at the Victoria hospital.

His thoughts drifted back to the funeral procession he had encountered a few days before. As the cortège passed him on the road, he had stopped and made the sign of the cross, bowing his head in respect, and it was then that he noticed that the two coffins in the back of the oxcart were laid out on a bed of fresh white laso.

What had been poignant about this procession was the scene just before the cortège passed him. As the rattle of the cart's wheels had come closer and closer, he had watched as the windows of the little wooden huts lining the two sides of the road had systematically closed one by one, in a quiet and orderly rhythm.

It was as if their inhabitants were trying to block out the reminder of death, as if they would be too exposed if their windows were left open. At the same time, through the gaping holes in between the wooden planks of those windows, he had sensed their eyes peering at the funeral procession.

He felt such grief then, as he had realised that this dreaded plague was not only killing the flesh, but the soul of his island, turning decent islanders into creatures hiding behind their closed windows, shaking with dread each time they heard the rattle of the oxcart wheels.

As he walked past the entrance of the botanical garden, his own sense of loss was almost overwhelming. He would have given all that he owned to be able to see her, to be close to her once again. Subconsciously, he found himself walking through the garden in the direction of the sanctuary they had shared, and he could feel her presence as he stared at the empty seat next to the small pool. He had not been back since the day the epidemic was declared, three months and nine days ago, and since then each and every day had been long and painful.

Had it only been the Christmas Eve the year before that he had listened with joy as her clear voice echoed around the church with those lovely Christmas hymns? Just a year since he had held her hand for the first time after midnight mass? And just over five months ago when he had kissed her on her birthday?

Can you feel me now? he asked aloud to the empty sanctuary they had shared. He was so near, yet so far from her. *Could she sense his thoughts? Did she still care for him?* He could not bear the thought that she would not survive this horrible time, and that he would find her name had been added to that long, dreadful list hanging on the church's door. *Please God, spare her. Be merciful*

Even as Louis prayed for the safety of Anna, at Beau Vallon, Albert's thoughts were likewise focused on his first-born. He had left work early and with nothing to occupy him, he found himself wondering how she was coping. He had heard whispers of how overworked the hospital staff was, with the hospital being packed with patients, and to judge by the ever-lengthening list on the church door, more victims every day.

How was she managing? Was she all right? From the time he was a little boy, Christmas Eve had always been an active day. In every corner of the village, pigs fattened during the year were heard squealing with the first light of dawn. Today though, silence reigned over the village, and Albert knew that this same silence was being repeated everywhere. The Seychelles were in mourning. There would be no celebrations this Christmas.

Albert had tried to remain positive throughout the epidemic. He had to believe that it would end and all would return to normal. He even managed to communicate his positive attitude to Christophe du Barré and they had combined forces in a union of optimism, just as they had in the past. Standing together firmly against the odds.

Whilst other plantation owners had cut back on production because nothing was being exported from the Seychelles, they maintained production levels, rotating existing stock in the sunshine and in the kalorifer to preserve them, and had built new sheds to accommodate the growing stock. Albert knew they were trying to ride out this storm in the best way they knew, by keeping themselves permanently busy.

Genevieve du Barré had also been keeping herself busy, spearheading the church's request for donations of bed linen for the hospital. In an effort to contain the virus, every dead patient were buried with their bed linen and clothing. Henri accompanied his mother on her buying sprees, acquiring large stocks of white *matapolanm* fabric from the Indian and Chinese shopkeepers in town, and with the assistance of a small army of seamstresses from all over the north of Mahé, Genevieve had ensured that the hospital remained well stocked.

From his vantage on the hill, Albert could see the approaching figure of the Police Constable climbing the small footpath towards his cottage. His heart froze as he noted the dreaded brown 'Envelope of Death' in his hand, the official confirmation from the Government to families, advising them of the death and internment of their relatives.

Breathe, he said inwardly, trying to force himself to do so. But he could not. He felt a great weight in his chest, squeezing his lungs in a vicious tight grip. *Oh Lord no, not Anna, not my beautiful daughter.* He knew he had to get to the footpath to intercept the Constable, to stop him from reaching his cottage, for he did not want him delivering the news directly to his family. No matter what, that was his responsibility alone. His legs felt like lead, his head spun in a near faint. By sheer will, he stumbled forward.

"Bonswar, Msye Savy," the Constable greeted him, staring into this pale and utterly desolate face with its dilated pupils. "Would you please take me to the house of Madanm Angeline Victoire."

Albert stood stock still, dumbfounded. He was breathless, clammy and trembling, staring at the brown envelope in the hand of this Messenger of Death. It took a moment for the words to fully register.

"Yes...yes, of course," Albert finally stammered, his heart pounding in his chest. "Please...follow me." The cold grip of the mortal shock slowly released its iron hold. Though he wished no ill on anyone else, he said a silent prayer of thanks for his own good fortune.

The smell of *karang* frying in freshly-extracted coconut oil wafted on the late afternoon breeze. Albert and the Constable made their way up the footpath. As they turned the corner around the boulder next to the *bilenbi* tree, they could see the smoke from the tiny outside kitchen rising above the banana trees circling the hut – dinner was being prepared.

They were greeted by a typical scene of a Creole plantation worker's way of life. But as Albert observed the quiet dignity of that scene which was about to be shattered, he sighed. He wished he was only here to collect the weekly contribution of eggs, vegetable and fruits that Angeline grew on a *mwatye* system with the du Barré estate. A few hens and their broods of chicks were rummaging around the yard, scratching the bare soil, searching for worms or insects, while two young reddish cocks were showing off their prowess, putting on a good fighting display for the pleasure of the hens, who seemed oblivious to their virile show.

One of Angeline's sons was sitting astride a *larap koko* near the kitchen, trying to get the flesh out of a halved coconut shell. On the small rock leading into the doorway of the hut, the imposing figure of old Madanm ti-Jean, Augustin's mother, sat with her legs very wide apart, her ankle length floral print skirt almost reaching the ground. She was busy prising the tiny round leaves off a big branch of *bred mouroun* on her lap and carefully depositing them in the *lavann* at her feet. She was a typical matriarch of the time, a respected, feared and fat figure, wearing a *servyet latet* and the unmistakeable loose *kazak* top.

She was sucking on the *priz taba* at the back of her mouth and spat the black residue next to the rock where she sat, while simultaneously ordering her grandchildren about, complaining about how lazy they had all become since their father had been hospitalised, and how he would be changing things with his cane when he came home.

"Bonswar, Angeline," Albert shouted.

Loud barks came from a dog who suddenly materialised from behind the hut, teeth bared and heading straight for the lower legs of the Police Constable. Luckily, the dog was restrained by the quick action of another of Angeline's sons, who had been tending to the pigswill bucket in the corner of the yard.

A barefoot woman with a naked two-year-old baby astride her hip, and holding a wooden cooking *lespatil* in one hand, emerged from the smoke-filled kitchen. As soon as she saw the Constable with his official envelope accompanying Msye Albert, her emaciated frame swayed involuntarily, a pallid tone settling on her frightened black face. Albert reached out just in time, catching the baby as Angeline's legs gave way. The Constable followed suit, catching her before she hit the ground. Heart-wrenching screams echoed all around them as they laid the fainted Angeline against the side of the kitchen.

Madanm ti-Jean had both her hands on her head and was turning around and around in the scattered *bred mouroun* leaves on the ground, stamping the yard with her bare feet, and letting her lungs amplify the hillside with the unbridled pain of losing a son.

Her anguished *kriz* summoned their neighbours, whose hurried and understanding faces emerged from behind every banana tree around the hut, ready to show their strength and unity, and their Christian beliefs and duties in moments of such terribly tragedy.

Even as her father was accompanying the Constable in delivering his dreaded news, Anna was on her knees, alone in the chapel at Victoria Hospital, praying to God for a miracle. During the past months she had confided her emotions and fears to him in her daily prayers, seeking strength and guidance.

But this day, this Christmas Eve, she felt different. Today she felt a cold fear in her heart. God's strength had sustained her as she stared at death daily, but in the early hours of this Christmas Eve, as she watched Augustin Victoire take his last, agonising breath, her fears, hurt and desires had all caught up with her. He was the first casualty from the du Barré plantation, a silent confirmation that the disease was among her family.

Over the past months, she had felt a guilty relief that none of the many new patients were members of her family. Then three weeks earlier Augustin was admitted, and the realization that no one was safe truly seeped into her soul.

Confined for such an extended period of time in the intensity of a hospital under quarantine, without seeing her family or her home, without being with Louis, and without getting her daily dose of 'soulful replenishment' from Beau Vallon's nature, all conspired to have a profound effect on her. Yet, for all the hardship, this period had also given her a space and time to reflect, to look closely at her own life and to see things in a new way. Maybe it was the daily dealings with death and the witnessing of human desperation, or maybe it was just the pain and suffering all around her that had prompted this self-analysis.

Whatever it was, it had served a dual purpose: it gave her insight and also helped her cope with her immediate circumstances. It allowed her to mentally detach herself from everything that was happening around her when she was away from the ward, and to concentrate instead on her own emotions and on her own probable future.

For the first time, Anna felt she understood that *love* - that four-letter word - was capable of creating so much havoc, pain and tender joy. She understood her feelings toward Louis. Sadly, her introspection also brought forth the reality of their relationship, and she realised that Louis saw her only as a friend, a special friend to be sure, but only a friend nonetheless.

She was someone to whom he could talk freely, someone he could trust. Many of her patients told her they found it easy to talk and to confide in her. Perhaps it was this quality that Louis responded to.

However, she felt certain that he did not harbour the same emotions and feelings for her that she felt for him. It was a great shame, to be sure.

Her feelings were such beautiful feelings to have for someone, all encompassing and pure, with a tenderness so profound it filled her heart and soul, her entire being, to overflowing.

But, at dawn today, when they had drawn the bed-sheet over Augustin's face, the fear that gripped her had been like nothing she had ever felt before. Louis was at risk. *He could be in this bed next,* she heard an inner voice say. Of course this was true, and it left her with a feeling of emptiness she could not describe. All she knew was that these feelings propelled her to the sluice room where she vomited the remainder of the black coffee that had kept her alert during her long night shift. Hot tears flowed down her face. *Dear Lord, please hear my plea. Please spare him, please let him live the beautiful destiny to which he was born.* She simply could not bear the thought that he might die. She was sure that it would mean the end of her life too, for she could not envisage a world without him – even if only as friends.

Despite her weariness, Anna had been unable to sleep during the day. Now, as she watched the sun's rays through the chapel windows and her night duty shift beckoned, she wondered how she would cope. *I will need your strength to manage tonight,* she whispered, *please help me to discharge my duty to the best of my ability.* Making the sign of the cross, she slid from the bench and knelt on one knee in the aisle and bowed her head to the altar. As she visualized His blessings on herself, she felt at that precise moment that her prayers were answered, and a solution became apparent to her.

With tears running down her cheeks, she walked solemnly to the altar, her whole being shivering with the enormity of her decision. She knelt on both knees in front of the Tabernacle and said aloud, *On this Christmas night, oh Lord, I pledge the remainder of my life on this earth to your service. I could never love another man and I will never know Louis' love, for our births and status are worlds apart. I beg you, Lord, to accept my pledge and keep him safe. I promise that I will take the Veil and dedicate my life to relieving the suffering of others. Please hear me, Lord, and grant me this mercy, on this the night of your birth. Please keep Louis safe from harm.*

The sky about Beau Vallon was fiery as Louis walked to La Residence, then straight to the atelier. Other than their oasis, it was only there that he could feel close to Anna, where he could look at his sculpture of her and recapture her image. He gazed upon that inspired work, expecting at any moment that she would smile at him and speak. He was surprised in his meditation by Marie, who had seen him go to the atelier and had brought him a mug of freshly-brewed coffee.

"Are you all right, Kinox," she asked, using the pet name she had given him when he was born. Since he had become an adult, she had used it infrequently. She was glad to see that it brought a smile to his face. He rested his hand reassuringly on her shoulder.

"Yes, I am fine, Nen Marie."

But she was not so easily fooled. She had seen just that kind of pain before, but for the life of her she could not recall where or when. Perhaps he was struggling with the news of Augustin's death, as was everyone on the plantation.

As Louis sat outside the atelier, sipping his coffee and gazing out at the magnificent, fiery sky, his thoughts were unfocused. It was a moment before he realized the voices he could hear were real, and coming from inside the atelier. Simon, the elder carpenter, and Yvon, his colleague, had come in to put the tools away for the night. Louis ignored their conversation until he heard Simon remind Yvon about his premonition, and it was only then as they spoke about Augustin Victoire that Louis first learned the sad news about the plantation's first fatality.

"I knew it," Simon insisted. "I knew she was the angel of death. Bad omens. Bad omens indeed."

"I saw her too."

"Yes, she came out from behind the bougainvillea bush in the garden…"

As he listened, Louis learned that all this had transpired on the night of the gala at the house, and that this *angel of death* had long, black hair and was dressed in white. When she ran across the garden, her feet never touched the ground, and all they could hear was low, moaning sobs as she floated toward the beach. And later, a terrible scream before she was swallowed by the sea. *Such foolishness*, Louis sighed to himself as he angrily dismissed their ignorance and superstition.

"Who do you think is next?" Yvon asked.

"You are right," Simon agreed. "Today, she took her first victim. There will be others. Maybe one of us. After all, we saw her…"

"You were right," Yvon said. "She was a bad omen. An evil sign."

Louis shook his head in disbelief. *Angels of death? Screams? Preposterous.* He dismissed the talk as being the result of too much baka. But then he remembered that Simon did not drink because of his diabetes. Suddenly, the hairs on the back of his neck stood up, and he jumped up and started walking toward the garden.

He had no idea where exactly he was going other than toward the bougainvillea bush, or what he expected to find. After all, four months had already passed since that night. He stopped suddenly as a shaft of the sun's failing light hit something on the ground. He bent to take a closer look. *What's this?* Tiny arms reached up from the blades of grass. He parted the grass and drew a quick breath. He reached for the small mermaid and, holding her carefully in his hand, he began to shake. *Anna, Anna.*

He looked toward the house. The view of the veranda was clear and unobstructed. His eyes widened. *No!* he cried out, seeing in his mind's eye what Anna had seen that night. She had seen him on the steps, and she had seen Marie-Ange de la Fontaine come to bring him back to the dance floor. He felt his knees weaken. *That* was the reason she ran. *Oh Anna, she was only a guest.* He wished he'd never come out to see the torches. He wished he'd stayed in the house. Aggravated, he turned abruptly to go to the beach. His arm scraped against the branches of the bougainvillea, and the thorns tore at his flesh, leaving two long scratch marks.

The last remaining bit of the sun was just visible over the horizon as Louis arrived at the driftwood. Christmas Eve, he thought silently to himself. It did not felt like it. He sat and gazed at the horizon as the last of the sun's golden rays were extinguished in the sea. *Talk to me*, he said softly to the small sculpture in his hand. *Tell me what you know, my beauty.*

The little mermaid looked back lovingly at him, her gaze prompting him to believe the evidence in front of his eyes, daring him to believe that his dearest wish was true.

Holding tightly onto the small sculpture, trying to let his emotions transcend that barrier of space between them, trying with every fibre of his soul to reach out to her, he so desperately wanted to hear Anna's voice. *Talk to me, talk to me, my love. I need to know,* he said aloud in the approaching dusk, *do you love me?*

Just then, the sound of the Saint Roch bells reverberated throughout the heavens. He heard in their pure peals the answer to his question.

"Yes! She loves you. She loves you more than you know."

Even as he received his answer, he felt the pain of uncertainty. Would he ever see her again? Would he ever get the chance to confess his love to her? The turmoil caused him to bow his head and weep, softly at first, then he let out all the anguish and pain of those last few months, as the absorbent sand of Beau Vallon hid his sorrows and sufferings.

The old hospital Matron wanted nothing more than to visit the chapel on this Christmas Eve. Her legs were weak, it was true, but she missed its quietude and peacefulness. Six weeks of pain and a sense of helplessness since the pneumonia first ravaged her frail body. More than once, she was sure that the Almighty was ready to take her, and the priest was called to perform the sacred rites.

But then the fever broke and her delirium abated. Her services were still needed here on earth it seemed, especially in this dire predicament that her hospital and staff were facing.

Now, as she arrived at the open doorway of the chapel, she was astounded by the vision that greeted her. Her legs almost gave way and she leaned more heavily on the two nurses supporting her. Before her, the white-clad figure kneeling in deep prayer in the front row of benches was oblivious to their presence. A sharp pain pierced her seventy-year-old heart. *How dare she, how dare an infidel defile the sanctity of my church?*

She shook in a violent rage. One by one, her ancient hurts and scars were reopened. She could feel them torn and bleeding, causing her raw, renewed pain. All those horrifying images and memories of her childhood traumas, all laid bare again.

She wouldn't put up with this abhorrent insult! No!

Please Lord give me strength to throw her out of your church, she heard her heart pleading. She leaned forward…out of nowhere, stopping her in her tracks, an invisible presence towered before her. Its power was so real and very deep. She sensed it with every fibre of her being. She felt its beautiful mix of deep love and pure peace, and was completely enveloped by its protective cloak. Her anger eased. She stood rooted to the spot, her mouth agape, the screams dying in her throat, trying to fathom this mystical phenomenon. And then she felt a sense of serene well-being…

The two nurses sat her comfortably in bed and she nodded a sign of appreciation, her hand gesturing them out of the room. All those tender and loving sensations were still vivid throughout her as she stared at the holy image of the Sacred Heart of Jesus hanging on the wall across the room. *Why Lord, why?* her soul pleaded.

With eyes closed, her mind returned to her native Irish village of Skibbereen in County Cork. The year was 1848 and she was only five years old. Ah, the images. Those horrible images! As distinct and vivid as they had been sixty-five years earlier. Her childhood was marked by hardship, pain, desperation and desolation. There was never enough to eat for her four sisters and five brothers, and everyone in the village, from her parents to the nuns and priests, looked skeletal.

The death and dying had begun in 1846. By mid-1848, she had lost her father, four brothers and four sisters to the potato famine. "They have gone to heaven," her mother sighed after each death, whether to reassure herself or her remaining children, she couldn't be sure. But oh, how she missed them. Particularly Mary, her elder sister.

Sixty-five years of prayer had failed to erase the memory of that night before Mary *went to heaven*. The look of desperation in Mary's eyes, as she had stared at that last morsel of food on her plate. "If only I had found the courage to give it to her," she cried to her soul every night since. "Maybe it would have been enough to save her life." She would never know and that uncertainty was to be the burden she would carry the remaining days of her life.

After Mary, there were only the three of them, two-year-old Peter, herself and their gaunt mother, Teresa. They shared a bed and, despite the hardship, it was reassuring to be so close together. Her tears were now streaming down both cheeks, drenching the white nun's habit around her face, as the images of the first day of August 1848 played in her mind's eyes. It was on that day that this heavy sword was placed in her hands and the onerous cross strapped across her back.

Peter always used to wake her, but on that day he had still been fast asleep, cuddled up against their mother, both looking peaceful. Leaning over Peter, she tried to kiss her mother on the cheek, but had jerked back quickly. Teresa's face was freezing cold. She was trembling now, as she remembered her screams and her desperate efforts to wake them. Then their neighbours had burst into the house. "They have gone to heaven," they told her, trying to take her from the room. All she remembered thinking was "Why did they not take me with them? "Why did they leave me all alone? and "Why is it so cold in heaven?"

When she took the Veil in 1861, Harriet Moore became 'Sister Patrick' in honour of the old nun who had nursed her back to health after her nervous breakdown and battle with pneumonia and malnutrition in 1848. That old nun had cared for her during the years of her childhood and adolescence, teaching her all she knew about nursing, giving her a platform which had kept her anchored during all these long years. Until this day…

She had learned to read and write at the convent, a privilege which the other poor, Catholic children of Ireland did not have at the time.

Though the Penal Laws of 1695, denying them the right to be educated, had been gradually repealed in the late 18th century, they were not completely removed until the Catholic Emancipation of 1829.

Even then, it was many decades before its full positive effects found their way to the poorest children of native Irish peasants. Education was a double-edged sword for Harriet. It liberated her, but also made her aware of the full scale of the atrocities perpetrated by the British upon Ireland. That knowledge combined with the traumas of the first five years of her life to harden her soul, making true love and forgiveness that much more difficult.

As a young nun practising nursing in the poorer community, she had seen the physical and emotional results of poverty and oppression and it had made that cross even harder to bear. Those who survived the potato famine bore the scars of the terrible infections they had contracted in those disease-infested workhouses, where whole families who were considered lucky to be admitted, were forced to take refuge after being evicted from their homes when the potato crops failed, and they were unable to pay rent to their wealthy landlords. Over one million less fortunate souls simply perished. Friends and families were forbidden by their landlords to take in the dispossessed. Living in ditches and burrows, forced to eat rotten potatoes and wild berries, they wandered with no destination. Their emaciated corpses were buried in mass graves, or simply left where they fell.

The horror of the Potato Famine was intensely personal for Harriet. She had watched every member of her family starve to death, and then to subsequently learn that an abundance of food was being exported from Ireland to England during those famine years, making wealthy landowners richer still, was just something she could neither forgive, nor forget. Britain had made its calculation and had determined that profits were more important than human souls. And the removal of the poor, by any means, was an admirable solution to over-population problems. God could teach love and forgiveness, but the reality of it would be much harder to achieve.

But now, this Christmas Eve, after carrying her hurt, anger and hate for sixty-five years, God was asking for more. He wanted her unconditional love. "See through my eyes," He whispered to her heart. She felt lost, her beliefs and foundations shaking at their core. In was then, in total desperation, she heard her soul cry out agonisingly to him.

Please help me, Lord, she prayed weakly. *I am too tired. Help me. It has hurt for too long.* She could feel that presence again, coming close, infusing her body and her soul. "Do not be frightened. Believe unconditionally."

Love works miracles. She surrendered to the presence and felt peace fill her. For the first time, she saw Patricia Kent as a human being, not as a Protestant, or a British subject. As woman on her own in life, very far away from her family and her home.

She was a good nurse. A wonderful nurse. She had demonstrated a keen mind, tremendous strength and devotion and hard work during the months of this epidemic. She cared for each of her patients with equal care and dedication, without regard to status or the colour of their skin. Patricia's strength kept the small team of nurses strong in the face of the horror they were all enduring. But what touched her most deeply was the devotion and care Patricia had given to her during those terrible weeks of her fight with pneumonia. Nothing that she had done in the past to make life difficult for Patricia had deterred her. She never faltered in her care, guiding her away from the gates of death.

Sister Patrick felt a new pain then, a sharp hurting pain – the pain of remorse. For now she could see Patricia Kent for what she was, a lost and tired soul, all alone, and like everyone else in need of God's strength and guidance on this Christmas night. *Please forgive me, oh Lord, forgive me, I am not worthy of your love.*

His answer came quickly. She could feel him reach out, removing the sword and the heavy cross from her. She felt his inner peace and love. So beautiful and so real. She knew then that it was finally all over. His forgiving heart had conquered her troubled soul.

Her relief was infinite as she cried one last time for all of them, for her parents and her brothers and sisters, and for those millions left to die on the altar of greed and selfishness.

After a day of meditation and prayer for a miracle on this Christmas night, old Père Valer stood still, high up in his pulpit, listening to the silence of his congregation below. All eyes stared up at him, wondering why he was starting the Christmas midnight mass with a sermon.

"My children," he began, as he blessed them with the sign of the cross, "Tonight, on this very special night of the year, we dedicate this mass and our prayers to Reverend Père Theophile, and the nuns, doctors, nurses and helpers who have been at Victoria hospital for all these past months, working tirelessly day and night, under horrifying conditions. And to what aim? To bring comfort and assistance to the suffering of our brothers and sisters who have fallen prey to this terrible plague. Let us all therefore pray to the Lord, on this night of his birth, so that he gives them his strength, guidance and courage to continue in their hard work".

As he spoke, Père Valer thought of the letter he had received from Sister Patrick describing the hardships he was now sharing with his flock. With each paragraph, the letter made clear that the hospital was facing a crisis due to a lack of nurses. "Please, look to your heart and prayers to find a way to help parents see the importance and dignity of allowing their daughters to become nurses."

He concluded his sermon by reading the name of everyone working at Victoria hospital during the epidemic and offered a special prayer for them, with particular emphasis on one particular nurse, a daughter of Saint Roch's church. Monia swallowed deeply as her granddaughter's name was acknowledged by the priest, and she turned her head back and glanced at Albert sitting on the bench behind her, next to Therese and his children. The glow of the candles reflected the tears in his eyes.

She turned back and felt her heart swell with two kinds of pride. Two days earlier, Ghislaine had written, announcing her first pregnancy. The news had brought some light in the darkness that surrounded them. Now, what she had endured as a black cloud on their good family name had just been glorified by the church, with the priest telling all parents about the virtue of nursing, and making a special emphasis when mentioning Anna's name to every member of this congregation. Monia felt truly blessed on this Christmas night. And it was not just Monia who reacted to Anna's name with powerful emotion. In the front row, close to the pulpit, where the elite of this parish sat, a young man in an immaculately tailored suit wiped the moisture from his eyes as Anna's name was acknowledged.

The two women in white came out of the chapel with arms linked, though the elder leaned on the arm of the younger for support. Midnight mass had been different this night, as indeed was everything else. The raised eyebrows, stifled coughs and expressions of complete disbelief that had greeted the entrance of the old Irish Catholic Matron and her English Protestant Assistant Matron as they came into the small Catholic chapel, quickly dissipated as the sincerity of their bond became apparent to all.

When Patricia had visited the Matron earlier that evening, the old nun had asked her to sit down. "What I have to say is very hard for me," she said haltingly. Patricia feared that the Matron was dismissing her, in the middle of the epidemic no less! But that fear was quickly eased.

"When I was a little girl, times were horrible," the Matron began, sharing with Patricia the story of her young years through her life right up to the revelation she'd had earlier that day. Patricia was as shaken as the Matron by the time the older woman concluded with the invitation, "I would be honoured if you would accompany me to midnight mass tonight, to celebrate with me and allow me to ask forgiveness for all I have put you through. I hope that you will find a way in your heart to accept my apology and to forgive me."

It was the true human spirit, that selflessness created of His own image which He bestowed upon the world from the beginning of time, that so illumined the sanctity of the small chapel that Christmas night.

Two souls, one Irish and one English. Borne of the pain and tragedies of two people, two nations and two churches divided in His name. He had set them free tonight…He had answered in his own unique way. No, not the end of the epidemic they all implored. But this…this was the miracle he accorded them on this Christmas night. The miracle of His birth was alive and flourishing on this tiny island that itself was struggling in pain.

The real spirit of Christmas reigned over the Seychelles.

The first yellow-green flowers greeting the slopes of Anse Royale had arrived in November the year before. Sprinkled all over the horizontal trellises and up and down the upright poles of *kalis di pap* which supported the thick and fleshy vines, this small manifestation made his spirit soar at the sight. What a gift! And arriving just a few months after his wedding, as a crowning glory to his biggest gamble.

Ignoring his mother's raised eyebrows, he had taken his young bride regularly to the vines the previous year, proud and happy to share this together. He wanted her to be with him to witness the changing tides of his family's legacy, to see his own ambition realized.

He wanted her to be with him as he took risks and reaped rewards. Had not his grandfather instilled this adventurousness in him? Had he not told him many times the story of his own gambles and adventures? He still remembered his eighth birthday, when Gran Père Olivier held his tiny hand around that soft and delicate flower, and taught him the closely guarded secret of this mystical plant. "They never understood it," he had whispered in his ear, referring to how the secret had eluded man's understanding for centuries, "but now you do."

Monsieur Olivier Maillet was an original Bourbonais. He disembarked on the shores of the Seychelles in the early part of 1853 accompanied by his wife, Aurelia, and their ten-year-old son, Andre. Other than his small family, he brought with him the precious cargo of cultivated vine cuttings from the neighbouring island of Reunion (Île Bourbon).

Olivier gambled everything on this new life in the Seychelles, bringing with him expertise and practical skills in the cultivation and processing of this lucrative and exotic crop. Edmond Albius, a young black slave boy, had mastered the technique in 1841, producing the 'golden pod.' In doing so, he had happened upon a secret which generations of gentlemen scholars of science and botany, as well as scores of aristocratic collectors, adventurers and governments had been trying to uncover, only to ultimately fail.

He had stood behind her on that crisp November morning the year before, holding her hand around the flower exactly as his grandfather had held his, showing her the care and attention she must exercise with each individual flower. Her nimble fingers had tenderly prised open the petals and soft lips of the flower, exposing its moist and secret interiors. She breathed in the gentle fragrance of the nectar-smooth tunnel beneath the thin membrane, which prevented the fertilisation process from occurring.

Using a tiny splinter of bamboo, he taught her to remove the membrane and, once done, to guide her thumb onto the tiny protruding male *anther*, pressing it into the gaping female *stigma*, initiating the copulation. When the process was concluded, he turned her round to face him and kissed her with a passion he'd never shown before, deliriously happy that in nine months time they would collect the fruit of their labour.

Three months along, the rows of vine-covered trellises stretched across the slopes of Anse Royale, heavily laden with bunches of green pods glistening in the early morning sunshine. Without question, it was the best crop the Maillet had produced. For several moments he stood there, feeling his grandfather's presence by his side.

He smiled a smile of quiet pleasure knowing that the success before him was not his alone. It belonged to both of them.

Vanilla was his passion from a tender age, his first love. He had learned from his grandfather who was equally passionate about this exotic orchid. It was not just their livelihood. It was their life's blood. There was a magical, entrancing quality to this plant, in the strength and character of its fleshy vines creeping gracefully up the tree props, in the intricate beauty of its sensual flower and its plump green pods.

Each pod is born out of a single flower which only opens for a few hours once a year and has to be pollinated by hand that same day. Then, the pods need a whole nine months on the vine to mature, plus another nine months for the drying out and processing. It was definitely labour-intensive and not a crop for the faint-hearted.

It had been five years since he approached his father with his new idea. Yes, it was a gamble, but Claude was certain he could make it a success. After much work, he finally convinced Andre Maillet to agree to what he proposed. Traditionally, vanilla vines grow on upright tree props. He had experimented with horizontal trellises connected between the tree props. A bold gamble, turning three acres of prime land into this new cultivation method, sparing no expense when cultivating the tree props in neat and tidy rows, so that the interconnecting trellises could be built properly once the young trees were about two years old. In his scheme there were no wasted spaces between the tree props, giving the vines twice the space to flourish, thus doubling the productivity and yield.

Three years earlier he had planted his cultivated vine cuttings, employing more labourers to ensure that the three acres of new vines were well cared for, with enough coconut husk mulching and the right amount of watering, as well as the systematic pruning of the tree props to generate the right balance of light and shade. The entire endeavour represented three year's tension. So much worry. So much doubt.

But Claude held his nerve, convinced he was on the right path. Then at the beginning of October the previous year, he pruned six inches off the head of each of the vines, halting linear growth and inducing the vine to flower.

It worked.

The feel of her hand on his shoulder brought him back to reality. He turned and smiled, as he put his arm protectively around Ghislaine's shoulder. She had had a glow since the midwife had confirmed her pregnancy in December. Their first-born was due in July, one month before the harvest, on the occasion of their first wedding anniversary.

They both felt joyful and fully blessed. Indeed, there were moments when they feared that they were enjoying *too much* blessing, knowing how others were suffering. Five months into the epidemic and there was still no sign of it ending.

But the Maillets, unlike so many others, had been fortunate with their crops. The harvest of August 1912 was sold to the agents in May 1913 and had left the Seychelles on the steamer in June. They were now in the final stages of conditioning the August 1913 harvest, which would be ready for sale in another three months time. Despite his sense of blessing, Claude understood only too well how precarious their future was. If the epidemic continued much longer and their crop remained on the shelves, they would be in dire financial straits, similar to the other plantations with monthly crops.

Even as Ghislaine stood alongside her husband on the slope of Anse Royale at Victoria Hospital, Anna's day was about to get worse. She was mopping the few remaining patches of ebony skin between the foul smelling scabs that littered Odile Toussaint's face and neck, hoping to freshen her and to bring down her temperature.

Odile's eyes held something different from the deep fear of so many of her patients. Her eyes were deep pools of sadness. She knew what was happening and she had surrendered to it, in perfect knowledge. She was painfully aware that her time was near. Why, even Matron was no longer severe and stern with her, but unusually kind. "God knows of all your hard work," she had said during one of her visits, "and how you selflessly cared for the suffering of others. You will be eternally rewarded, my child." During the previous months, she had been on

Anna's side of the epidemic, standing with her colleagues, nursing hundreds of patients.

No more.

Her only sorrow was not being able to say goodbye to her loved ones, not being able to see them one last time, and the knowledge of their own agony at never having said a proper goodbye to her. Her only, very small, consolation was the promise Anna had made to personally deliver her last wishes to her parent.

Odile wanted them to know of all her hard work during this epidemic, but above all, how much joy and fulfilment nursing had brought into her life, and how she hoped they would be proud of her as a member of that elite team who fought the epidemic.

At exactly three o'clock in the afternoon of 20 February 1914, Nurse Toussaint took her last breath. She was the first member of the nursing staff to die in this epidemic.

There were four women at her bedside at that final moment, one Irish, one English and two Seychelloise, and despite all the professional ethics and protocol, there were tears streaming down their faces as they placed the white sheet over her head.

Matron placed her right hand on Odile's head and whispered, "*God speed, my child.*"

Outside the hospital, in the villages scattered around the island of Mahé, the other effects of the quarantine were making themselves known. With no steamers visiting the island for almost six months, staple commodities such as sugar, rice, flour, lentils, onions, garlic, soap and pepper, were running desperately low. Government rationing had helped a little, but now the Seychelles was poised for its worst nightmare, a famine in the middle of an epidemic.

Deep sadness haunted the tropical breezes, and a sense of total isolation and fear prevailed. Everyone on the island had lost a relative or a friend to the epidemic. No one knew who would be next. All had cast aside their normal friendliness and warmth, and had grown wary of their neighbours, looking for signs and symptoms on every face encountered.

As always, it was the poor who suffered most as circumstances grew worse. Most labourers working the plantations on an already meagre wage saw their working hours halved, and in some cases they were laid off altogether, because crops were not being exported.

Things were desperate indeed, with the British Government struggling to manage only with the assistance given by the network of Catholic churches and its priests. Their influence over the better-off members of their parish saw the coconuts lying wasting in the fields finding their way to the cooking pots of those who had nothing. At the same time, surplus stocks of salted fish and breadfruit were distributed by plantation owners; nothing was allowed to go to waste.

A surge in beekeeping saw an increase in production of honey as a replacement for sugar, whilst cassava *galet* and *penpen* were popular replacements for both rice and flour.

But by far the boldest enterprise to surface out of this tragedy was the small sea-salt factory on the south-east coast of Mahé. Agricultural labourers who had been laid off were employed to collect sea water, which was then exposed to the sun in flat containers, until nature evaporated the liquid and a thin layer of salt crystals could be scrapped off the bottom.

Salting was the only way of preserving fish for local consumption and export, and the makeshift factory was even able to supply some of its stock to retail shops all around the island. Laid-off labourers also found employment in the island's only soap factory whose demands had increased tenfold. There they would collect seaweed for burning with wood chippings, and then combine the ash from them with coconut oil to produce the crude-looking soap bars.

It was a concerted effort from all sides, but there was still a great fear hanging over everyone.

How much longer will the epidemic continue? How long will the food stock last? How many more people are going to die?

Even as the islanders of the Seychelles agonised over their future prospects, in the denseness of this lush tropical oasis, the spirits of their forefathers smiled in quiet contemplation. They had known these islands from the very beginning, when they were still in their virgin state, before men populated their shores, and they were even more bountiful today than they had been on that first landing in 1756. Over those 158 years, their rich soils had seen the introduction of many lucrative new species which had served to enrich their original flora. Today their inhabitants were on the verge of finding out exactly which one of those successful species would prove to be their ultimate lifesaver in this dire moment of their very short history - the breadfruit tree.

These magnificent trees grew in abundance all over the islands, growing to a height of fifty feet and each with a crop of hundreds of fleshy globes over a twelve-month period. Its fruit had a potato-like flavour and texture, was rich in fibre, starch, vitamins and minerals, with a weight of around six to nine pounds when mature, and could be prepared in a variety of ways, making it one of the most versatile crops they possessed.

The trees were also prized by the islanders for the quality of their wood in furniture manufacturing. Steeped in a rich history stretching from the shores of Tahiti to the islands of the Caribbean and beyond, this tropical tree had caused men to revolt, and had brought tragedies on the high seas. This tree saw Captain William Bligh forcibly evicted from HMS Bounty in 1787 and cast adrift in a rowboat in the middle of the vast ocean. He had been accused by his crew of wasting the vessel's precious water stock in his determined efforts to keep the 1,015 new plantings that the Bounty was transporting fresh and alive, at the peril of his own crew, a story which gave the humble *l'arbre a pain* its own place in the annals of history.

In the years to come, it would stand out as one of the most beneficial of decisions taken on that day in September 1913 by all those who had sat around that long table. On that day, the Governor's office made it illegal and a punishable offence for *'anyone to be caught cutting down any breadfruit tree.'*

A simple decree, with a mighty result. This tree was spared, and in turn, it saved the lives of hundreds of desperate islanders.

By mid-March 1914, the medical personnel grew certain that the signs were real, and not mere figments of their hopeful imaginations. Still, they remained silent, frightened to be too optimistic. Finally, Sister Kent broke the spell.

As the morning staff read the handover report to their colleagues, she called attention to the graphs and the well-kept statistics she had carefully compiled.

The pattern was clear. Still, she cautioned about raising hopes, as it could be only a temporary lapse in the virility of the virus. "It is a tricky disease," she noted soberly, as if anyone in the hospital needed to be counselled about the epidemic's nature. No, not until the last remaining crust had disappeared would they dare to give real voice to their hopes. A momentary failure of concentration could be catastrophic. The doctors and nurses were determined to protect each other right to the very end, resolute in their decision that no more lives were going be lost to this terrible scourge.

But the darkness seemed to be lifting. The long nights of vigil and prayers had finally found their way to heaven, just like the nursing care, dedication and devotion had helped heal the mortal flesh, and the human spirit had found the strength to fight back. Where there had been only fear in the eyes of the people on the island, now there was a ray of sunshine. Word was out. The hospital was being fumigated and disinfected. Could it be? Could the epidemic finally be over? The Seychelles dared to smile once more.

At midday on 30th March 1914, in well-orchestrated and beautifully co-ordinated unison, the Catholic and Protestant churches of the Seychelles shared in their first communal initiative. From all over the island, the chorus of church bells merged their joyous peels for the first time in the history of these islands. The epidemic was finally and officially over. The bells rang with a message of victory and triumph, but above all with a message of peace and love.

His love. His Churches. Both celebrating together.

CHAPTER 10

A New Dawn

During the followings weeks it was impossible to escape the sense of euphoria that everyone felt with the release of such a tremendous burden. There was undisguised relief, gratitude for surviving, and great joy as family members were reunited. Along with a deep sadness newly-imprinted on the souls of those who had endured these endless months, there was also a sense of resilience, of renewal that was a legacy of that dreadful time.

Now, on this last day of April, a month after the epidemic finally ended, this strength and resilience was plain to see in the sun-drenched, beautiful town of Port Victoria, where its inhabitants stood alongside each other in the largest gathering in the history of the island.

Old Père Theophile, dignified in his brown cassock and leather strap sandals, emerged gracefully through the arched doorway of the cathedral and into the late morning sunshine. Under the gaze of all of the Christians, he walked solemnly down the wide steps. On his chest he held the same wooden cross that had accompanied every single one of them on their last journey. The bells of The Immaculate Conception, the Patron Saint of Port Victoria, rang out a sombre funeral march as the holy man led the long procession march in the direction of the Mont Fleurie cemetery. It was time to bury the dead properly.

The Bishop of Port Victoria, Monseigneur Leon des Avanchers, led the 'Service of Remembrance' in honour of the 195 smallpox victims.

Their names and the parish they inhabited were read out ceremoniously, with special emphasis on Nurse Odile Toussaint, who was remembered and revered for the sacrifice of her young life in the service of others.

The service was an emotional catharsis for the people of the island and it touched every heart amongst the congregation. They had each suffered through the same nightmare, each and every one had endured the dread of not knowing if they would be next to succumb. For the black-draped relatives of the victims, it was a particularly emotional and painful episode. Yet there was also comfort, for they were now finally participating in a proper funeral ritual, something they had longed to be able to do during those harsh days, to be able to lay their departed to rest and to start in their healing process.

At the top of the little hill, Père Theophile stopped and opened the wooden gate which led to an enclosed, isolated part of the cemetery.

Under strict instructions issued by the medical authority, the Government had ordered all graves of the smallpox victims to be away from the rest of the cemetery and so this area had been fenced in with a locked gate. A drastic measure, true, but one deemed necessary to ensure that none of the graves would be disturbed or re-opened to bury another person, for it was believed that the virus could survive for centuries in the soil.

Turning around, he looked upon the sea of mourners spread out all the way down the little hill. They stood still, waiting. There followed the mass of ordinary Seychellois who had come from all corners of the island to pay their final respects and to show their solidarity, to offer their silent testimony that the spirit of the island and its occupants remained unbroken.

Dotting this ocean of mourners were the bouquets of vibrant tropical blooms they carried, adding colourful resplendence to the midday sky. But the gentle expressions of sadness and remembrance reached out to the old priest, and he carried the weight of that sadness in his heart. He knew the power of his role and his office to these people.

He stood before them as an iconic presence, poised at the top of the hill, ready to guide them to the place he had laid their loved ones to rest. He was the final link, the representative of God who had been there for their loved ones; the one who had given each of them a Christian burial.

As he heard their pain, he felt a tenderness unsurpassed for this grieving flock, for unknown to them, this tragedy had also guided him to his own *raison d'être*. It had been decades since his master had led him to these shores, but it was on those solemn and grim days when he had escorted the oxcart and bare coffins to this silent hilltop, and gave each poor soul their final blessing and Christian burial, that he felt his own divine reason for being. It was then that he understood why he had been sent to these tiny islands.

On this day, his heart rejoiced. Lifting his eyes to the clear blue sky, he thanked his Maker for having chosen him for this task as he blessed the people with the sign of the cross.

Three weeks before the memorial service, Anna, beginning a week's holiday the day before, set off from her home at Beau Vallon to visit Odile Toussaint's parents at Anse Faure, on the east coast of Mahé.

Her sad journey had been determined by her promise to a dying Odile, one which she wanted to honour before all else. "Mer...mersi mon piti," Msye Edmond Toussaint said in a proud and trembling voice, reaching out and holding Anna's hand in both of his. Then he lowered his eyes. "I will heat the coffee," he continued, glancing at his wife who had remained still and silent throughout.

Anna slipped her hands from the old man's and approached the old lady, amazed at the family resemblance between mother and daughter.

"Madanm Toussaint," she whispered as she settled on the small stool next to her armchair, "Odile wanted you to know how much she had enjoyed being a nurse and what a great fulfilment it brought to her life." The old lady nodded her head gently, two tears falling down her face. "She loved you both very much and she wanted me to tell you."

Madanm Mauricia Toussaint remained still, pride and grace defining her features. Then, in a broken whisper she said, "Oh God, why did you take my only child, Odile…"

At that point, she lost herself to her grief, her hands grasped to the sides of her head in desperation. Anna put her arm tenderly around the old lady's shoulder and held her as she cried for the loss of her only child.

After coffee Anna said good bye to the old couple, pleased that they seemed to have been touched by her visit. As she made her way back to Port Victoria, she reflected on how human nature clings to that last connection to life. She was the last person Odile had seen. The Toussaints could tell that she was close to Odile, and had been trusted by her. This seemed to have brought them comfort, and she had also been able to put their minds at rest, reassuring them that Odile had received the last rites, and that the end was very peaceful, surrounded by her colleagues as well as Matron herself.

After nearly seven months of confinement within the walls of Victoria hospital, Anna relished each step of her long journey, walking freely along the beautiful seaside coast of east Mahé. A white seagull hovered in the clear sky above her. The journey to Anse Faure from Beau Vallon had taken well over two and a half hours. On her way there, her thoughts were on the message she was to deliver.

Now, on her return, she enjoyed the verdant scenery, the lovely tropical sunshine and the cool sea breeze. So many months so close to death had a way of making one appreciate being alive, of being able to enjoy nature, so abundant and true.

There you are, she smiled at the seagull who had just swooped past her, *following me to Beau Vallon, are you?* The imposing boulders and lush vegetation of the hills seemed to tumble straight into the sea.

Very few patches of flat land existed and the main road, which had been carved along the shoreline where the ocean met the hills, was really nothing more than a retaining wall of massive granite and filled with red clay which had hardened over time.

There were no sandy beaches like Beau Vallon on this side of the island, and the waves from the sea lapped the granite walls of the road. At high tide, the waves would often rush right over the road altogether, soaking the vegetation on the other side and drenching anyone who happened upon the road at the time. Half a mile out to sea, a white band of frothy bubbles was visible, crowning the area where the blue waves met the sharp head of the coral reef, the silent protector of this section of Mahé.

As she left the village of Pointe Larue and arrived near the church of Saint Andre in the picturesque little village of Cascade, Anna stood gazing at the mystical image of beauty and majesty rising in precipitous grandeur, that guarded this little church. The sheer slopes and untameable peaks of age-old granites, and the tangled growth of their green forests displaying white canopies of albizias in perfect splendour, were a feast for the eyes. Yet, for all the magnificence of the mountain's peaks, it was at the foot of the church of Cascade where the real sense of awe produced by this mountain could be properly felt and appreciated. There, the illusion that she was sprouting almost right from behind the church was palpable; the mountain evoked a sense of complete domination over the tiny village at its feet.

One of the original landmarks of Catholicism in the Seychelles, the church of Saint André, Patron Saint of fishermen, had been completely rebuilt in stone at the beginning of 1900, transforming it from the simple wooden chapel the first Catholic missionaries had built in honour of the Saint in 1882, into an imposing monument perched high on the hillside on its own granite pedestal. From this commanding position, it overlooked the Cascade river roaring down the hillside, flowing over boulders and between trees and vegetation before gathering into a wide and calm lagoon bordered by the granite walls of the main road. With a big scramble for freedom at the mouth of the small tunnel running underneath the wooden bridge of the road, the river continued its spectacular dash for the open sea on the far side of the road.

On the water edge of the lagoon, the big wooden wheel of the watermill creaked with the force of the river, satisfying the water demands of the small coconut coir factory perched on the bank, where the island's supply of ropes, mattresses and mats were made.

The washer-women, *fanm larivyer*, occupied the opposite bank of the lagoon, their skirts hiked up to their underwear, standing knee-deep in the cool mountain water. Amongst this group, it was traditional to 'whisper' a juicy piece of gossip at the top of your voice to your friends at the far end of the bank, for the members of this circle were indeed the village's own 'radio bamboo,' the mouthpiece of all gossip and everything else happening in their community.

All news was analysed and debated according to its merit, criticised or applauded as appropriate, but in every case it was embellished further, to make it extra tasty before being spread around. No secret was safe once the washer-women had wind of it.

As Anna climbed the rocky steps leading up to the church, she could sense their eyes following her. She was a stranger in this part of the island, and she had no sooner been spotted than the speculation started on who she might be, which part of the island she might be from and, far more interestingly, what was she doing here on her own? No chaperone!

Anna, in her way used to the curious eyes of others, simply ignored them.

The interior of the church was pleasantly cool. In the enveloping silence, every footstep echoed throughout. The air was impregnated with the wafting aroma of incense and burnt candle wax, mingled with the lingering perfume from the beautiful frangipani and roses arrangements around the altar. A reassuring sense of divine peace pervaded the church of Saint Andre. The memories of her last visit to this place three years previously returned to her, contrasting with the sense of peace she felt this day.

Their adventure then had begun with the cock's crow. In the pristine air of the early morning hours still heavy with dew, they began their long journey, walking from Tonton Lionet's home in Saint Louis to the church of Saint André in Cascade. Mère Monia, Ghislaine and she had all been dressed in their new frocks, for it was a very special affair. Islanders from all corners of Mahé as well as the neighbouring islands of Praslin and La Digue would be coming to attend, for it was the annual feast of Saint Andre. Celebrated every year on the last day of November, this important occasion in the Christian calendar of the Seychelles was presided over by none other than the head of the Catholic Church himself, the bishop of Port Victoria, Monseigneur Leon des Avanchers.

Passing through the villages of Les Mamelles, Petit Paris and into Cascade, the festive ambience increased as more and more people joined the throng, all beautifully dressed in bright and cheerful colours. The occasional rickshaw creaked through the crowd on the narrow, coarse-clay road, loaded with the 'well-to-do' members of society also heading to the church. The entrance to the village was decorated with green coconut leaves hanging horizontally on bamboo posts, creating a green fence of welcome. Colourful blooms of bougainvillea, frangipani and flamboyant were tied along the railings, displaying their bright beauty to everyone joining in the celebrations. Every tree and every tiny hut along the village road also boasted green ferns and bright tropical flowers.

The first view of Saint Andre was visible as they came around the last bend in the road. What an enchanting picture! An everlasting imprint teeming with wonder and nostalgia. Perched high on the rocky slope, she glittered in the early morning rays of the sun, her gigantic emerald mountain standing etched against the pale beauty of the sky behind her, whilst at her feet a massive freshwater lagoon simmered in silence.

On the ocean in front of her, a flotilla of boats and pirogues of various sizes bobbed at their moorings. Beyond the frothy band of bubbles of the coral reef, two schooners with white sails were also visible, their human cargo being ferried ashore by various pirogues small enough to be able to pass through the narrow channel cut out in the reef.

It was a magical portrait, enhanced by the crowds of faithful in their colourful Sunday best, and all the beautiful tropical flowers and coconut leaves decorations. There were also hundreds of triangular and square flags of all colours, floating proudly from bamboo posts adorning the slopes up from the main road and all around the wall of the church's ground. The *paroisse* of Cascade were showing their reverence to their Patron Saint in a blaze of colour.

The celebration of mass lasted well over two hours, but the most memorable part of the occasion came when Monseigneur Leon des Avenchers led the long procession out of the church and down the rocky steps to the seafront, accompanied by a chorus of lovely hymns that echoed throughout the village. The voices from hundreds of *fideles* complemented the efforts of the choir of Cascade's church, showing their happiness and enthusiasm with a devotion in honour of one of the island's greatest Patron Saints, imploring his blessing and protection on all the fishermen of Seychelles.

Embarking into a small pirogue whilst dressed in the long flowing robes and regalia of a bishop was no simple task. Everyone crossed their fingers as the head of the Catholic Church of Seychelles, with a remarkable grace and serenity, manoeuvred himself to sit tall and proud at the very head of the pirogue as he was rowed out to where the fishermen waited patiently in their boats for this yearly benediction. As his pirogue moved throughout the silent flotilla, his right hand could be seen dipping again and again into the holy water receptacle as he blessed them all with the sign of the cross. Ashore, lining the roadside and the rocky steps to the church, the hymns continued with an even greater fervour.

Anna felt refreshed as she came out of the church and stepped into the midday sun, pausing briefly near the edge of the wall to admire the scene before her. The bay was bare today, only one small pirogue rowed back to shore. In the distance Anna could see the outline of Port Victoria.

The green lawn around the church was as deserted and silent as the bay. Three years earlier, it had been a hive of activity with dozens of stalls made of bamboo posts and thatched with green coconut leaves doing a roaring trade with the crowds of the faithful, all only too eager to joyfully spend all their hard-earned rupees for the benefit of the church's fund.

It had been a joy to tour those colourful stalls, surrounded by the bustling and happy crowds. The aroma of home-made delicacies sent tantalising messages to every taste-bud, reinvigorating all the senses after such a long and tiring journey, and a particularly lengthy celebration of mass.

On one stall, an array of soft and viscous nougat, made from freshly-grated coconut in caramelised red sugar and flavoured with nutmeg and vanilla, sat appetisingly next to an assortment of fruit jams made from bananas, paw-paws and zanmalak. The neighbouring stall was heaped full with *coco rouge* being prepared for drinking by a squatting villager with a big machete and a matching smile. Due care had to be exercised so as to carefully place the lips on top of the hole in the coconut, preventing a new, clean frock from getting wet with the coconut water, whilst simultaneously trying to remain 'ladylike.'

Everywhere one turned, people were eating, drinking and chatting. The longest queue had been in front of the savoury spice stall where the aroma from the mounds of deep-fried *samousas*, filled with hot vegetable curry, or spicy fish, dominated the breeze. These competed with the platters of *gato piman* that left the tongue burning for a few minutes, yet never deterred anyone from asking for a cornet of the equally spicy *granm*. So many stalls and all so different! But the sugar-cane stall was the most intriguing. Hundreds of pieces of juicy sugar-cane, vital for the taming and appeasement of the fire in those hot mouths that had just visited the spicy stall next door. And at the rear, well beyond the gaze of the priests and *God forbid,* the bishop, mugs of the potent *baka kann* were raking in more rupees than any other stall, all neatly controlled by two permanent look-outs, whose winks and gestures would direct the next customer to their turn around the back…

There was something for everyone. People mingled, strangers introduced themselves and sat in some corner of the church's veranda, or in any shady spot. They could be seen partaking of their own bowls of *plo*, a delicious preparation of rice with salty sausages and pork cooked with herbs and spices in a hot curry sauce. They would be spending their money on a nice sweet dessert after lunch, maybe on one of the sticky *moutay* or a couple of ripe pumpkin or sweet potato fritters. Or, maybe they might throw caution to the winds and go all out for one of the delicious *moukat bannan*.

These were a must for these occasions, Mère Monia had told them. Wrapped in green banana leaves and cooked slowly over a *ben mare*, the concoction of ripe mashed bananas mixed with cassava flour and flavoured with nutmeg, cinnamon and vanilla, happened to be one of the most expensive desserts from the sweet stall.

Maybe the purchase of a nice pair of embroidered headrest covers from the stall with its delicate and fine needlework would be a good souvenir from the proud Catholic ladies of Cascade. It did not matter how or where one spent one's rupees, it was all for the same good cause, all offered with such pride and joy by the host village who wanted to ensure that everyone who had travelled such long distances to share in this celebration would return home happy and filled with good memories.

Anna smiled as she remembered that day. A sense of nostalgia came over her, for that occasion had been matchless. She remembered how proud Mère Monia had been of the two of them. "My two granddaughters," she introduced them to acquaintances and friends. One such couple had been Monsieur and Madame Andre Maillet of Anse Royale.

A coincidence? Maybe yes, for it could have been just fate. On the other hand, perhaps there was a devious side to Mère Monia that had eluded them. Had the feast been a ruse to present Ghislaine to the Maillets?

Her answer came as an all-over tingling, as she visualised again this scene of three years ago, and she knew then that she was right; it had been the latter. Throwing her head back she roared with laughter, her voice joining the loud peels of Saint André's bells as they announced midday.

It was almost one o'clock when she reached Mont Fleurie, and passed the entrance of the botanical garden. She paused as the one thing she had been trying to suppress so as not to have to deal with its agonising consequence, suddenly filled her thoughts. She felt herself shaking to the core as it demanded to be acknowledged, telling her there was no way out of her dilemma. Her legs were heavy as she moved along the familiar footpath, each impending step taking her closer to final reality. Her heart ached, as all her empty tomorrows rose to meet her face to face. It occurred to her that this was the final farewell; she was on her way to say adieu to her one and only love, to spend one last nostalgic moment of remembrance at the oasis where they had shared the most precious of all her yesterdays.

The garden was silent and peaceful, colourful blooms perfumed the air, the distant chirping of birds was faintly audible. On the surface, it seemed just the same, but she could sense that the place was greatly changed.

It was as if an emptiness plagued the heart of this luxurious refuge, a void that mystified her as she shivered with apprehension in the warmth of the afternoon heat. She felt as if this abundance of nature could actually feel the weight of her pain, as if it shared her innermost conflict and tragedy and understood the reason for her visit. She felt humbled as the soul of this place reached out to her and touched her troubled heart. She sighed gratefully, knowing she was not completely alone, that she would never be alone. She looked around, knowing that the gentle power of this place would always be there for her, always faithful. All she had to do was believe in it.

She continued forward until she turned the last corner from their secret meeting place. She felt suddenly weak and had to lean on a boulder for support. Her breathing was hard. The words of her sworn oath now beckoned. It was time to honour the pact she made with God in that chapel on Christmas Eve. It was time to face her destiny.

Seven months. Seven long months of turmoil and pain, of anxiety and fear. However, his deep faith in his God and the pure feeling of true love in his heart had served as a lifeline, carrying him through the long nights of aching solitude and the equally long days of painful existence. Finally, it was over. Or was it? The immediate life threat was gone, but his anxiety and fear persisted. How had this long phase of tragedy shaped her? The pocket watch in his hand read exactly one o'clock. One hour to go.

Maybe today will be the day, he thought as he replaced the watch back in his pocket, pacing anxiously around the little pool. For each of the past eight days, since the epidemic ended, he had come each afternoon and kept a two-hour vigil at their oasis, hoping and praying that she would come. Yet again, as on the seven previous days, all that visited this place with him was the echo of silence.

He was still alone, still waiting.

Maybe she is keeping away on purpose, he thought, sitting down by the small pool. He feared that the painful episode from the night of the ball had conspired with these past horrible months to traumatise her. Or worse, he feared that she had decided not to see him again. He brought his hands to his face. The thought was too painful to bear.

When he could think again, he cursed the limiting rules of their society. The rigid structures of their lives were so damning. Even so, he remained conscious of the sensitivities involved; the last thing he wanted was to cause her any more grief. Still, he *had* to find a way. *I must speak with her again!* He looked up to the brilliant blue skies. *Please help me, Lord,* he implored the heavens. *I cannot live without her.*

A sound caught his attention. Gentle footsteps on dried leaves. He straightened. He sensed her presence even before she took that last turn around the boulder and came into view. And then suddenly, she was there, standing before him. Though she looked straight at him, at first her eyes they could not believe he was actually there.

They both stood frozen, silent, waiting.

She looked to him to be very pale and extremely sad, as if she carried a load too great for her to bear. But oh, so beautiful. She could not believe that he was really there, before her, in the flesh.

The seconds continued to tick away, and suddenly, he moved. Without a word, he closed the space between them, took her trembling body into his arms and held her fast.

"Oh my God," he whispered, not conscious of speaking, "I have missed you so. I love you. Do you know? I love you." He held her tighter still, by his tight embrace communicating his fear that he would never see her again.

The sound of his voice, and the power of his words, filled her heart. She abandoned herself to his powerful embrace. She could not speak. She could barely breathe. However, from somewhere deep in her soul, sobs sprang forth, wracking her body against his. And then she too was proclaiming her love and her fear.

"I didn't know if I would ever see you again," she cried.

Their proclamations of love intermingled so that it was impossible to know when one voice began and the other ended. He continued to hold her as she cried. He caressed her hair and kissed the top of her head. "I am here. I am here," he said over and over, reassuring her that their moment of fear had passed.

I will always be here," he promised, letting her know that from that moment on she would not be on her own, and that his love for her would live to the end of their days.

As her tears subsided, she raised her face, her eyes seeking his, but it was their lips which magically met, brushing gently at first. He tasted the saltiness of her tears and then, as the kiss grew more passionate, he tasted only what he would later describe as pure love. The intensity of the moment consumed them and their bodies and souls exulted in a new physical togetherness which moulded them for all eternity into one heart.

Who knows how much later it was when they sat side by side at the edge of the little pool, one of his arms draped firmly around her shoulder, her head resting in the curves of his neck. She sought to draw strength from him, to find the courage and the words to tell him what she knew she must tell him. She wanted only a few minutes more; a few minutes more to live this love a little while longer.

"Louis," she whispered finally, "I am not free to love you."

She felt the grip of his hand on her upper arm, turning her to face him. "Anna, are you promised to another man?" he cried, his face a mask of anguish.

She shivered. "No!" she cried. "No, not that. I could never…I would never love another man." She dropped her eyes. "But yes, I am promised to another life. I made a vow to God that I will take the Veil." Having uttered those words, she refused to raise her eyes to his. She refused to be witness to his suffering. How she wished that there was a way out from her fate.

For his part, he could not control the trembling of his body. He could not fathom that he was to lose her forever. He knew now that she loved him as he loved her. This was all too cruel…surely the God they both prayed to could not reserve such a destiny for them. What God of love would cause those who loved him to endure such pain?

"There is a way," he said, his voice desperate and broken. "There *must* be. God will show us a way."

For days Louis agonised. He prayed. He begged God for guidance and deliverance. Like Anna, he made promises to forgo his privileges if only he was offered a solution. As he made his way back to their oasis that afternoon, their last meeting was vivid in his heart and imagination. Anguished by her revelation, yes, but also filled with pure love. That she had dedicated her life to God, so as to save him from the epidemic! During the terrible months of that disease, he had prayed to God every day for her safety. But he had not shown the courage or strength to offer his own life or status for her safety. What she had done was selfless and pure, and he was humbled by it.

As he arrived by their little pool, a familiar shape wrapped in brown paper bulged in his pocket. He rehearsed what he wanted to say over and over again. When he finally was able to speak his words to her, he was greeted with utter shock, disbelief and complete happiness.

"Well?" he asked, waiting for her to say something, but all she did was stare at him.

For her part, she could not believe what she had just heard. "You are prepared to do all this for me?"

"You are the best thing that ever happened to me, the girl I will love for the rest of my days. Yes, I will do all this and more for you. I will do anything for you."

She trembled like a delicate leaf in his arms. She laid her head against his chest and listened to the steady beat of his heart. "Thank you, my love, thank you for finding the perfect solution.

I am so honoured for everything that you are prepared to do for my sake, to know that I will be allowed to continue nursing, even after I become your wife." Tears rolled down her cheeks. "Thank you."

There was no doubt what society and tradition expected of him. A man of his status, the son of a rich landowner and entrepreneur, would be expected to marry within the elite of the island, to someone of his own class and upbringing. That had been his immediate concern when he considered his parent's reaction to his decision. Would they accept the daughter of their overseer as his bride, or would they shun him if he went ahead without their blessing? This had been of no small concern. His entire future resided with his family name and business. All the land and resources were tied in together but, more important, there was his great love and respect for his parents and his brother. He trembled at the prospect of having to choose between them and Anna.

He was relieved as to his material future when he remembered the bequest made by his maternal grandfather, Monsieur Paul Duval. A substantial sum of money had been left to both Henri and himself, which they would inherit directly on their respective twenty-first birthdays, the legal age of maturity, and his was only months away in September.

Material well-being was one thing, the love of his family another. He wished with all his heart that his parent's love for him would not force him to choose.

His parents were only one concern. There was the matter of Anna's parents as well. They would have no choice but to object to the union once they knew of his parent's disapproval. After all, their livelihood was dependent on the goodwill of his family, and they would not risk offending them and their longstanding association. As Anna was only coming up to eighteen, she still required their consent to marry.

Of course, the more pressing and worrying aspect had been Anna's vow to God. How could she honour that vow and also be his wife? Père Valer gave him the answer. He had been in a deep prayer all alone in church in the middle of the day, and had only noticed the presence of the old priest when he had felt a hand on his shoulder. "Come my son," indicating that private corner next to the altar. Omitting Anna's name, Louis had unburdened his anguish to this old priest, his head bowed against the wooden lattice division of the confessional box like a man who could see no way forward. After a deep period of contemplation, followed by a very thoughtful and studious prayer, Père Valer had informed Louis that no matter how difficult it would prove for him personally, and for his social status in the community, he must allow her to continue practising nursing.

"At the very least, she must fulfil that part of her promise to God," the old priest had said solemnly. "Remember, God knows all our hearts, hears all our prayers."

He smiled at the young man. "Remember too, that the love of a man and a woman is as sacred as the Veil. The most selfless action in God's eyes is when we offer our own life, our own future, for the one we love."

His smile widened as he promised Louis he would pray for an amicable solution. "And try not to worry," he added, "I know just how much your parents love you."

"I have something for you," he said as he unhooked the golden chain and medallion he was wearing, looped it over her head and fastened it securely around her neck. "I can't…" she began to protest. But he placed his finger against her lips to hush her concern.

"This is a very special family heirloom which I inherited from my mother on my eighteenth birthday, and I would like you to keep it safe for me, until the day when I will give you our official engagement ring. For now, just think of it as a token of my love and our betrothal."

She could not believe what was happening. She had never known such happiness. For several moments, she simply rested her head in the curve of his neck, listening to the rhythm of his heart and the gentle sound of his breathing.

She could barely believe the joy surging through her. The audacity that he loved her as much as she loved him, that they could actually enjoy a wonderful life together.

"Oh, I almost forgot," he said cheerfully as he shifted next to her, "I have something else for you."

"Something else?"

And then, as he presented her with the wrapped mermaid, she was suddenly laughing and crying at the same time. "Oh Louis, you have found her," she sighed, holding the little mermaid once again in her hands. She was just as beautiful now as she had been the year before on her birthday.

It was a beautifully sunny May morning. She stood serenely in the arched doorway of the Saint Roch church, her white ankle-length dress reflecting her purity and beauty. Delicate flowers from the circular garland of *laliyan de me* crowned her veil, adding an aura to her calm and peaceful expression. All around, colourful flags floated in the soft bay breeze, and bunches of equally vivid blossoms of bougainvillea and green ferns adorned the grounds, adding a festive dignity to the old church.

"Almost done," Therese said as she rearranged the flower garland over her veil yet again.

She barely felt her presence. Her attention was held by the altar, the centre of masses of flowers and candles, but in particular it was the statue of the Virgin in the small alcove to the right side of the altar which held her gaze.

An arch-shaped structure of green ferns and delicate white roses bordered the alcove. Dozens of white candles illuminated the space, giving a glow to the tenderness and love radiating from the Virgin's face.

She turned then and gazed at the expressions of joy and pride gracing the faces of her family members; everyone was so thrilled for her. But it was her mother's expression that struck her deepest. Therese's eyes were brimming with tears of joy as her mother's happiness caused her own heart to swell and rejoice. Even Mère Monia's eyes were filled with tears as she stood proudly next to her son. The enormity of the morning dawned on her slowly. This was the start of a new life for her, a life which she was certain would be fruitful and blessed.

There was a quiet happiness in the faces of the congregation, all dressed in their Sunday best. As one, they turned and watched her as she paced slowly up the aisle, her two hands held together in front of her chest in a gesture of prayer and adoration, with the small white rosary which Mère Monia had given her two weeks before entwined between her fingers.

This morning she would receive 'the Body of Christ' for the first time, and then in the afternoon she would reaffirm her beliefs and devotion to the Catholic Church in front of the whole congregation, something which her parents and godparents had done on her behalf when they had brought her to church for baptism nine years before.

Then she would be anointed with sacred oil by the Bishop himself, a sign of her Confirmation into the Faith. To the echoes of the beautiful hymn '*Je me consacre a vous,*' she would kneel in front of the alcove of the Virgin Mary, take the white garland from her head and place it at the foot of the statue in a gesture of adoration, and ask for the Virgin's blessing on her life.

On the new road upon which she was poised to travel, she would need the Virgin's prayers and support as she became a young adult and embarked upon her chosen vocation to become '*Sœur Chantal,*' the first member of the Savy family to take the 'Veil.'

For as long as Chantal could remember she had been passionate about teaching. She loved to teach her siblings prayers and songs. Even so, during her lessons in catechism in preparation for her First Holy Communion she had felt something else, something more glorious. Observing the patience of the nun in giving the lessons, taking note of her dedication and passion, she had witnessed a moment of grace. The purity of teaching went beyond the life and dress code the nuns observed. Not from anything but the most humble grace, they commanded a special form of respect from everyone, a respect they had earned by surrendering their lives to the service of God and other human beings. In that moment, she knew she had found her destiny.

As her godfather, it was Tonton Lionet's privilege to host a feast for the family after the First Holy Communion session of the morning.

By the appearance of the dishes it looked as though Tante Florence had far surpassed herself. Although the rest of the family enjoyed the feast, Chantal ate little. The food was delicious, but her thoughts and appetites were elsewhere. She listened as Therese told everyone for the umpteenth time about the day Chantal told her she wanted to become a nun, and how proud and blessed she had felt then. Mère Monia spoke proudly of her own conviction that Chantal would be doing a great service for the community and the Church.

"To teach all those poor children," she sighed, her voice filled with respect and love. Then she turned to the gathered family and reminded them how much society was indebted to the nuns for providing an education to future generations. Tante Florence noted that there was a shortage of nuns on the island.

Chantal noticed that even her father and two elder brothers looked at her differently today. Yet it was the affection and tenderness in Anna's embrace outside the church that had touched her the most, when she had kissed her on both cheeks and given her a lovely white prayer book and a small holy image of the Virgin Mary. "You will make a wonderful nun and an excellent teacher," she whispered into her ear. "It is a blessing to be able to follow your heart and to make a positive difference to the lives of others."

Several weeks later, on a balmy late afternoon in early June, the Seychelles' flowering trees perfumed the air with the delicacy of their bloom and a cool soothing breeze caressed the coastline. The island was at peace with its beauty and serenity. It was so nearly perfect that it seemed impossible that the dreadful fear of the epidemic had ended only two months earlier.

Patricia Kent dismounted from her bicycle and parked it against the shop front. She glanced at the small, securely-fastened wooden window and smiled at the ingenuity and business drive of the shop's Indian owner, who had obviously found a clever way around the official Sunday closure of all shops on the island. It was common knowledge in the village that should one need something urgently on a Sunday, a couple of knocks on the side window was all that was required, although most often the weight in the paper cornet was lighter than if one were to purchase the same item any other day of the week.

The shop's double wooden doors facing the main road were its only source of light and ventilation. They were open between 5 a.m. and 8 p.m. every day except Sundays, whatever the weather. The doors were adorned with two massive 'U-shaped' metal hooks, always decorated with various species of bloated and red-eyed fish hanging from pieces of ropes, swarmed upon by an army of flies.

The owners squatted in a circle in the grounds next to the shop, drinking away their last cents as they gambled with cards, contentedly allowing their family dinner to rot.

Inside the shop, the flame of a tiny coconut oil lamp flickered from a wooden shelf in the corner, casting a dim glow on the golden face of the miniature god statuette with several arms, and all the offerings of smoking incense sticks, pieces of fresh coconut and yellow marigolds scattered on the shelf.

The odour from the incense sticks mingled with the smoke from the oil lamp, overcoming the appetising aroma coming from the variety of peppery spices stocked by the *malbar*, as the people of the Seychelles had fondly named their Indian traders. Behind his waist-high wooden counter which ran across the width of his little shop, stood the barefoot and nervous Msye Vellu. His fingernails were dirty, and red *betal* stained his mouth. He was dressed in a set of white *senbou*, long ago stained to a smoky beige by constant wear.

He snapped at the ever-obedient Madanm Vellu who jumped to do his bidding, fake gold bracelets dangling on her arms and ankles, a red thumb-mark in the middle of her forehead, and her tummy bulging yet again with one of her numerous pregnancies, all the while holding the latest tiny *vellu* astride her hip.

Like most of the wooden buildings in the Seychelles, the little shop had no ceiling and the beams supporting the roof were exposed, which proved very useful. The heavy, square wooden beam supporting the roof structure was also an anchorage point for the pair of weighing scales suspended in chains right over the counter, the pride and joy – and most important tool – of any shopkeeper. Atop the counter, numerous containers were heaped with fried *samousas* filled with vegetable curry and *gato pimans*.

Chickpeas stir-fried with onions, chillies and cumin were also always available, their aroma enticing anyone who appreciated the hot bite of the small Creole chillies.

Next to them, two glass jars containing a variety of colourful *sikredoz* and fried *moulouk* gleamed in the dim light, whilst on the floor behind the owner stood a variety of gunny bags filled with rice, lentils, *zanberik*, peppercorns, onions, flour and other dry goods. Alongside these there were three large wooden wine casks that currently housed the village's supply of coconut oil, brown sugar and salt. Two smaller casks held the fiery, red curry powder and yellow, turmeric powder, both essentials of the Creole curry.

At the far end corner of the shop, rolls of plain and printed cotton fabrics leaned against the wall alongside the wooden yard measure, completing the picture.

"*Biskwi sale, silvouple*," Patricia said in broken Creole.

A customer's request always brought a broad smile from Vellu, exposing all the redness of the *betal* in his mouth and on his lips. But Patricia, well, she was special.

He clasped his hands in a gesture of adoration in front of his chest as he lowered his head in a formal welcome, extremely happy that this very distinguished, white customer, an English lady, was gracing the floor of his little shop.

Patricia had only recently become acquainted with the hard and salty biscuits. She had sampled one during the dark days of the epidemic, when fresh bread was non-existent. To her surprise and delight she had taken an instant liking to them, and in the weeks since had tried without success to get her house-keeper, the extremely reliable and overly protective Marie-Ange, to get some of these biscuits for her. But it appeared that in Marie-Ange's opinion the biscuits were part of the poor people's diet, certainly not fit for an English lady of her rank. With one excuse after another, she had failed to bring the biscuits into the house.

And so, as she was cycling by the shop, Patricia found herself unable to resist the urge to stop and get them herself. She smiled as she watched Vellu wrapping her biscuits in brown paper. *Marie-Ange is in for a big surprise*, she thought to herself. Patricia genuinely liked Marie-Ange and knew that she had been lucky to secure her services. Not only had she come highly recommended, but she had been part of the household when she had acquired the tenure of the lovely colonial bungalow on the slope of the hill overlooking the ocean, at the far end of Anse Etoile's tiny and picturesque seafront village.

In the little room behind the shop, Patricia could see Vellu's wife squatting next to the burning charcoal *reso*, her bulging tummy almost touching the wok as she stirred its contents vigorously, sending the aroma of the spiced curry wafting around the shop. Her children, of various ages, sexes and sizes, played happily, seemingly oblivious to the danger of the wok and burning charcoal overturning and causing the entire shack to go up in flames.

Patricia took it all in – the sights, the family, the smells. It all put her in a very happy mood as she left the shop. She placed her bag of biscuits in her basket and then mounted her bicycle, conscious of the importance of the little shops as the lifeline of every village on the island. The shops stocked everything from needles and spools of white cotton thread to buttons and laundry soap bars, curry powder, charcoal and salted fish. In addition to these necessities, they also stocked a handful of luxury items, such as boxed Lifebuoy soap, tiny glass bottles of Eau-de-Cologne and Fleur D'oranger, small jars of Mentholatum ointment and tins of powdered Ovaltine. The Indian and Chinese merchants were the island's retail network, their goods purchased from the handful of importers based in Port Victoria and transported along the coastline by oxcarts to their shops.

As she rode, the gentle breeze blowing through her hair, Patricia felt very happy and pleased.

Later in the afternoon, as she took comfort in the old Creole canvass armchair on the wide veranda overlooking the ocean, she sipped her tea, quite certain that there was nothing more satisfying than a cup of Ceylon tea brewed with care.

As she gazed at the ocean, she thought about how her view of the world had changed in the recent past, particularly since the epidemic. In truth, she had been truculent and impatient in the past, the day-by-day demands sapping her of all tolerance. But now, she felt at ease. Satisfied. The last piece of the puzzle had fallen neatly into place and now she could start afresh. She felt that all the things which she dreamed of accomplishing on this island were now possible. With Sister Patrick's blessing and backing, she had been given a free hand to revolutionise the healthcare system.

The turning point had been Christmas Eve, when Sister Patrick had asked for her forgiveness. Advanced in years now, and weakened by her near-death experience with a bad bout of pneumonia, Sister Patrick had decided to take a back seat and remain as Matron in name only, with the occasional visit to the wards when she deemed necessary.

Her reverie was interrupted by the approach of her gardener, old Msye Dugasse, who wanted to show her the new cuttings of bougainvillea he had just acquired. "Where to put them?" he enquired, seeking her thoughts even though he, like she, was fully aware that he had already chosen the location for them. Like Marie-Ange, he was another staff member whom she had acquired with the property. He was a master. An artist. The slope to her bungalow was a canvas of carefully co-ordinated colours. Around the small lawn in front of the bungalow, exotic, tropical blooms perfumed the air, adding to the picture.

"Marvellous," she sighed.

A schooner glided along past Sainte Anne's island, heading towards Port Victoria, whilst two black pirogues rowed in the opposite direction, heading out to the fishing grounds for the night's session of bottom-fishing. "Just marvellous," she sighed again, taking another sip of her tea.

From the wide, sun-bleached veranda of her thatched wooden bungalow, she gazed at Sainte Anne island straight in front of her, at the entrance to that secure area in front of the port, and the other small islands of Île Moyenne, Île Ronde, Île Longue and Île aux Cerfs stretching out in a horizontal curve to the right. All so beautiful in this late afternoon light. Patricia felt a comfort now, realizing that the Seychelles was her real home.

These magnificent islands, with their temperate climate and simple, friendly people, were now all that she needed in the evening of her life.

For a split second, she wondered if David would have been happy living on this island. She smiled, realising he would have been happy anywhere so long as they were together.

She closed her eyes and let her head rest back. Her thoughts drifted to and fro, becoming focused when she smelled the appetising aroma coming from the dinner being prepared in the outside kitchen at the back of the bungalow. Grilled fish. She smiled at the waft of her favourite dish, knowing it was an atonement of sorts from Marie-Ange, who had registered her displeasure about the biscuits a bit too directly when she had arrived back at the bungalow that afternoon.

Patricia thought about the first time she had tasted the Creole-style, grilled red snapper. It had been so spicy that she thought her mouth was on fire. Over time, rather than fully adapt to the spice, Marie-Ange had been convinced to use less-strong chillies. They had since found a happy medium, and now she fully enjoyed the dishes, although Marie-Ange added additional chillies for herself, spreading them over the fish before she ate.

Patricia missed little from England. These islands had an abundance of everything - well, almost everything. A nice Sunday joint of lamb with crispy roast potatoes, sprouts and carrots was one such dish that did not exist here. Cheese and butter were also now distant memories. However, it was a nice bar of Fry's milk chocolate and the occasional big bowl of strawberries and fresh cream that she missed most. She still yearned for the glamour and sophistication of London's West End theatres. It was the one thing which tropical islands like the Seychelles, no matter how beautiful, could never replace.

With a sigh she went to wash her hands for dinner. As she placed her hands under the overflow from the water cask at the back of the bungalow, she marvelled at the clever network of bamboo, *ladal,* which fed fresh stream water directly to her bungalow from far up the gorges of La Gogue's mountain. This was the islanders' ingenuity at its best, using local products readily available. Although a practical way of getting water directly to the household, it was also quite costly in terms of maintenance and fees and not a luxury which many houses in the Seychelles could afford.

After a delightful dinner, Patricia's thoughts were once more focused on revamping the healthcare system. In particular, she thought about some good news she had received earlier, news that related to Anna. She first noticed a change in Anna when she returned to work after the epidemic. Patricia initially assumed that her new demeanour echoed everyone else's – a result of relief and happiness that the epidemic was finally over. But clearly, the continuing blossoming Anna exhibited was due to something more than relief. She practically glowed. Something about her reminded Patricia of her time in the desert, when she lost her heart to David.

The more she observed Anna, the more she became convinced that something similar was affecting her. She felt a conflicting sense of joy for Anna and a heaviness at witnessing an experience she would never again know. But she could not be sure, and the uncertainty bedevilled her. Just this morning, when she bumped into Anna in the pantry, she decided she could no longer be unsure. Her desire to know conspired with Anna's need to finally confide in someone.

Prompted by little more than a simple, "Anna, how are you? Something seems different about you lately..." Anna poured out her heart. Her feelings about Louis du Barré. His proposal. The impossibilities that they were determined to overcome. Their long wait until September, when he came of age. Patricia listened closely, at once delighted for the young woman but dismayed at her inevitable loss of a very wonderful nurse.

"Louis and I have spoken about my vow," she went on, surprising Patricia. "He has agreed that I will continue as a nurse even after we marry."

That piece of news nearly knocked Patricia over, for it was unheard of that a man occupying his status would allow his wife to continue to tend to the sick. But as she sat in the comfort of her sun-bleached canvas armchair, with a glass of French brandy in her hand and the twilight caressing the curves of the trees all around her, she basked in the significance of her good fortune. This news made it all so very clear. She really could achieve what she had set her heart on doing when she landed on this island four years earlier. In Anna, she had found a mirror image of herself, and she would be able to mould her in the certitude that her own influence and training would live on in this pair of capable hands long after she herself was gone. It was too wonderful a feeling to describe, too deep an emotion to fathom.

Earlier that same morning, things were quite different for Monsieur Gustave Benezet at Le Chantier's boat yard. On the pretext of scheduling minor work on one of his schooners, he saw for himself the progress on du Barré's second schooner which, according to the yard's owner, was to launch in September. In a remarkable show of restraint, he smiled politely at the news. Inside, he was churning with indignation. He continued to fume throughout the morning, his thoughts growing darker with each passing hour. He knew that he had only one course available, but as he looked into the anxious eyes of his sons, he could only hope they would prove to be strong and resolute as he when the time came.

He had been clear about the way forward. "We shall plan it down to the last detail," he said, his voice urgent and reassuring. "No mistakes. There is no margin for error. Our survival depends on complete success." As he outlined each son's responsibilities he emphasized more than once the need for absolute secrecy. "Not a word to *anyone*."

He tried to assuage their uncertainty by reassuring them that their predicament was not of their making. "But regardless, it is there now, and it is not going to go away by itself. We have every right to protect our livelihood from such marauders," he said passionately.

In the next room, purposefully removed from the *men's discussion*, Madame Gertrude Benezet stood with an ear against the door listening to her husband's every word, and she was also fuming. Like her sons, she was hardly won over by her husband's argument. Her female survival instincts were in full bloom at the notion of such peril threatening her family.

Her husband was barely halfway through his plans when she had formulated an action plan of her own, complete in every detail, with the same end result as his, only much different in approach and character.

On the pretext of visiting her seamstress, Gertrude left early the next day, clutching her handbag containing a secret stash of rupees – the result of years of siphoning from the housekeeping allowance – determined in her plan. Two hours later, after struggling along the almost non-existent footpath, she arrived breathless at the thatched hut at the top of the hill.

She entered the tiny hut, stepping into a dark and airless space, so low in height that she had to stoop to enter through its only door.

Her heart pounded as her eyes adjusted to the dim light, and she surveyed her gruesome surroundings. Witchcraft and black magic stared back at her with cold, unblinking eyes. She made a face in reaction to all those foul odours in the hut. She wanted nothing more than to flee this place, but she did not. Determined, she sat on the coconut trunk stool by the only table in the room, her wet palms trembling in her lap as the black shape, with its ghostly white eyes, stared at her. She could no longer flee even if she wanted to. That evil presence seemed to keep her locked in place now.

"What do you want from here?" a soft, hoarse voice whispered.

Before she could speak, the voice began to shriek. "Rupees! I want all the rupees in your bag. Give them to me!" Two bony fists banged the table in front of her, as her trembling hands sought to retrieve the money from her handbag.

By the time she emerged from the hut, she had despaired of ever seeing sunshine again. But there she was, in the sunlight and fresh air, arching her back into its upright position and staring straight ahead.

As she walked, she could feel those eyes on her back, watching her from the darkness of the hut, almost expecting any minute that those cold and bony fingers would suddenly grab hold of her from behind and drag her back into that horrible room.

She trembled with fear at what she had just done, nearly losing her footing as she hurried down the footpath, wanting nothing more than to leave it all behind. She knew that her actions could never be undone, and that the du Barré family was now doomed... *One day I will have to answer to the Almighty himself for what I've done. One day, when my time finally comes.*

Her journey back felt like a long walk along *the path to hell*. With each step, she replayed earlier events, the ghostly eyes, the hideous tasks she performed, the foul smells which even now lingered in her mouth, nostrils and on her clothes and hair. But it was her hands that were most offensive. Even after scrubbing them several times in the stream flowing by the footpath, they still held the smell of rotting flesh. Her thumb still bled badly despite the handkerchief securely tied around it. The entire episode had taken about an hour, but felt like a lifetime. As she walked, she repeated like a mantra - *There was no other way. There was no other way.* She was determined to protect her family and its livelihood – at all costs.

The most terrifying moment had been when the wrinkled and bony old fingers placed four tiny wooden coffins in a row on the table in front of her. Each was about seven inches long, complete with wooden covers which the old witch had removed before handing them to her. "Go," she said, pointing to the containers in the corner of the hut. "Bring me the contents."

Gertrude returned with thick, gooey muck, the source of she didn't wish to know. Back and forth from the containers to the table she went, placing the stuff in each of the coffins. The last of the containers had been in the darkest corner, next to a bed-like piece of furniture. As she bent to dip her fingers into the mixture, eight pairs of eyes stared back at her from under the bed.

Then came an unearthly hissing the likes of which she had never heard before and hoped to never hear again.

It was at that moment, as all the stories she had heard of this evil old witch told by her neighbours and workers proved true, that she felt her own warm urine running down the length of her trembling legs. She had wet herself. Such indignity!

Gertrude sat back on the coconut trunk stool in her wetness as the witch placed the coffins inside a circle drawn from a piece of charcoal.

The witch then added all sorts of concoctions – bits of finger nail, hair, animal teeth, human bones, rusted nails, wood barks, and strange oils from tiny bottles, as well as four tiny pieces of paper with the name 'du Barré' written seven times on each.

The old witch folded the papers over several times as she chanted, spitting on each of them before placing them into the festering contents of the coffins.

Just when Gertrude thought it was all over and done, the bony fingers had grasped at her hand across the table, holding it firmly over the coffins. With a sharp knitting needle, the witch stabbed her thumb in four places, causing her blood to spill onto the table and into the coffins. Amidst the piercing and throbbing pain, with the old witch squeezing her thumb for even more blood, she saw a white smoke rising from the coffins as her blood mixed with its contents. Then, with a cry that reverberated around the hut, the old witch slammed the lid on each coffin. Without another word, the old crone gestured to her to leave.

Two days later, a small sliver of moon rested in the cloudless skies over the mountains and valleys of Baie Lazare, its faint glow like the stroke of a silver pen against the pitch darkness of the late hour. Whilst the island slept, one lone crouching figure was in the blackness, lurking alongside an unmarked grave, humming as her wrinkled fingers placed the four tiny coffins deep within the soil.

Of all those who lived on the island, she was the only one who knew the anguished soul that inhabited this grave, for he had been her first attempt in creating a *dandosya*, an *undead*. The ritual had gone spectacularly wrong and she had lost his animate being, but his soul had remained as her property. Now, from beyond this very grave, he was still hers to command at will. Standing dutifully around the grave, her other *undeads* grinned as she placed the coffins into the soil, for they had seen it done before and knew only too well what was to come. Their devious minds rejoiced in anticipation of the arrival of new slaves, for it was their only source of pleasure. They looked forward to preparing the shackles, chains and whips for the grand occasion. It would be their privilege to administer all the perverse acts to the newcomers on a constant and unremitting basis until they lost all sense of who they had been, and were forced to embrace their new status as *living dead* – eternal slaves to the one and only master.

There would, of course, also be the joy of remorselessly working the newcomers to the point of exhaustion, and restricting food and drink to the point of demented starvation, whilst watching their bodies wasting away. Piece by piece, they would then be forced to collect and place the rotting body parts and flesh in the foul smelling containers, until the transformation was complete and they shrunk into small and evil looking creatures with ghostly eyes. Just like them.

Two weeks later, in the pre-dawn hours of 15 June 1914, he arrived. Weighing an impressive eight pounds and screaming at the top of his lungs. Ghislaine had endured twelve hours of labour, twelve hours during which Florence and Sonia had done their best to allay the worries of Claude, who had paced the veranda non-stop while consuming too much black coffee for his own good. But, in the end, all was well.

Olivier Maillet was the image of his father, a mop of tarry black hair crowned his round little face, complemented with a pair of equally black eyes. Naming the child had been easy. They had decided on the name months earlier. Olivier for a boy, Monia for a girl. Names for the two people who had marked both their lives.

Monia smiled as she watched Anna cradle Olivier in her arms. Anna's composure was different. Something had changed in her since the end of the epidemic, *a maturing*. It was as if she had entered the epidemic as an adolescent and come out as a mature young lady. As she considered this change, her old eyes travelled to Ghislaine. Her joy illuminated her face. Motherhood suited her. Monia felt pride and love fill her heart as she watched her two granddaughters, realising just how special they were. How different and yet how alike, and how blessed she was by them both.

Monia had sought a chance to have a private moment with Anna. She was hoping to share an inner conflict which had been burdening her for months now, to try to explain it in her own words, and hopefully to get Anna to understand and maybe to forgive her. Monia recalled too easily the terrible months of the epidemic; she could still picture the panic that animated each person's expression. She felt a tightening in her breast as she remembered the pain of so many as they witnessed the names of their loved ones being added to that distressing list on the church door. She shuddered, recalling her younger son's anguish as he lived each day with the knowledge that his first-born was in the middle of it all.

She had tried to be strong for him, to remind him of the importance of what she was doing, and how a mere slip of a girl of seventeen could actually make a difference. She quickly realised that her words were more directed to herself than anyone else. She was too set in her ways.

She had been cruel and had sat by and watched as her beloved granddaughter's heart had suffered from being spurned by her. It was only during the epidemic, when Anna was constantly at risk, that she felt remorse for her behaviour. She prayed then, prayed to God with all the fervency of her being to be given one more chance to look into those beautiful emerald eyes, and to tell her how proud she was to be her grandmother. Today, ten days after the birth of Olivier, she had her chance.

It was that very confession she made to the younger woman, as they stopped halfway on the journey back. As Anna heard the words fight their way from the old woman's lips, she trembled with emotion. Soon, they were both crying and hugging each other tightly. As the Indian Ocean lapped against the granite walls of the east of Mahé's main road, they both knew that they had lived a moment that would last their entire lives. For Anna, Monia's confession felt like a weight had been lifted from her shoulders. She hugged her sobbing old grandmother to her chest, caressing the top of her head, swearing her forgiveness and love for the older woman.

It had also been a day of discovery and immense joy. Anna's fear of matrimony and childbearing, this hard and painful burden she had feared would enslave her, seemed to have disappeared. Louis' declaration of love had changed everything…it had been replaced by something else, something tender and warm, something beautiful. Holding tiny Olivier for the first time, Anna had felt a strange emotion surging through her being.

As she had cuddled this tiny bundle close to her heart, she momentarily loss the sense of place and time, as she felt the joy and fulfilment which would one day come, when she would hold Louis' first born in her arms. The intensity of the love she felt for him had overwhelmed her then, and she had not sensed the tears strolling down her face, until they dropped softly on Olivier's tiny face and he blinked in surprise.

They had shared the sanctuary of their oasis for almost an hour and now, knowing they could not remain, they both dreaded their imminent departure. 'Goodbye' had become more and more painful. Her head rested against his chest, his arm draped around her shoulder, protecting her within the strength of his body. A special kind of peace echoed around the garden as they savoured those final minutes. This special place was also experiencing their happiness.

Since he had declared his love for her nearly two months earlier, they had shared moments of tenderness and passion in the seclusion of this enchanting garden, moments that she had never dared to dream she would experience. His dedication to his vision of their future together kept her strong and she had been able to draw from this strength, especially when she lay awake in her own bed with her sleep unable to conquer her terrible fears. All she needed to do was close her eyes and imagine being next to him, let her heart reach out and feel his love…and calmness and peace descended upon her.

On 30 June 1914, Sister Kent put the finishing touches to her plan. As she finished, she sat back in her chair, deeply satisfied. She could envisage it all so clearly, the benefits that would accrue to the lives of the ordinary islanders and how her legacy would live on for good. She sighed deeply, feeling great anticipation.

As she enjoyed her moment, her thoughts turned to Anna and to how the challenges of this new initiative would remould her nursing future. It would be difficult, but she was a strong and confident young woman who would embrace these new opportunities. She had already shown this strength during the epidemic, in addition to her unwavering devotion toward nursing. Sister Kent had no doubt that Anna was the perfect person for this important task.

She had youth and passion, and she had her future-husband's blessing to continue nursing. Now, due to the distress of the epidemic, they also had the backing of the Catholic Church and all of its communities. This, allied to her personal influence over the ruling members of the British Establishment who held the purse strings, created a perfect combination.

As she reviewed the duty roster, she saw that Anna was due to start a two-week night duty shift the following day. *No, no,* she sighed to herself. *That will not do.* She needed Anna to work the morning shift for the foreseeable future. That would give the two of them time to start working on her plans. She made the necessary change in the roster, giving Anna a day off the next day, followed by all morning shifts. In high spirits, she crossed the wide veranda from her office and strode to the female ward, only to discover that almost all of the nurses on the morning shift – including Anna – had already left.

Crestfallen, she was left to entrust a nurse yet to leave with the message about the change to the duty roster. "Do you understand?" Sister Kent asked her, looking into her clouded eyes. "This is important."

"Yes, Sister," the young nurse said, although neither her expression nor her voice made it seem that she did.

Glancing at the report the morning staff had just handed to their colleagues on the afternoon shift, Sister Kent could see that at least three-quarters of the patients in the ward suffered from preventable diseases. Lack of proper personal hygiene, non-existent sanitation facilities, contaminated water supplies, exposed storage of cooked food, flies and verminous parasites, and the lack of proper education among the vast majority of the population, all contributed mightily to needless diseases, suffering and death.

She was certain that a restructuring of the healthcare system could change this once and for all. Of course it would be an uphill struggle to convince the British Administrators of the benefits of her plans, but she was confident she would be able to win them over.

Her hope was to target the women of the island, mothers and homemakers who were responsible for the children, and were also bread winners in their own right. She envisioned a network of home-visiting nurses providing basic education, along with de-lousing and de-worming initiatives, and an immunization campaign. Making progress with the men would be more challenging, but she was certain that with Matron's intervention they would be able to use the influence of the plantation owners and the Catholic Church to get through to this section of the community. *It is simply deplorable that so many men are dying from preventable diseases like Leptospirosis.* She knew that the source of this was due to the local supply of home-made brews that became infected by rats urine. Vendors considered their brew still drinkable even if they had just scooped out a dead rat from the exposed containers. She thought of the suffering that the agricultural workers infected with the tetanus bacillus endured before they died, for no other reason than they worked contaminated soil whilst they had an open wound on their hands or feet.

Tragic, just tragic. And all avoidable with minimal effort and proper education. I must succeed, I must.

CHAPTER 11

The Silhouette of a Sailboat

As Anna took the last curve in the road, the sun hovered on the horizon, diminished but unbowed, and the whole bay of Beau Vallon glowed in the orange and red sunset. At times like these she was convinced that the entire spectacle existed only for her. *So beautiful*, she sighed contentedly.

This was the best eighteenth birthday present Beau Vallon could have offered in the absence of Louis. The Alouette had gone on one of her overnight trips to Île du Nord the day before and had plainly not yet arrived back on Mahé, for he had not turned up for their regular rendezvous. She felt sad when she realised that he would not be coming, but had made her way to the hospital to start her night duty shift. Once there, she was told that the duty roster had been altered the day before. Somehow, she had been the only person not informed of the changes, and had lost her only day off for that week as a consequence. She was annoyed.

"Nurse Savy," Patricia called out as Anna left the ward. After apologising for the last minute changes to the duty rota, Patricia briefly explained her plans and visions to Anna, whilst determined not to give Anna a chance to fully assess the enormity of the task. She handed her a brown envelope. "This letter is to inform your parents of the changes to your working hours, and don't not worry, each phase will be covered one step at a time." Anna had accepted the letter with a smile, her lost day off suddenly forgotten. Her heart rejoiced at this exceptional news.

That she was to be at the forefront of these massive changes, working side by side with Sister Kent, was just the best gift ever. The best eighteenth birthday present.

It was a relief too that she would only work morning shifts for the foreseeable future. She had not been looking forward to the two weeks of night duty shifts. As she quickly made her way back to Beau Vallon, a new sense of jubilation now marking her birthday. Her nursing career had just taken the most exciting turn imaginable – she felt truly blessed.

Looking at the bay now, bathing in this glorious kaleidoscope of colours, she felt happy and relaxed. Its beauty always revitalised her and made her feel alive. Closing her eyes, she drifted into a wonderful sense of peace and warmth as she imagined Louis being there next to her, feeling his love and strength.

Indeed, it was this beautiful sight which greeted him as he arrived at the driftwood, just as the fading light of the sunset cast its glow on the most peaceful scene he had ever come upon. She looked so serene. The light. Her beauty.

He had to pinch himself to be sure he was not standing inside his own dream. He felt his heart swell with love. He could barely believe what she had come to mean to him in these two short years. He was so happy that, for whatever reason, she was not at work tonight for he had been so desperate not to have missed their rendezvous. He blamed the last minute cargo that Île du Nord had decided to transport to Mahé for throwing his carefully planned trip into chaos. Even if he had tried his utmost to get the Alouette back on time, the winds had not been favourable. Yet looking at her now, he realised that this was the way in which fate had meant them to meet on this day, in exactly the same place and with the very same grace as when he had first set eyes on her two years earlier.

In her dream she could feel his presence. It was such a beautiful feeling. The sky was losing its fiery glow now, turning into shades of grey and blue. As the song from the martens in the branches of the bodanmyen trees died down for the night, she knew it was time to go home. Reluctantly she opened her eyes and, for a split second, she thought she was still dreaming as she gazed into his face. She blinked and reopened them, only to see him smiling down at her.

"You're here!" she cried out.

"Yes," he said. "I am here."

Her smile was brighter than the setting sun had been. She could not have been happier. He was here with her for their anniversary and her birthday after all, and she had the most exciting news to tell him!

The slither of the new moon shone in the night sky, but all else was lost in the dark shades of night. Then, one by one, the stars twinkled in the darkness. The breeze turned cooler. He held her closer to his body. She felt his warmth and could feel their hearts beating together as one. He leaned down and kissed her.

"Bonne anniversaire, ma chérie, Je t'aime trés, trés fort."

As he whispered to her, she felt as if her very soul might melt with the intensity of her emotions. No additional words were required. They had each other and the beauty of the magnificent sanctuary created by the night. They held one another and let their emotions speak silently as they gazed out at the bay. As the moments passed, something new arose, something that had not inhabited their sanctuary before. A faint stir of fear, of apprehension. Like a wisp of a cloud in an otherwise blue sky, it did not sully the intimacy of their moment, but it was there nonetheless.

A slight shiver travelled through her as he ran his hand over her alabaster skin. Despite his own desire, he moved slowly. He did not want to scare her. Kiss by kiss, caress by caress, he removed first one garment, and then the next, until she lay in the sand before him beneath the gleam of that small crescent, beautiful and desirable.

This body which he had worshipped in his dreams and which he had sought to recreate into a wooden sculpture, was now at long last beside him. For an instant, he feared that he was simply living within a dream until a soft sigh, a moan of pleasure, escaped her lips.

The gentle waves brushed the sand. The breeze rustled through the leaves of the trees. The powdery softness of the sand cushioned her body as she relinquished her every inhibition. She felt the fire of his own exploration even as her own hands discovered the body of the man she loved, each ones touch intensifying the other. She trembled. She felt as if she was wavering on the edge of a delicate, intense and passionate sensation as he began to trail down her body, kissing first the side of her neck and then down her chest until his lips came to rest on one of her breasts. Driven with passionate urgency, he took her nipple between his lips and suckled at her puckered flesh.

"Oh," she sighed in an expression of unbelievable pleasure.

The warmth from his lips, while centred on her nipple, quickly radiated down over her abdomen, finding its intense and wet centre between her legs. She trembled with passion as his hand and mouth continued their exploration, sending ripples throughout her body. She felt herself floating, as though she had become moist heat. The intensity of his caress and kisses was so potent, so pleasurable. She was on the edge, and it was bubbling, bubbling over...

"Oh, mon chéri," she cried out, "Oh Louis." The throbbing wet centre between her legs overwhelmed, as all the build-up intensity reached its climax and she experienced her first orgasm. Waves and waves of intense pleasure took hold of her entire body.

His mouth on her breasts, his caresses, magnifying the whole pleasure, her heart and breathing racing frantically. His hand pressed against her thigh, his fingers stroked that wet centre, setting her ablaze yet again. Suddenly, the evening air chilled her moistened nipple. He was once again kissing her as he positioned himself above her. His hardness pushed against her as his knees pushed her legs wider apart.

She cried out when she felt a sharp, throbbing pain pierce her. He kissed her passionately, drowning out any other cries. She did not think that she could stand any more – the pain and pleasure mixing so intensely as to drive her completely mad. Beyond this madness, she could hear his declarations of love. She could feel their perfect union.

"Je t'aime, Je t'aime," she cried out.

There were moments after they made love that she did not feel that she could move, so sated and satisfied was she. But soon, they were in the warm waters of the Indian Ocean together. He washed the sand from her skin and her hair. She pressed herself against him and kissed him, baptised by love and the warm, salt water. He was behind her, holding her tight.

She could feel that heat rising within her again, as his hands caressed and stroked her. She turned to face him, weightless in the water as he lifted her. Her legs wrapped around his waist. He slid into her, filling her, thrilling her. It all felt so right, so beautiful…she felt nothing but happiness and joy.

The dawn of the new day found them cuddled in each other's arms on the soft fleshy leaves of the patatran creepers. They opened their eyes to look upon one another at the same moment. They smiled. As they kissed they knew their bond was complete and eternal.

Her joy was such that she was quite certain she was broadcasting what had happened to everyone she met throughout the day, a thought which concerned her and made her colour.

Only that night, in the Savy's family cottage, in the privacy of her own bed, with the lights turned off, had Anna at long last been able to relax, to fully consider the events of the longest and most meaningful day she had ever had. Only in the cool darkness of her room had her thoughts come together, as she saw once again all that had led to the night before.

Had it been fate or coincidence that had brought them together in exactly that same spot, or had fate played a hand just as it had two years previously? It didn't matter, of course. The urge to stay there had been too strong and too powerful, and she had been totally and utterly powerless. Anna was not alone in being unable to stop thinking about those events. Louis too was completely engrossed in his thoughts. If he ever doubted her feelings for him, the previous night erased those doubts. She gave herself totally and without any prejudice. She proved her love, and he felt a greater love for her now than he had ever thought possible.

Two days later, Anna and Patricia were finally able to sit down for their first session. Anna's parents had received the letter from the Assistant Matron explaining that due to a program of reorganisation within the healthcare system, Anna would be working morning shifts only, and would be receiving additional training in the afternoon in preparation for the implementation of the program. Anna had been a bit surprised, as well as very excited, when Sister Kent shared with her the changes she envisioned, and how she thought it would enhance Anna's nursing career to be at the forefront of those changes.

"I do believe that your contribution will prove invaluable in the future," Sister Kent told her, with a great deal of emotion.

Until that moment, she had not suspected that Sister Kent had such confidence and trust in her.

"Thank you," said Anna, with full modesty.

In truth, over the past two days she had been concerned about the meeting, and all of the good changes to come.

Her life, her love…it all seemed too good to be true. She had been scared that somehow something would materialise and take it all away. Patricia had quickly read Anna's fears and been just as quick to reassure her.

"You are in a wonderful position," she said, reminding her that her future husband had agreed to her career. "Now, I need your help to make a difference to the lives of all the ordinary Seychellois people." She leaned closer to Anna. "They need you, my dear."

Patricia had tried to prepare carefully for her meeting with Anna. What she had not prepared for was her own feelings as she spoke to the younger woman…she felt strangely maternal, as if as she was speaking with her own daughter. That feeling both thrilled and unnerved her. More and more, she had found herself looking at Anna and wondering what her own daughter would have looked like. Would she have had a passion for nursing, or the same cornflower blue eyes as her beloved David?

There had been times when she had to turn away. It was almost too painful to have such imaginings, but other times her mind drifted in more pleasant ways. Now, as she spoke with Anna, she found her thoughts returning to the deserts of Khartoum, to her one and only love, and to the tiny six-month-old foetus, her only child, taken so tragically and laid to rest just like her David, on the shores of the Nile.

As tears welled in Sister Kent's eyes, Anna understood that her feelings were animated by something more than the nursing career. This strong and powerful woman clearly had something within her that she needed to address, and for some reason she had chosen her to trust. Anna leaned across the table and took the older woman's hand in hers.

"Are you all right, Sister Kent?"

Patricia's eyes widened as she looked at the younger woman. Then with a sigh, she confessed to Anna her deepest secrets. To her relief, it seemed to be the most natural thing in the world, to share these things with Anna. Still, the things she spoke of caused her deep grief. For decades, as she had struggled to continue with life in England and then in the Seychelles, she had carried the pain of those two graves on the shores of the Nile with her always, able to share her burden with only one other person, her beloved Charlotte. Now, with this young woman holding her hand, and looking at her with emerald eyes which seemed to hold more wisdom than most mature adults, she knew she had finally come home. She was safe at last.

Tears rolled down Anna's cheeks as Patricia's story transported her to a time and country she had never known. The utter sadness of what she was hearing was overwhelming.

Losing the one person you love most – she felt she couldn't breathe at the thought of losing Louis – it was devastating. But to lose your only child as well! She was certain that she would not have been able to bear it.

She looked at Patricia with renewed and deepened respect. This was a very strong woman indeed.

It was 30 July 1914. A few short weeks before the launch of his beautiful schooner and his very important birthday on the twenty-second of September, when he would come of age and inherit in his own right. Progress had gone well with La Sirène. Everything was exactly on schedule. His relationship with Anna and their night of passion on her eighteenth birthday seemed to have brought them even closer. As he made his way up the path of the botanical garden to their rendezvous he could hardly believe all the wonderful things that seemed to be coming together in his life.

Louis loved Anna's new schedule. It meant he was able to see her every day, save her day off. The change had proved to be rewarding for her as well, she seemed to have gained in her conviction and confidence in nursing. He enjoyed seeing this side of her, as she had shared with him her enthusiasm for the future of the healthcare system and explained the plans and goals of the re-organisation. He could not help but smile as he listened, proud and moved by what these things meant to her, and that she would be at the forefront of so many positive changes.

Her sails became visible in the late hours of 30 July as the Dauphin glided quietly around the northern tip of Mahé. The bay of Beau Vallon welcomed her to the harsh reality ahead. Rolland Benezet was at the helm of his schooner, glaring with intensity as the words of his father echoed in his thoughts, *Remember my son, it is our livelihood we are protecting.* With those words, Gustave had embraced him in a strong and powerful farewell hug. Rolland's hatred was deep and true. He had chosen his crew with great care, strong and sturdy men who had been in their employment since they were young lads, men who owed their allegiance and obedience, and who would not think twice about risking their very lives.

As it turned out, their task proved remarkably easy. Boarding her as she lay low in the water, her hull packed to the brim with a cargo of copra, cinnamon and patchouli, was effortless. The men paused only briefly. Their eyes were accustomed to the darkness as they moved silently on her deck, each to their allocated task, stopping only at the sound of loud snoring coming from a corner of the deck.

He is quite old and expendable, without a family, Rolland told himself, knowing the man's fate already. *No one will miss his passing.*

He drove his blade through the sleeping figure, bringing the snoring to an abrupt end. A brief, gurgling took hold of the night's silence as he gestured to his crew to continue.

The red glow from the burning Alouette illuminated the night sky as the four strong swimmers boarded their own schooner. The same breeze that fanned the flames glided them from the scene of their crime. They had been successful. Rolland's thoughts turned briefly to the other half of the plan, to his father and brother and the nearly-completed schooner in the boat building yard, and he wondered if everything had gone to plan there as well. Fortunately for the du Barrés, the launch deadline of the 22nd of September saved La Sirène from that fate. Gustave and his son had to abort that part of the plan to 'torch' her, when they found boat building yard carpenters working the night shift in their attempt to meet the deadline.

Dife! Dife! Dife!

Anna heard the cries, and opened her eyes when she realized that she was not dreaming. Her father and brothers rummaged noisily through the bungalow and then, in a parade of loud footsteps, dashed out of the front door. She leapt from her bed and went to the window. She saw the red glow on the bay. Before she could even think, she was running down the footpath barefoot with only one thought in her mind – Louis. She found the beach crowded with plantation workers, staring in disbelief at the sight before them. Still others were busy pushing the black pirogues down the beach and out toward the burning Alouette.

She looked everywhere in the chaotic and panic-driven scene. The dogs running wild, barking in the direction of the blaze. Women weeping. Men shouting. The heavy breath of something more terrible, in its way, than the epidemic had been.

The ferocity of the flames sent the cargo's thick, oil-based black smoke over everything and everyone, its charred pungency overpowering the delicate scent of the bay. The burning Alouette continued to creak, moan, sigh and sizzle despite the buckets of sea water used to douse her. Meanwhile, more and more people crowded onto the beach.

In the middle of it all, she spotted one black pirogue heading back to shore from the Alouette, and at the head of the pirogue she could see his face. His bare chest was exposed to the night's air. Even from afar, she could see the tension in his body, as if he was trying to propel his pirogue in one swift row back to the beach. She didn't know what was going on until he caught sight of her and shouted, "Anna, we have a man injured!"

The nurse in her immediately took over. "Shawls!" she called out, reaching for the shawls immediately thrust in her direction. She quickly prepared a makeshift bed on the sand, a place upon which to lay the patient. Then she directed two onlookers to bring their torches closer so she could examine the injured man.

A moment later, bare-chested Henri, covered in black soot and blood, ran up the beach to her while carrying old Msye Julien in his arms, leaving a trail of bright red blood on the pure white sands behind him. The people formed a protective border on both sides of him as they looked on in horrified disbelief. More shirts and shawls were handed to Anna, everyone trying to do *something*, anything to help.

She quickly and professionally examined the old man's wound, tracing its length from his neck, down his chest and horizontally across his stomach, exposing part of his intestines. She tried to assess the degree of blood loss which continued unabated despite the shirts tied securely around him.

She raised her eyes to Louis, her look conveying the message she knew nobody wanted to hear. Despite the fact that the old man still had a faint pulse there was little she could do, little that anyone could do.

Anna knelt down on the sand and placed the old man's head onto her lap. "Monsieur Henri," she said, "please press down here." She knew that the pressure would accomplish nothing, but that it would at least allow Henri to think he was doing something to help. But there was nothing more anyone could do. All that was left was to hold the old man tenderly, and hope that in his final moments she could offer a little comfort, maybe help him to regain his faith in humankind and to forgive the perpetrators of this horrific act.

"Out of my way! Out of my way!"

She looked up to see the imposing figure in his brown cassock suddenly materialise, panting loudly from running the entire length along the beach from the church. The priest knelt alongside her, the tobacco smell on his breath strong despite the stench of smoke all around. "Is he still with us, my child?"

"Oui, Mon Père."

Kissing the wooden cross hanging from the thick white rope around his waist, he immediately started to perform the Last Rites. The crowd joined in the prayers. Anna, however, kept her hand on the patient's pulse, lost in a world of her own. Her eyes scanned the hills and mountain of Krev ker, where more plantation workers became visible in the flames of their torches, zigzagging in the darkness, the contours of the footpath dictating their descent as they hurried down to the beach. There was a cruel beauty to the image, despite the devastation all around her.

To her eyes, those flames were reminders that there was still goodness in human nature, despite the evil so manifest that night. The flares reminded her of the fireflies that graced the trees outside her bedroom window. Her thoughts were on those fireflies when she lost his pulse. The prayers had yet to end, but she kept her hand securely on his wrist as she imagined his spirit freed from his tortured body.

Indeed, it *was* a powerfully touching scene that greeted Julien's spirit as it came forth. His head was resting on the lap of a beautiful young girl. Even with her hand on his wrist, he knew the secret which only the two of them were sharing. She had known exactly when it had happened, but had not betrayed his passing. He noted the anger and agony in Henri's eyes, and he had felt an enormous sense of helplessness knowing he would not be there to help him. There were the tears streaming down Marie's face, the one woman that he had loved all his life, who now stood trembling in grief. He wished now that she had not been so stubborn, that she could have found a way to forgive his witless indiscretion so that they could have had a full and happy life together. But that was now all ended. His life on this earth was over.

Only his God, and the visions of his forefathers beckoning, remained. Whilst everyone else watched the scene on the beach, ensuring that Julien received his last rites before leaving this earth, in her heart Anna had been saying prayers of her own for the old black man on her lap. She prayed both to Almighty God and to nature that this old man had loved so much, asking them to guide him on this final journey and to grant him a peaceful resting place for all eternity.

CHAPTER 12

Suicide and Rewards

There was no shame in acting out of character, not that day. Even a people baptised in the fire of the epidemic deserved consideration that day. For the 4th of August 1914 was a day unlike all others. The First World War had just been declared.

Who knew how to cope with such news? The future itself was thrown into a turmoil that was impossible to fathom. From the most privileged to the poorest, Seychellois society was terrified. The outcome of this war for their small colony of the mighty British Empire was uncertain at best. This was not like a smallpox epidemic where necessary measures to isolate and treat the sick until the infection had been eradicated were available. This was a global affair over which they had no influence. They were isolated in the middle of the Indian Ocean, far from the protection of any British mainland bases. Alone, the islands had no defences.

Foreseeing the war being fought on the seas as well as land, plantation owners feared cessation of steamer services, and hence no outlet for their export crops. Merchants could see their stores becoming totally empty and their profits dropping to nothing. The illiterate labourers in the fields feared everything. Perhaps even more frightening, they all had nightmares of the same terrifying image, German warships attacking their small and defenceless islands, bombarding them and destroying everything under the protection of the British flag. The distances separating the 115 islands which formed the Seychelles, spread out over the vastness of the Indian Ocean, meant that they could be attacked and destroyed individually, with no means of raising the alarm or getting any form of assistance.

In the aftermath panic which gripped the islanders when the declaration of the War was announced, it was only the resolute attitude of the British Establishment that managed to pacify, mobilise and unite everyone to the greater good. Just as with the epidemic, dire circumstances forced them to join forces with the French descendants and the Catholic Church, to focus on the immediate and long-term plans for the well-being of the Seychelles during this war, and what active role the Seychellois should play on the world stage itself.

The establishment and its allies threw themselves into planning, arranging and management mode. New rules and laws were immediately adopted to minimise the hardships on their subjects, plus efforts made to find ways of sustaining their fragile economy during the conflict.

The initial hysteria which saw scores of people taking to the hills for protection against a German invasion, and the widespread looting of livestock and foodstuff in fear of a famine, was now subdued.

Instead, all efforts were targeted on the protection of the islands, along with grand-scale endeavour of food crop production to sustain the needs of the population. A defence committee was set up to oversee the proper workings of everything, from firearms training of the police force to the recruitment of civilians as special constables, and the construction and manning of a chain of lookout posts throughout the islands. The panic had eased.

English, French and Creole stood shoulder to shoulder as allies against the tyranny of Germany. Some of the more patriotic descendants of the French settlers were seen draped in the French *tricolore*, boarding the steamer out of Mahé to the heroic cheers, songs and tears of farewell from their families and friends. Both French and English flags were waved in pride for their young heroes on their way to join the English forces in the trenches of France. They would defend, to their last drop of blood, the land of their forefathers.

They might only have been a handful and from a tiny colony, but their patriotism to both France and England was indisputable. The fact that they were fluent in both languages would prove to be extremely valuable in the muddy trenches and in the countryside of France, where the locals had difficulty communicating with their khaki-clad allies from across the channel. The Seychelles efforts would leave their mark on history.

Henri felt as though his world was collapsing. Five days after the murder of Julien and the arson on the Alouette, war was declared. In many ways, the murder and arson cut deepest. The atrocity had enraged both his family and the law-abiding communities of the Seychelles, and had seen the Head of the Police Force personally heading the investigation, sparing no manpower in his efforts and pursuit of those criminals. Unfortunately, the declaration of war had thrown the investigation by the wayside, with precedence being given to preparations for a possible German invasion.

Henri was not so easily deterred. His rage at this insult to his family, and at the vicious murder of his beloved mentor, remained unwavering. He was determined to see those responsible hanged, and to keep this case in the limelight irrespective of the uproar, fear and extra activity that the onset of the war had produced all over the island.

He sat across the desk, facing the stern figure of Mr Stanley Collins, the British Commissioner of Police, as he read the du Barré's offer of reward.

His mind drifted back to the days immediately after the arson. The charred wreckage of his beloved Alouette rising like an ugly sore against the clear azure waters of the bay. Even now, he could smell the gagging odour of burnt copra, cinnamon, salt fish, and the burnt wood which had once been his precious schooner. His rage had not left him, nor had his bitter sadness for the loss of Julien.

I will avenge your death, dear friend, he had vowed silently back then, promising that he would not stop until he found the criminals and brought them to justice.

Indeed, his anger grew daily, until it became obsessive. Now, on this first day of September 1914, one month after that horrific incident, he prepared to play his trump card: a reward of *one hundred rupees* for any information that led to the capture and conviction of the culprits. It was a huge reward, beyond any that had ever been offered before, and enough to make whoever earned it quite comfortable. Henri hoped it would distract attention from the happenings in Europe; it was something that he had to do, and he could not rest until it was done.

Gustave Benezet had marked thirty-three dark days and torturous nights. Days and nights of anguish that he knew would never end. The nightmare was here to stay. He would never be released from its grip. He was doomed for all eternity. He had been numb in the weeks before it happened, convincing himself that he had no choice, that circumstances had taken the decision out of his hands. He had not considered the consequences. But now, as he looked at the face staring back at him in the mirror, he could see too plainly the ravages of the past month. Deep, dark lines etched into his tanned face, black circles around the eyes which exhibited an unfathomable dullness. His eyes were opaque and lifeless, overcoming the luminous rays that had always spurred him on, that had been his power and strength before that fateful night. That light was gone for good, and he felt dead inside.

Unlike his face, his hands still looked strong and rugged, like those of a hard-working man. But in his mind's eye, he could see the stain of innocent blood oozing from every pore, reminding him that nothing in this world was ever going to wash away that night. His family and all their generations would feel this curse, for his actions had tainted them for perpetuity with the blood of an innocent man.

His was a heavy burden to carry, one he feared he would be unable to sustain for much longer. His heart ached as his thoughts turned to his first born.

The little boy with a mop of red curls whom he had held in his arms over three decades before, and who had since turned into the spitting image of himself, was now in the mortal path of the hangman's noose. And it was his fault. He was guilty of arson and murder along with an even greater sin. Failing as a father and protector, he would be his own son's executioner.

Damn Christophe du Barré! Had it not been for du Barré's greed things would have continued as normal, and everyone would have been happy going about their own businesses, the Benezets on the seas and the du Barrés on the land. But no, rather than this peace and harmony, he had been backed into a corner, with no way out. So he had resorted to desperate action to secure his livelihood.

But now? The weight of his deed and its consequences was slowly taking the life out of him. With news of the reward, he knew that he did not have much time left and that he needed to make a decision right away. The declaration of war early in August had granted him a kind of reprieve, as the general uproar and fear had shifted all focus away from the arson and murder. But with news of the reward, interest was back on his devilish deed. Once again, his arch-enemy had managed to back him into a corner, and this time there was truly no way out. *One hundred rupees,* he whispered to the face staring at him in the mirror. *My life for one hundred rupees.* He trembled as he imagined for the first time the grip of the hangman's noose pressing against the sides of his throat, crushing the protruding ridge of his Adam's apple.

Later that same day, Christophe du Barré was at his desk, blotting the excess ink from the second letter to his sister since the declaration of the war. He prayed that his beloved Monique would listen to his advice and waste no more time in finding transportation from France to the Seychelles. With news reaching the Seychelles of the German army's atrocities in France, he had ended his letter with a sort of joke, emphasising that it was now the right time for the holiday which she had promised she would take one day to introduce Philippe to the tropics, and to give their mother another chance of experiencing their beautiful islands. He replaced his neat and extremely handsome feather quill to its prime position on the beautiful family heirloom, an elaborately carved and glossy writing desk made from *bois noir*. This was a very special piece of furniture his grandfather had commissioned on the birth of his own father, and he always used it with great pride and care.

His thoughts returned to events here at home, to his old friend and mentor whom he missed very dearly, whose tragic passing he regretted so much. He had been particularly concerned though with the anger and pain in Henri's eyes since the incident.

He knew Henri was finding it difficult to deal with the reality of this cruel act, so to some extent, the offer of a reward was his way of helping Henri. Over the last four weeks, he had felt helpless as he had watched Henri's desperate attempt to keep the investigation going, and he was now quietly hoping that this reward would bring the desired results.

The one positive thing about this whole tragedy, that had greatly touched him, was how everyone on this island – with the obvious exception of the perpetrator of the arson – held him in high esteem. Letters of sympathy were still arriving, and friends as well as acquaintances had flocked to La Residence to express their anger and disgust.

All of his clients had even gone to the loyal extent of keeping their products dormant in their warehouses whilst they awaited the launch of his new schooner. He was extremely glad that in three week's time the cream of the du Barré's future fleet would sail triumphantly out of Port Victoria. He had every intention of making sure the patience of these faithful clients was justly rewarded.

Whilst Henri had been reeling at the atrocity, Christophe remained focused on the bigger picture, on new ways of showing his enemy that they would not be defeated. First, he decided that the Alouette would be rebuilt. He smiled as he made a mental note to announce this decision at the launch of La Sirène. It would make an apt parting tribute to Julien, as well as a positive new initiative for Henri. Just as important, he would commission a third, and possibly a fourth, schooner in the near future. He was determined that once and for all, he would be in control of the transportation system of the Seychelles, to never again find himself at a disadvantage with his clients in not being able to provide them with a reliable service.

Of course, he was no different from anyone else on the island, in that he feared for the future. War loomed in frightening ways. But, as with the dark days of the epidemic, he decided that the only way forward was to focus on the bigger picture, on the world that would exist after the war ended. He knew that it would be important to maintain prudent and consistent production throughout the conflict so that his business could carry on when things did return to normal.

Unlike the epidemic when the Seychelles had been quarantined from the rest of the world and no steamers would call at Port Victoria, these circumstances were different. Services would become affected, but the world would still want to trade, albeit not as frequently as they might have desired.

By careful stock planning and continuing his business as normal, whilst others grew uneasy and cut back on production, he would stand to make the most out of a very bad state of affairs. More important, his plans would keep him active and occupied, a good way of riding out the storm.

He had never been a man to do things by halves. He believed this was the right course of action, the right time to conquer the market completely, and to repair some of the damage and hurt. He would bring out the latest and fastest schooners, and let everyone see that he was a serious force to be reckoned with. And in so doing, he would be striking his enemy where it would hurt the most - in his wallet.

The outbreak of the war meant different things to different people. The inhabitants of the Seychelles were indeed a real pot-pourri of nations, from the black Africans who formed the majority of the population, to the handful of white Europeans from France and England, plus a few Asians from both India and China.

For one person in particular, it brought contradictory feelings, divided and torn loyalties. On the one hand, Patricia felt the huge natural lure to her native homeland, and a deep patriotic need to be there. On the other hand, she knew that the vigour of youth with which she had been blessed three decades earlier when she volunteered for active duties in the Khartoum Expedition, had long since deserted her. Now, at the age of fifty-seven, part of her doubted her ability to make a real difference on the battle fields, while another part was confirming that all her experiences, especially with the nursing of troops, was what the war efforts really needed.

Then, of course, there was this small island community which four years ago had welcomed her, had given her such beauty, peace and security, and had appeased her yearnings for the new sense of home. Was she capable of giving it up to satisfy the sense of obligation and duty to her homeland? She remained undecided. If the Germans turned out to be even half as barbaric as the Arabs she had witnessed in the desert, then the likelihood of this small population being completely eradicated was very possible. Despite the warmth of this September afternoon, she shuddered inwardly as the horrific images she thought she had vanquished from her memory suddenly reappeared in vivid clarity, taking her back to a time that she had hoped she would never, ever revisit.

She trembled as she imagined her tiny hospital with its scarce supplies and manpower trying to cope with such an onslaught. She felt the futility. What would her beloved David have advised had he been here with her? Her thoughts were interrupted by a gentle knock on her office door.

"Yes?"

A moment later, Anna walked in. As soon as she saw the young woman, Patricia smiled. She knew then that she could never abandon this island. She could not leave them to face such a possibility on their own. She was needed here, and she would not allow her dreams for the future here to go unfulfilled. More, she did not want to be parted from Anna, this young girl who had come to mean too much to her. The Seychelles was her true home now.

Anna would remember this September day as well for a very different reason. For the past couple of weeks, she had been feeling unwell. She had tried to ignore her malaise, putting it down to the tension that the war in Europe was already causing everyone in the Seychelles, especially the nurses.

Any fighting on the island would mean a great many patients with all manner of wounds, and the nurses all feared being overwhelmed. However, over the last few days, Anna felt progressively worse, and this day was particularly bad.

She was lethargic during the morning shift, and now, as she settled with the notes from the previous day's lectures, a violent stomach cramp caused her to run to the nearest toilet, where she vomited. When she returned to the desk, she apologized to Patricia, who looked at her sudden pallor with some concern.

"I've not been feeling well these past few days."

"Maybe you should try to eliminate different things until you isolate what's bothering you?" Patricia suggested. She was about to add that maybe Anna should see the doctor when a sudden shiver went through her. Once again, she found herself back in the desert of Khartoum and to that day barely five weeks after the death of David. She had been in such terrible grief. She could think of nothing else but him, and had even found herself silently praying that a stray bullet would find her so that they could be united once again. But the stomach cramps which began soon after his death kept bending her over in pain. They were getting worse with each day. Her colleagues had no option but to march her to their field doctor for medical attention. And just like that, the dark days that followed David's death were given a hint of hope. Maybe she could envisage a future after all. She was, as it turned out, over two months pregnant.

Looking at Anna, her heart raced with dread of this same possibility. She held her voice steady as she asked, "When did you have your last menstrual cycle?"

The question confused Anna at first but after a moment's thought, she replied.

"The middle of June."

As soon as she spoke, she understood the significance of the question and the answer. A heavy silence followed. Patricia could see the turmoil growing in Anna's eyes. Patricia too felt panic rising in her own throat, but she needed to stay focused, to protect Anna. She wanted to be able to tell her that all would be okay, but she knew that would be a lie.

It should not matter, she told herself, knowing that the plight of one frightened girl in the middle of all that was happening on the island and across Europe, should not be important.

But she knew that the truth was the exact opposite. Events such as these were simply not permitted. This would have a profound effect on Anna and her family, bigger than any effects a world war were ever likely to have on them.

Three decades earlier, her own pregnancy had been the spark that she badly needed; knowing she was carrying David's child had given her renewed strength. But her circumstances had been so different. She had left her parents' home in the countryside of Surrey when she was quite young, her wish to pursue a nursing career in London being frowned upon by neighbours and friends. Her parents distanced themselves from her, removing her completely from their lives over the years thereafter. She had been on her own, financially independent, and in charge of her own life when she had become pregnant, and at that moment in her life it had felt like a pure blessing. That reality could not be for Anna. The frightened young girl of eighteen in front of her, just now coming to terms with the possibility of pregnancy and its real consequences…all she could possibly see was her world collapsing from underneath her. Patricia felt so helpless. "Do not jump to any conclusions yet," she said softly. "I will need to give you a proper examination before anything can be confirmed."

Louis held her, kissing the top of her head and trying to reassure her of his devotion, trying to reach her. He knew she needed to know it, to hear it, but above all, feel it.

Anna had arrived at their oasis in floods of tears. He begged her to tell him what was wrong, but for the first few minutes, she was unable to speak. He didn't know what to think. All he could say was "Whatever it is, don't worry, we'll make it work."

However, he was not prepared for the truth she was to confess to him through her tears. He was stunned. At first, speechless. But then after reining in his own feelings, he managed to calm her then reassure her that nothing was ever going to change the way he felt about her, and that they were going to face this unforeseen problem together.

How small and vulnerable she seemed. He held her even more tightly. Then, lifting her face, he kissed her tenderly.

"We'll always be together. No matter what," he promised her.

He led her to their favourite spot by the small pool. Now, watching the shadows of the sun dipping within the branches of the tall trees encircling them, he knew it was time to say goodbye. He longed to go on holding her like this, so that he could protect her from all of the pain and heartache that was heading their way. But instead, he had kissed her gently on her head once again, whispering softly, "Je t'aime, ma chérie."

In the darkness of her room, Anna curled up in a foetal position, hugging her pillow against her chest for comfort, trying for a few brief moments not to think. Such a luxury was not to be hers tonight.

Walking to Beau Vallon, her whole body had felt numb. Everyone she met on the way seemed to have a look of disapproval on their faces, as if they knew what she knew. Then, the awful moment when she arrived home. She had to summon all her resolve not to break down, but to pretend that she was suffering from stomach cramps and a headache. Her mother unwittingly made her feel worse when she commented, "That time of the month is always painful for young ladies."

She was too ashamed to look her mother. She suffered already for the pain she was going to cause her parents, and the stain on their good family name. She was certain that her mother would be able to read the truth in her eyes, that she would know of the terrible sin she had committed.

She could still feel the hands of Sister Kent as she had carefully examined her abdomen earlier that afternoon. The embarrassing and probing feelings of the internal examination. Anna had herself examined others that way, but then it had been only part of her nursing duties. Her patients had been married women, happy to be in the 'family way.'

As she was herself examined, she prayed it would be a false alarm. Surely it took more than one night of passion to become pregnant? But she knew different.

The walk from the hospital to their oasis became nigh on impossible as the seriousness of her predicament became clear, and she was able to foresee the devastating implications for herself, for Louis, and for their parents. The pain, heartache and guilt grew and grew. She felt the weight of her sin, and saw how her actions would hurt those whom she loved so much. *My fault. All my fault.*

Louis swore his undying love for her. But what about her family? What about the community where she had grown up? He said that nothing had changed. In three weeks, he would turn twenty-one and would be in good position to go ahead with their plans.

"We can get married. I will always be there for you and our baby."

His words reverberated in her thoughts. This was real. She was going to have a baby. Their baby. The maternal instincts which she felt earlier that afternoon, when she had heard him say 'our baby' for the first time, were overwhelming her once again. Her hands went to her abdomen, in a gesture of protection and of complete and utter love for their tiny unborn offspring.

Louis' night was just as unsettled as Anna's. In addition to the news that she had delivered to him that afternoon, he had to focus on the plans and details of the next three weeks. His all-important birthday. These new circumstances now made his initial plan even more urgent. Time was of the essence. Everything had to work. There was no room for failure.

He had recovered from the initial shock of the news. Although still reeling from the enormity of the task ahead, the romantic part of him rejoiced at the thought of becoming a father. As he imagined his own child in his arms, he saw that it was his own father who held the answer to all his problems, the one person who would be able to help them. Louis knew he would have to get his father's blessing, and permission to get married right away. This would be no small or easy matter. Again and again, he rehearsed how he was going to approach him with this problem, so that he was guaranteed the desired result. Even coming of age and inheriting in his own right, he did not want to be isolated from his family for he loved them too much to let that happen. He sighed deeply. He knew the pain that this news was going to cause them.

He determined that the morning of his birthday would be the time to approach his father, as he would be in an exceptionally good mood at seeing him turned twenty-one, as well as being proud about the launch of La Sirène. Once he had his father's blessing, he knew that his mother would follow suit. If there was anyone who really had any influence over Anna's parents, it was certainly them. They would ensure that Anna got her parent's blessing to marry, and that she was not cast out in disgrace, disowned from her family. His parent's blessing would be seen as a public endorsement of their acceptance of Anna as their daughter-in-law, a new member of the du Barré family. In turn, this would no doubt have some positive influence on the church, and on the community as a whole, a result of their high standing and privileged position in society.

He was under no illusions. His was a daring plan, but it was the only one he could think of that made any real sense under the circumstances. With this comforting feeling of hope and optimism, and a heart full of love for the beautiful young girl carrying his baby, he eventually fell asleep.

Whilst Louis was taking comfort in the peace that sleep was offering him, elsewhere on the island the lookouts scanned the horizon, their focus concentrated on the horizontal line being illuminated by the light of the full moon. No German war ships could pass unobserved. Their efforts were important to everyone, and they felt privileged to be playing such a great and important role in the war efforts. Black labourers such as they, with monotonous jobs, rarely got any sense of fulfilment, but this work was different and was offering them recognition in the eyes of everyone. Seychelles' first line of defence had been entrusted to them!

It was rewarding to see what Germany's tyranny had provoked on these tiny islands. As the French and English were now allies, fighting side by side in Europe, the people of the Seychelles had also decided to lay their past to rest, and to unite under one banner. It might have taken them a hundred years to get to this point, but this entente between those French descendants and their British rulers was now as clear as the blue skies over those lovely islands. The Seychelles had finally become a *real* British Colony.

Gertrude Benezet had struggled to maintain her composure ever since that dreadful day, which she could still not get out of her mind. Although the past three months had proven to be the worst of her life, terrifyingly difficult and anxiously long, she tried her best to go about her daily routine as if nothing had changed. But now, she was feeling betrayed. It seemed everything had been in vain.

She had overheard her husband telling their sons that the new du Barré schooner was being launched on the twenty-second of the month, and that all of their clients were putting on a show of solidarity by refusing to use any other schooner to transport their goods in the meantime. She had been keeping her ear to the ground these past three months, listening to the local gossip for any breaking news, waiting and hoping day in and day out for weeks now, that the spell of the old witch doctor would start performing its magic. But to her growing frustration, nothing damaging had happened. Even the outbreak of the war, it seemed, had not have any adverse effects on the du Barré family and their business.

Looking at the scars on her thumb, she shuddered as she remembered the pain, fear and humiliation that she had endured, and the lingering scent of putrefaction that she had been unable to wash off her hands these three months. She had put her trust and faith in the powers and reputation of that old witch doctor, and in the dark forces that were capable of accomplishing miracles. Her thumb had healed now, but every night the pains had felt like that first day, sharp and throbbing. She had borne it with dignity, knowing that soon things would start going wrong for du Barré and his businesses. A personal sacrifice she had to endure for the well-being of her family.

Now, as she listened to her husband talking about how much money they had lost and how worried he was about the reward that was being offered, she knew that all her efforts had come to nothing. The spells had not worked. The launch of the new and modern schooner this month would finally destroy their livelihood. It was then that the truth dawned on her, and that made her even more enraged. The du Barré family was under the protection of another, more powerful witch doctor! Of course!

There were many on the island. This was the reason. It had to be! They had gone to a more powerful witch doctor. And why not? They were wealthy. They could certainly afford the best.

All her evil efforts had been in vain.

On the 7th of September 1914, four very nervous and dishevelled shipmates presented themselves at Port Victoria's police station. In a rushed and confused outburst which left the Police Constable behind the front desk perplexed at first, they managed to convey their intended message. They had information about the arson and murder and would like to talk to the person in charge about the reward that was being offered.

They had gone over and over their story since the very early hours of that morning, when they had set out over the dew covered hills and through the dawn chorus valleys of the coastline of Mahé, to get to Port Victoria. They had convinced themselves that the reward was theirs by right, and they were ready to go through whatever was required to collect it. They pressed their thumbs in the ink pad and applied them forcefully onto the empty space at the end of this long, official looking document which the stern Constable had just finished filling in on their behalf. It was their due. A gift that would never present itself again in their lifetimes. All they had to do was to bend the truth a bit, wipe their own slates clean. None of the incident was not of their making. They had merely obeyed orders. Blame belonged to the decision-makers.

The form completed, they sat quietly on the hard wooden bench in the corner of the Police Station's reception area, awaiting the arrival of the British Officer in charge of the case. As they sat there, each of them imagined the plot of land, the comfortable house, and the life of ease which this generous sum of *twenty five rupees* – each man's cut of the reward – would buy them. They would be landowners. They would be emancipated. Yes, their futures seemed rosy indeed.

Gustave Benezet's mug of coffee gave off its strong aroma, adding to the village scent that was gently perfuming the light breeze. It soothed him, reminding him of simple pleasures which he had always taken for granted and which now, in this final hour, he was appreciating for the first time.

The whole scene in front of him seemed brand new, every little detail suddenly alive with colour, smell, sound and beauty. From the silvery grey coat on the small *troutwel* walking along the wooden rail of his veranda's balcony, to the vivid, red beauty of the bougainvillea blossoms hanging from thick fleshy stems that had entwined themselves around the veranda's posts. He had been looking at these things for the past fifty-nine years, but had never really *seen* them.

A peacefulness had settled over him since he had come home from the beach, devoid of the burning anger, fear and pain that he had been feeling over those past days.

He had struggled in making this decision, but now that it was made it was as if things had been taken out of his hands. He had noted the absence of those four shipmates this morning and had known instinctively where they had headed, and why. It was done. He was no longer in control, and he felt at peace. He was now aware of everything around him, the small things in particular, conscious for this very last time that he might not only say goodbye, but be able to take all these images and sensations with him.

His gaze turned to the two open doors, revealing the interior of his beloved home, the one place where he had always felt safe. From here he had watched his two sons grow into strong men, just as his father had watched him, so many years before. He sighed, filled with the memories he would always treasure, and that no one could ever take away. Even at this eleventh hour he could still feel the passion which had ruled so much of his life - his one and only love, the sea, and this vast and beautiful part of the Indian Ocean. His heart sank as he realised that he would never again know the exhilaration of navigating the ocean, his footsteps would never again be heard echoing on the deck of any of his schooners.

It had been a difficult farewell early this morning, as he had watched both of them sail out of the bay of Baie Lazare for the last time, their sails ballooning as they took to the seas, each skippered by one of his sons. His heart ached, but he was aware of the beauty of the image, and it was this memory that he would now take with him on this new journey, to its bitter end. Everything else in his life had been unimportant, performed out of a sense of duty or expectation. A meaningless blur of years that he had sailed through without pausing to look around him, without recognising the details as he was doing today. Sadly, it was too late to appreciate what he had taken for granted for so long.

The tops of their felt hats were just visible, with the proud insignia of His Majesty sparkling with authority in the brightness of the September sunshine as they made their way up the slope of the hill to his house. The barking of neighbouring dogs accompanied their progress, announcing the arrival of strangers.

From his vantage, sheltered on the veranda, he could see their five faces, official, ready and willing to perform their duty as the law of the land commanded. His hands shook slightly as he uncorked the small bottle, pouring its content into his coffee mug, never taking his eyes off their approach. In one, quick gulp, he swallowed every single drop of the vile tasting black liquid.

With his eyes still upon them, the sound of their boots announcing their arrival in his yard, he sighed deeply and placed the mug on the table next to the three letters addressed to his wife and two sons. Then he stood up, ready for the unknown journey ahead.

It was only then that a pale and tear-stricken Gertrude, her long, flat hair tied in its usual round chignon on the top of her head, appeared in the doorway. Her eyes darted from his face to the coffee mug and to the letters on the table. She needed no words to know what he had done and why. She looked at her husband and with her clear expression, let him know how proud she was of his bravery, and how she would cherish his memory to her dying day. No goodbyes. No expressions of sentiment. She did not expect any. He was doing things in his own way, as usual. That had been their life together. From the beginning and now to the end.

With the same arrogance with which he had lived his life, Gustave Benezet gruffly acknowledged the five constables standing at the bottom of his stairs by holding out his hands to be shackled. He made his way down the steps for one last time, stepping into the bright sunshine with his head held high. The piercing, blue English eyes stared in unspoken disgust. They dared Gustave Benezet to show some remorse for this hideous crime, but he was unmoved. He signed his confession in a swift and audacious gesture, elegantly inscribing his full name and title under his signature. With that flourish, it was done. Rolland was now safe.

Island gossip twisted the story a fair amount. Before the ink was dry on Gustave's confession, the island knew of the four *good* sailors who had done their Christian duty in telling the truth about the murder and arson. Without mention of the reward money, their actions became a grand, humanitarian gesture. They were good. Benezet was evil.

The story on the island had him resisting the police officers who had come to arrest him, but how they managed to overcome him in the end. How the very shrewd British Commissioner of Police had used his skill to get him to confess. The narrative was set. It was island gospel. And not just an embellished story, but an historic occasion indeed. For it was not every day that a white man would hang for the murder of a black man on the island.

At 5.30 a.m. on the 8th September, Constable Lafortune completed the final task of his shift, giving a mug of coffee to the prisoner. He was glad to be going home soon. Throughout the night and the in early hours of dawn, a small crowd had been gathering along the street, their lanterns and flaming torches keeping vigil, all waiting for a view of the murderer.

They wanted to see him sweat and shamed as he was taken in chains to be charged with his crimes and sentenced to death by hanging. Although patient for now, the police anticipated a much larger and angrier crowd later that day. Officers would be required to ensure the safety of the prisoner on the short walk from the station to the Supreme Court building, and that journey which looked to be increasingly challenging.

Constable Lafortune entered the cell with the coffee, and immediately blew his police whistle. The shrill sound pierced the confines of the small building in the silent early hours, the coffee from the mug in his hand splashing all over the floor. More high-pitched whistles reverberated far and wide around Port Victoria, their insistent tone urgently summoning assistance. There had been no response from the prisoner. The black liquid had worked its dark magic according to its schedule, just as the old witch doctor had said it would. Gustave Benezet of Baie Lazare had already met his maker and had denied the island his final walk of shame.

CHAPTER 13

The Roar of German Metal

$\mathcal{B}$right sunshine and a gentle breeze welcomed La Sirène to the open waters of Victoria on the 22nd of September 1914. With her white sails ballooning in the late morning of the equinox, Louis felt her rise with ease, responding to his command and facing the incoming wave with air and grace. Despite the painful absence of Julien, the family had decided that for this one day they would not allow tragedy to mar the joy of the occasion – the coming of age of the younger son and the launch of this elegant schooner. As she glided gracefully around the tip of the northern coast of Mahé and the bay of Beau Vallon appeared in the distance to greet them, the sound of the lansiv announcing her approach echoed in the stillness.

Henri had to brace himself. The emotion that the heavy shell evoked was too real for comfort. He could feel Julien's presence next to him, as he had been back when the Alouette was launched. This was the triumphal entrance for La Sirène, a renewal of pride and hope after that savage death and arson. It was an effort to ease the pain that had scarred both his family and their community, which even the suicide of Benezet had been unable to heal. Floating gracefully on the sea, La Sirène would fill the gap left by Julien's death, a send out a message of survival against the odds. It was what Julien would have wanted.

Crowds of plantation workers and onlookers waved from the beach as the flotilla of black pirogues rowed out to meet the new member of their fleet, each sounding their own lansiv as a sign of welcome and joy, their music echoing through the peace of this elegant bay. Although no one could prevent the tears they shed, it was with joy that they sought to soothe the pain of the tragedy that had taken place only a few weeks earlier.

Old Père Valer was standing at the head of the first pirogue, a reassuring figure etched against the pale blueness of the sea, the breeze billowing his cassock and making him look larger than life. As his pirogue circled the new arrival, his right hand dipped again and again into the receptacle of holy water, blessing La Sirène with the heavenly protection of his Master, and welcoming her into the service of the community.

The journey from Beau Vallon to Silhouette Island had been exhilarating for Louis. Now, as he observed his family and guests gathered around the antique dining table and Père Valer offering the blessing before the meal, his thoughts turned to Anna and to the conversation which he had had with his father that morning.

His father had reacted with surprise when he asked for his blessing and permission to get married, surprise which was compounded at his further request for his father's personal intervention and assistance.

In halting, stuttered words, he had tried to explain how complicated and urgent things become, and how he was unable to rectify matters on his own, particularly where the young lady's parents were concerned. There was a moment of silence which felt interminable to Louis. Then his father delivered his answer in the form of a very big hug, reassuring him that he would do everything in his power to ensure his happiness and that of his prospective bride.

"You know how much I love you, and how proud I am of you. Now, today is a very special day for you, as it is for all of us. Let us discuss the details later when we return from Silhouette Island." Louis could not have felt happier or more relieved at his father's response.

The clinking of his father's wine glass brought him back to the present. "To Louis, and La Sirène."

Everyone's glass was raised. "To Louis! To La Sirène!"

The joy of the toast was followed by a moment's silence for those fighting in Europe, and then a heartfelt toast to the life and memory of a very dear friend and mentor. Finally, Christophe surprised everyone when he announced that he had given his blessing to Henri to build a new 'Alouette.'

La Sirène returned to Mahé from Silhouette during the morning of the 23rd of September, and immediately started to load the cargo that had been sitting in the shed at the Port for weeks, pending transportation to Île du Nord. She would sail the next day, and it would mean an overnight stay on the island as there was now a backlog of cargo which needed to be loaded onto the schooner. This would be a time-consuming process, giving the whole round trip a two-day span, and it would mean a late arrival back on Mahé on the twenty-fifth of the month. So Louis left Captain Francourt to supervise the final loading and hurried to his rendezvous at the botanical garden.

It had been an eventful and heady few days during which Anna had never been far from his heart and his thoughts. Right now, he was desperate to see her before his departure to Île du Nord, otherwise, it would be four days without seeing her. Far too long a time under the circumstances. As he made his way up the path, his heart raced with excitement and the anticipation of holding her again in his arms, telling her the good news.

Hearing his reassurance that all would be well gave Anna some small shard of hope. She did not dare to fully believe that all would be well, but she allowed herself to think that maybe, just maybe, there was a ray of light at the end of the darkness she felt within her heart.

On numerous occasions she had heard from both her parents just what an honourable gentleman Christophe du Barré really was, so now listening to Louis she took comfort in that knowledge. She dared to believe that he was not the kind of man who would go back on his word, that he would indeed do everything possible to help them. Louis' continuous declaration of love for her and their baby, his promise that their families would not be dishonoured, his certainty that all would be well, served to convince her that there was indeed a future for them after all. She found strength in all of his beliefs and promises. He was all she had. All she ever needed.

His caresses and embrace were long and lingering, conveying their heartfelt messages. "You must remain strong," he told her. "Believe in me."

"I do," she said, looking into his eyes. "I do."

"I will be with you forever," he promised. "Always remember that."

She cried when it was time to say good bye. Their parting kiss was tender and very emotional as she savoured that final moment in his arms. In truth, the only time she felt safe at all was in his embrace. She clung to his words, to his love, to the promise that his parents would help convince her own to forgive her and give the couple their blessing. Perhaps all would be well again in their peaceful, perfect garden.

Louis steered La Sirène towards the open seas, a very proud Captain Francourt at the helm alongside his young charge, as the first light of dawn was visible beyond the small islands guarding Port Victoria. The long years of Francourt's marriage had been barren. Never having been blessed with children of his own, he took great pride in witnessing Louis' growth. He could not have been more proud if Louis had been his own kin.

In the twilight of his life, Francourt knew he had been privileged and honoured to have Louis and Henri in his life, to be able to bestow upon them his experience from years at sea. Indeed, the love that he felt for the sea had been passed to both of them. He swelled with joy and pride at having been the architect of that love. No sons could have honoured him more.

For his part, Louis felt a sense of pride and joy as he sensed the schooner respond to his commands. Despite her full load, she felt light and smooth, easy to control. He was eager to enter the open seas, to feel the waves caressing her new timber, to enjoy the salt sprays, and to lose himself in the magic of her white sails billowing in this early morning breeze.

La Sirène's inaugural trip two days before had been a great event for many reasons. It reaffirmed the family's pride and strength in the face of adversity, a triumphant celebration of the life and memory of Msye Julien and a celebration of his twenty-first birthday. The trip to and from Silhouette itself had been very pleasant, especially the welcome that La Sirène had received when she had sailed into the bay of Beau Vallon for the first time. The echoes of the lansiv brought a feeling of joy to his heart. But that journey paled in comparison with this special day - La Sirène's first commercial trip. Her true maiden voyage.

As the last rays of the sunset cast their glow over the island, Louis stood watching the last pirogues head back to shore for the night. The offloading of cargo from Mahé had been completed. Now La Sirène sat higher in the water, her white hull more visible, showing off her streamlined curves and contours, and her white sails drawn down, leaving her intricate riggings visible. Two flags fluttered on her masts, one French and one English, reflecting her true allegiance.

Louis had come ashore and, strolling along the length of the powdery soft beach, he headed towards the granite boulders with his thoughts no longer on the sea but on Anna and their unborn child.

Though joyous, the events were unexpected and had changed the timetable for all his plans, forcing his hand and leaving him with very little time to act. Even with his father's assistance things could not be rectified in their entirety. There was no way to avoid the inevitable shame attached to what had happened. Even his position and privilege could not do that. On a small island, where everyone knows everyone else and truth and subtlety often lost out to excitement, such news would travel fast. Anna's reputation, as well as that of her family and his, would be tainted by this stigma.

The truth was that there would be no traditional 'white wedding.' The church offered only a simple midweek blessing in cases where the bride was already in the 'family way.' It saddened Louis that Anna would not enjoy the rite reserved for a virgin bride. He felt he had robbed her of something very special and that feeling pained him. Even if they forgave him, it would be hard for his parents as well. To forgo an elaborate wedding for such a simple ceremony would be a serious let-down for them. But whenever his thoughts were saddened at the negative consequences of their actions, he remembered the blessed and positive one — they were going to have a baby. He would be a father. He wondered if his child would be a boy or a girl. Sometimes he imagined the baby so convincingly that he could *feel* the tiny bundle of the new child in his arms.

He had been resting against the boulder for a long while. Indeed, when he made his way back along the beach, the stars were already out. As he walked along the sand, he felt good. It had been a long and satisfying day, one which would live in his memory, his first trip as master of his own schooner. He reviewed his plan for the days ahead. Depending on the winds, he should be home well in time for dinner the following night, which would give him a good night's rest before resuming the all-important conversation with his father the next day. He believed his father would not let him down. Hadn't he already promised to do all in his power to assist him?

It was just after noon the following day when La Sirène sailed from Île du Nord. She was sitting low in the water once again, her hull packed full with the months of cargo that had accumulated in the stores. Captain Francourt had been very satisfied with the way Louis had organised the storage of the cargo, distributing the weight very professionally, giving the right balance and pitch for La Sirène's journey back to Mahé. All was well.

They were about two hours from Île du Nord when the skies began to cloud over, turning the bright afternoon sunshine into the dim light of dusk. The wind picked up, whistling powerfully in the schooner's sails and propelling her at great speed across the growing waves. The swells were bigger and rougher now, and breaking more erratically. The sky was now dark.

"A passing cloud," Louis said confidently to the Captain when the first flash of lightning illuminated the gloom, sending all eyes skyward. To a man, they listened and counted with anticipation for the crack of thunder to follow. It came with a very loud bang its roar rumbling through the darkness. Then the heavens opened, pouring rain in furious and pelting repetitions that lashed mercilessly at La Sirène, now bereft of her grandeur and looking very small and vulnerable in the menacing ocean.

The driving rain, thunder and lightning continued non-stop for over an hour, and Captain Francourt grew more and more concerned as he saw things taking a turn for the worse. There was something about this sudden change in the weather that he found troubling. A part of him acknowledged the unpredictability of the ocean, but another part of him felt something else. He kept his concerns to himself as he stood at the helm next to Louis, ready to take over should the need arise.

The waves had grown to a frightening size and were crashing violently against the sides of La Sirène, tossing her from side to side and drenching her deck.

Her sails were stretched to capacity, testing her new riggings to their limit. In the flashes of lightning, the crew of the vessel could be seen scurrying around the deck, trying to protect the cargo that was stored in her hull. Louis' voice remained composed and calculated even as their predicament worsened. With absolute authority, he delivered strong and firm commands in between the waves and the roars of thunder, keeping the crew actively occupied. At the same time, he struggled to keep La Sirène steady, riding all the huge incoming waves.

The roar of powerful motors could not be heard above the howling of the winds and the crashing of the waves, nor the dark and enormous outline of the enemy vessel visible until it was almost upon them. Like a terrifying vision from a nightmare, tons of ugly, menacing steel emerged like a phantom out of the darkness, bearing down on them. The screams from the crew were lost in the horrific loud noise as it devoured the whole front section of La Sirène and those within her. The wound came to within a few feet of the helm where the young Sailing Master watched in utter horror as the whole frontage of his schooner disappeared. It had all happened so fast, without warning, with no chance to change course, taking both the Captain and Louis by surprise.

As the helm gave way and the torrent of water rushed in at them, they stood together as the steel directly over them prepared to devour the second half of La Sirène. They exchanged a final glance, and in this brief moment everything moved in slow motion.

"I am proud of you," Francourt called to Louis. "I could not have done anything differently myself."

For his part, Louis felt no fear or panic, only a profound and painful regret. As the water crashed over them, he cried out in excruciating agony, "Anna, oh mon Dieu, Anna."

They descended slowly, down and down. Francourt was bleeding desperately, with blood seeping from his chest and arm. All around them, the broken and bloodied bodies of the crew, limbs, torsos, heads with eyes wide open in shock horror, tumbled in a slow motion, underwater descent. Francourt became aware of Louis nearby, deeply immersed in the turquoise ocean that was now stained with red, deep where the waves could not get to them, heading for the softness of the seabed.

Above them, the dark shape of the metal giant went over them as though they had never existed, as though they had only been a little twig floating in a vast storm.

There was blood pouring out from the side of Francourt's chest and arm. Just in front of him he could see the body of Louis drifting towards the seabed. Francourt was nearing unconsciousness, but an unknown strength surged through his body, propelling him to reach out and grab Louis and arrest his descent to the deep.

He began to swim upwards, dragging Louis' heavy body with him, and feeling as though his lungs might burst. And then, with a strangled cry and gasping for breath, he found himself at the surface.

The waves had calmed. There was debris all around. They narrowly missed a piece of what used to be the main mast, tossing about in the current. The rain had abated, and the sky was starting to clear. Then, as a ray of sunshine broke through the clouds, he saw her face, the beauty and vitality of which had mesmerized him since he had first set eyes on her at the boat building yard.

She was floating towards them, complete with a big chunk out of La Sirène's bow. He took strength from the vision of her. After several attempts, he managed to lift himself and Louis onto that piece of wreckage, laying him flat on his stomach against the back of the mermaid, his head resting on her neck and hair, securing his arms tightly around her chest. He tore off his shirt, using pieces of it to tie Louis securely to his beloved sculpture. When he was done, he gazed at Louis, satisfied with the last possible service he could have rendered to such a brave and beautiful young man, for they were definitely meant to sail together for all eternity.

Even as he finished lashing Louis to the sculptured image of his love, he could feel his own strength ebbing away. He knew he had little time. He glanced up to see the massive metal ship roaring away in the distance, its German flag flying proudly from its mast, oblivious of any concern for the destruction it had left behind.

He lowered his eyes as his breathing grew shallow. He was grateful, at least, that his last efforts had allowed him to bring Louis' body back to the surface. A final, true act. And then the alluring sea called to him, the love of his life beckoned him to his final rest. There was satisfaction in that as well. He knew in his heart that his eternity was not meant to be anywhere but with her, down there in the deep. *Adieu, mon fils,* he whispered to Louis in his last breath, as he slid gracefully into the depths of the Indian Ocean.

CHAPTER 14

The Aftermath

While the dawn of the 24th of September had seen the departure of La Sirène to Île du Nord, it had also seen the arrival of the monthly steamer from Europe. Her arrival was a welcome sight, for everyone had been dreading the possible reduction, or even cessation, of the service altogether due to the threat of the German warships patrolling the surrounding oceans. Her arrival meant the shops would have stock for another couple of months. Most importers had doubled their usual monthly order on the instructions of the Government, a precautionary measure just in case there was suddenly a big gap in the frequency of the voyages to the Seychelles. The plantation owners with export crops were also relieved to see her berth within the confines of Port Victoria, for it meant that their products were going to buyers in India and Europe and hence they would be able to stay in business. The fragile economy of the Seychelles would be maintained, for now at least.

But perhaps more than the economy, the steamer was important for its other cargo – mailbags from Europe. The postmark of Woolwich stood out on the thick brown envelope that the clerk handed her, prompting Patricia to sit down at her desk before her anxious hands opened the envelope. Charlotte Craddock's handwriting was as elegant as the lady herself, the graceful Matron of the prestigious Royal Herbert Military Hospital. Although small in stature and of a stocky build, she possessed the refinement, poise and charm of a true English lady.

She had succeeded Patricia five years previously, after having served as Assistant Matron for a number of years, but they had known each other for over four decades, as both had trained together at the Florence Nightingale School of Nursing.

Whereas Patricia had always been the adventurous type, Charlotte was just the opposite, preferring the comforts of England to the enticing allure of faraway shores. Yet in their professional capabilities they had been the perfect match, just as their all-encompassing friendship had seen both of them supporting each other when personal tragedies had struck at different stages in their lives. For nearly five years, Patricia had kept abreast of changes in the medical world, as well as happenings in London, through her lifelong friend. They exchanged monthly letters filled with gossip about the differences in their diverse worlds, and reminisced about the times they had known together in Woolwich, the three decades they shared as nurses, enjoying the special and distinctive qualities of this garrison town bordering the great River Thames.

Each time she read correspondence from Charlotte, Patricia could recall the second-floor apartment they shared in Plum Lane, on Shooters Hill, where – from a height of 432 feet – they enjoyed a panoramic view of the river and its industries. She sighed now, recalling the beauty that winter brought, wrapping everything in its white blanket; the Royal Artillery Barracks, the Naval Dockyards and the Royal Arsenal, along with Beresford Square, where tradesmen and women plied their trades.

She could almost hear the voices around the market stalls, with everyone out to get a bargain, and those horse-drawn open carts loaded with a mountain of bales and drums coming from the ferry, jostling around the crowds. Woolwich was an example of a town where the very rich and opulent lived alongside the ordinary and the disadvantaged, where comfortable horse-drawn carriages, horse-drawn trams and the poor shared the streets.

She sighed as these memories and so many more flooded her thoughts. She brought the envelope to her nose, breathing in the scent of Charlotte's perfume, faded from the letter's long journey. It reminded her of so much. Then with the letter-opener she sliced open the envelope, anxious to read this first letter from Charlotte since the onset of war.

As she read, it was plain how much had changed since the last letter, when *war fever* was sweeping every corner of London. Now, the tone of her letter was more sombre. It spoke of how the declaration of war had descended into a kind of slow motion, with the reality of its actual existence slowly registering on every face, a quiet and composed air of resignation taking over from the excitement of the previous months.

*I helped to organise the first contingent of British nurses who left for France on the 12th of August...*Charlotte wrote. As Patricia read these words, she felt herself wishing that she could be there, receiving her own kit and getting ready for embarkation. But she knew she could not be – she was needed here, now more than ever before.

Elsewhere on the island, sitting under the shade of his veranda with its view of Beau Vallon beach, and bathed by the soft breeze blowing in gently from the Indian Ocean, Christophe du Barré was staring at the two envelopes from France, uncertain as to which he should read first. The long and immaculate handwriting of his mother, Madame Marie-Antoinette du Barré, was still as elegant as ever. Age it seemed, had not robbed her of this very ladylike skill. *My God*, he sighed to himself, looking at the writing on the envelope and realising that the following year would be her eightieth. *Perhaps this is the incentive that might persuade Monique to bring her to the Seychelles once again.*

He opened her letter, read her greetings, and then was amused as she went on to describe in no uncertain terms what she would personally like to do to those Germans. He smiled at her spirit.

But then, the remainder of her long, thoughtful letter left him feeling quite sad, as well as deeply disquieted. She described the defeats suffered by the French army in some places, despite their valiant fighting, and the atrocities that were being inflicted by the Germans on the ordinary civilians afterwards. Churches that harboured civilians were set ablaze. Corpses were left in the roads and gutters, rotting where they had fallen as the living fled the onslaught of the German army. The pages trembled in his hands as he feared what could happen to his mother and his sister if he could not convince them to come back to the Seychelles. The countryside of Bordeaux and Agen was away from the frontlines for now, but if the war was to escalate that could change.

She concluded her letter with descriptions of heroism and bravery of some ordinary men and women who had defied the Germans by returning to their villages to help those injured and to bury their dead.

Despite all that is happening, everyone in France believes in the French army, and no matter how bad things might seem, we remain convinced not only of a victory, but of a reversal of the humiliation which France had suffered in the 1870 war against Germany. The restoration of the Alsace and Lorraine territories, which the Germans had taken during that war, would be the glorifying reward for everything they were now going through.

Monique's letter shared her mother's tone, but with a different perspective; it emphasised what was happening with Philippe since the outbreak of the war.

Philippe Burkhardt had been born in Muret, near Toulouse in the South West of France, in the summer of 1855. His mother, Juliette Gonthier, the only child of Edith and Sebastien Gonthier, the village's baker, had a shotgun wedding six months earlier to the blue-eyed German immigrant, Rudolf Burkhardt, much to the annoyance of her parents and the whispers of the whole village.

But Rudy, as he came to be known in the village, was a hard worker and came to earn the respect of everyone, including his in-laws.

He learned the art of *boulangerie* to perfection, much to the happiness of Juliette and their growing son, Philippe. The first real sign of trouble began fifteen years later, in July 1870, when war was declared between France and Germany. Once again, he was held in suspicion as the villagers waited to see what he would do next.

Rudy volunteered his services as an interpreter for the French army, leaving Muret in August 1870, two days after Philippe's fifteenth birthday. He died on the 28th of January 1871, at the hand of his own countrymen, when Paris fell to the Germans after a prolonged siege.

Philippe had kept to this day the Letter of Commendation which Juliette had received from the French Army afterwards, and which she had treasured until her own death in 1880.

Unlike his parents and grandparents, Philippe did not go into the bakery business, but had preferred the art of winemaking. Working his way through the countryside of Bordeaux, he had learnt not only the production side of winemaking but the culture of the vines as well. It was whilst on a trip to Agen, a small neighbouring town close to Bordeaux, that he had become interested in the vast plantations of prunes, a speciality of the area, and had then switched his expertise to this new crop. He was forty-seven years old in 1902 when he married Monique du Barré, a forty-four-year-old Seychelloise of French descent who had bought a farm in Agen adjoining his own to try her hand at the cultivation of prunes. They had not looked back since.

It seems as though history is repeating itself, Monique wrote. *Philippe now finds himself with a problem and is not sure how he should go about affirming his allegiance to France.* Her words troubled Christophe. He realised that Philippe had no right or obvious path to follow, every way he went would have some sort of repercussion.

Knowing his sister, he knew she would stand by him through thick or thin, and damn the consequences. Given the circumstances, it would be easy for French people to hate anyone with a German parentage or connection, especially in the midst of the brutality they were experiencing.

Christophe realised that Monique would not leave his side, she would want to be with him. He did not know how to advise her or what to do next. He could not possibly ask her to abandon her husband in his desperate hour, nor their livelihood and all of the local people who depended on their employment at the farm. He found himself whispering a silent prayer instead, hoping that God would protect his sister and her family and that they would not have to pay with their lives for their patriotism. As he considered his sister's letter, he felt a burning hatred toward the Germans. Even though he had never set foot in the land of his forefathers, part of him felt the eternal bond that even distance could not sever.

The sky had turned to a very dark grey as he lifted his head. The lovely sunshine that had been illuminating the beautiful early September afternoon was hidden. The day suddenly looked as dark and menacing as he felt. Silhouette Island, which had been in his view a few minutes earlier, was lost, shrouded in thick blankets of mist travelling straight towards the bay of Beau Vallon. Christophe watched its silent, steady approach. In the space of a few minutes, the afternoon light turned into the dark colour of a very late dusk. Everything seemed to come to a standstill.

The storm arrived with ferocity, the thunderous echoes of its strength reverberating and shattering the silence that had preceded its arrival.

It came straight towards Christophe and then, inexplicably, halted within inches of where he sat under the open veranda, as if it had come up against an invisible wall right in front of La Residence. For several seconds it hovered in this one spot, holding his gaze, almost as if it was trying to communicate with him. The storm seemed to dare him to believe that there was no escape from its destructive power.

The pause lasted for a minute, maybe two. But then suddenly, it shot forward, lashing forcefully at him, drenching both him and the furniture. He scrambled out of the canvas armchair, trying his best to protect the two letters in his hands, whilst the accompanying winds whistled overhead, sending the lace tablecloths and head-rest covers from the furniture whipping up around the veranda.

The storm tore at the branches of the shrubs and tropical flowers in the garden, now lying horizontally, flattened by the pressure. In the ensuing flashes of lightning, the housemaids, who had been caught by surprise with this sudden change in the weather, struggled with the ropes that secured the long rattan curtains along the veranda, doing their best to unroll them so as to keep the wet floor and furniture from further drenching.

Two hours after the storm had hit Beau Vallon, Albert was inspecting the damage and mobilising his labourers. Only one roof from the labourer's huts had been blown off completely, although several other huts had sustained damage. The estate suffered a heavy loss of coconut trees – scores had been uprooted. The labourers had lost pots and kettles from their open outdoor kitchen, and the vegetable garden around the huts had also taken a beating; bamboo trellises complete with the vegetables they supported, littered the ground. A few of the labourers who kept bees had their hives overturned, and there had been some damage to stocks as well. The stacks of salt fish that the labourers had been unable to gather into the shelter of their huts in time would require plenty of future sunshine and attention to prevent them from going mouldy.

It would be days before the mess was cleaned up. Still, it could have been worse. Such a violent storm, and out of season! But no livestock had been lost, a great source of comfort both to the labourers rearing them, and to the estate.

Silence reigned over the three members of the du Barré family as they sat at the dinner table that evening, each contemplating the ferocity of the storm that had come out of nowhere. Lasting only about two hours, it had lashed out cruelly, almost with a sense of vengeance.

Even if they were all thinking of Louis and the late arrival of La Sirène, none of them voiced their concern. After all, such storms were normal in the shipping trade and there was nothing to worry about whatsoever...

"It is a shame about all those trees that we lost today," Genevieve said, trying to start a conversation. But it was slow progress. They were each conscious of the empty seat at the table and all wishing there was a way of finding out whether or not the schooner had left Île du Nord. At the same time, they reassured themselves that La Sirène was a strong and sturdy schooner with all the latest riggings, capable of withstanding any storm. Not least, Captain Francourt was onboard with Louis, another positive thing. The trip from Île du Nord to Mahé was only a matter of a few hours – it was not as if they were coming from one of the far outer islands. The storm had lasted for a very short time. They must have bypassed it somehow. A few hours delay, nothing more. La Sirène would arrive the following morning. No reason to worry.

The family continued with their dinner, slowly sipping the delicious French wine imported for their pleasure. But despite the peace of this family time together and all the advantages which were available to them, there was a powerful sense of unease. Even as he ate, Christophe was thinking of something else.

He was remembering what he'd seen in that storm, a strength and cruelty at its core that he had never seen before. The storm had been trying to tell him something, but he was unable to decipher it. Sipping the full-bodied red wine from Bordeaux his mind turned to Monique. She was now condemned to stay in France. The anger and rage he felt against the Germans were vivid once again. He wondered then if the message in the storm was a warning of what was to happen to his sister and mother – after all, he had been reading their letters when the storm suddenly appeared! He wished old Julien was still alive. He would shed some light on this. And then, his own hatred of Gustave Benezet flared anew.

Henri had not been at Beau Vallon when the storm hit, having spent his day at the boat building yard. He could tell how ferocious it had been from the devastation he saw when he returned, a vision that was enriched by the description that Marie shared in great detail as he sat sipping his coffee upon his return to La Residence. It worried him that La Sirène had not returned to Mahé that evening as scheduled, and he had waited until almost dusk at the Port, talking to the old sea salts who hung out around the quay, waiting for a boat to hire them for a trip or helping with the loading and unloading of schooners.

They counselled him not to worry. They had no doubt Captain Francourt had sat out the storm and was going to stay the night at Île du Nord. The Captain was an authority at this Port. Each of these men had sailed with him at some stage or another in their lives, and were quick to offer their praise of him. Still, he felt uneasy as he glanced at his brother's empty seat.

He told himself he would return to the port at first light, for if they left Île du Nord in the early hours of dawn then they would arrive back early, and he wanted to be there to greet them.

He excused himself after dinner, not joining his parents in the lounge. Instead, he made his way to the beach where he tried to calm his mounting unease.

It was a beautiful, star-filled night. Slowly, a feeling of peace infiltrated his soul, soothing his mind as he looked out at the dim shadow of Silhouette Island across the bay, knowing that Île du Nord was close by out there. Although invisible at night, being much smaller and lying some three miles further away from Mahé than Silhouette, it made Henri feel closer to Louis. He was not alone in gazing in the direction of Silhouette Island.

From her first floor bedroom window, a lady also had her eyes fixed on the island across the bay, her birthright. The remains of both her parents lay side by side on the little hill, looking out at her across the bay, watching the life she had created for herself as the wife of the lovely man whom her father had chosen for her. In her heart of hearts, Genevieve knew that they would be looking out for her youngest offspring as well, and ensuring that no harm came to him, for they knew just how much he meant to her. They were the only ones, apart from her chambermaid, who knew of her deepest and darkest secret, and of the most terrible sacrifice she had had to make in order to stay alive. She was sure that they both understood why she had done it, why she had had no other choice. She had to choose life over death.

At dawn on the 26th of September, Anna was making her way to the hospital in Port Victoria. Her early start meant she had little contact with her parents and siblings each day, and they therefore had less chance of discovering her secret, a reality for which she was deeply grateful.

This day she was particularly happy, knowing that Louis had returned the previous night and she would be seeing him this afternoon after work. But she also felt mounting apprehension as she contemplated the day ahead. It would be very important for them. During their last meeting at the botanical gardens before leaving for Île du Nord, Louis had told her that he would be continuing his talk with his father this morning, which meant that everything would be out in the open.

Christophe du Barré would know that she was the girl whom Louis wants to marry, the pregnant daughter of their overseer. A girl who was going to leave a black mark on their good family name.

The thought of this played havoc with her fragile stomach. How would they react to having her as a daughter-in-law? She had to stop to lean against the trunk of a cinnamon tree for support. She was trembling after her third session of vomiting of the morning. She'd thrown up three times and it was not even six o'clock yet. It was going to be one of those bad days.

Anna could feel the heaviness of her abdomen as she straightened up. She had started to feel conscious of it for a while now, and even if part of her was afraid of what this day was going to bring, another part was relieved that she would not have to live with this terrible lie for much longer. She would not have to hide her growing tummy under layers of petticoats and hope that no one would notice that she was gaining weight, just as she would no longer have to keep averting the eyes of her parents and siblings.

She picked a couple of cinnamon leaves from the branch directly overhead and wiped her mouth with them. The aroma of the cinnamon permeated the morning air, and brought a much needed and soothing effect to her empty stomach. Gazing around, she saw the damage the storm had caused. She had been at work when it happened, but everywhere around her the evidence of its passage was apparent – it must have been very powerful indeed.

Henri hurried to Port Victoria that morning, continually checking his pocket watch. He estimated that he would arrive at the quay by around ten a.m., the same time he would have expected the schooner to arrive. His path was sometimes blocked by the aftermath of the storm, trees lying across the road, and boulders and soil that had come down the sides of the hills in landslides. He was vaguely aware of these obstacles, but his mind was focused on one vision only - the flags of La Sirène proudly fluttering on her mast in the early morning sunshine as she made her graceful entrance into Port Victoria.

He felt an ache in his stomach when he arrived to find the quay empty of all but a few barges and pirogues bobbing at their moorings. He walked to the end of the quay and stood silently at the edge. He squinted his eyes against the morning sunshine, peering out at the long horizontal line in the far distance, searching for any sign of an incoming sail, but there was only silence and the scent of a salty breeze. He did not notice one of the old sea salts from the day before approaching him.

"We will have sighting of her sails before noon, Gran Msye, do not worry."

Henri turned and looked at the old man.

"I will keep watch for her approach," the weathered salt said sincerely.

Henri nodded, acceding to the deep bond of seafarers. He knew that the lateness of La Sirène was of as great a concern to this old man as it was to him. Henri realised that for this wrinkled and barefoot old-timer, this port and all its activities was the very essence of his life. This fraternity, with its unwritten codes of conduct handed down through the generations of seafarers, still controlled and united all who had ever ventured on the ocean.

Henri was deeply moved by these thoughts as he made his way towards the boat building yard at Le Chantier.

The sincerity in the honest, black eyes of the old man as he had offered his services had touched him in a way he had not expected. He was filled with gratitude for a man whose name he had only just learned, someone who had always been just another face in the background of the quay.

He wished that his old Julien was still alive. He felt a great need for his wisdom and strength right then. *I miss you, my old friend*, he thought silently. He could almost hear the little grunting noises he used to make, and imagined him shaking his head in an affectionate way, as he used to each time Henri would not grasp or decipher something which to him was simple or straightforward.

"Always apply a little bit of intelligent perspective to an emotional problem, son," he could hear him whispering, as if it had only been yesterday when he had stood next to him on the quay as he waved goodbye to the beautiful sixteen-year-old girl who had agreed to be his wife in five year's time. It was only a year ago now, on the 7th of September the year before, when Danielle and her family had left the Seychelles after their holiday and he had stood at the quay and watched the B.I. taking her back to her homeland in Mauritius. So much had happened since then that it now felt it was a long, long time ago.

A few days after their departure, the Seychelles had plunged into a smallpox epidemic which lasted over six months and killed almost 200 people, leaving behind not only the open and visible scars, but the internal ones of fears and vulnerability. Then two months ago, he had seen a man he respected and cared for die a horrible death inflicted by a coward. The images of his beloved Julien lying bleeding and mortally wounded, and his Alouette going up in flames, had not left him. The arrest, confession and suicide of Benezet had done nothing to alleviate his anguish.

And then, only a few days after the arson and murder, the news of the First World War was announced. A catastrophic event for Europe, and the lives of his grandmother, uncle and aunt now in grave danger.

It had been a catalogue of cold and cruel events, with so much suffering and pain to try and adjust to in such a short space of time, only relieved by the proud day the previous week, when Louis came of age and La Sirène was triumphantly launched. Life had been so hopeful and beautiful in August 1913, but now that felt like such a long, long time ago. He could still remember the first time he had set eyes on her, when he realised he had found the one person with whom he wanted to spend the rest of his life. Danielle de Ravel had touched his heart in a way no other girl had, and he wished that he could just close his eyes now and go back to that time. *Je t'aime, mon amour.*

Through the pages of her letters over these past months, he had come to realise just how fortunate he was to have her love, for despite her young years she had a sense of maturity and understanding which overwhelmed him. It was her great strength, wisdom and integrity that had helped to sustain him during the terrible days after he had lost Julien, and whilst he was battling to get justice for his death.

Even during the first six months of their courtship, when she was aware that the Seychelles were under quarantine with no ships calling at her port, so he would not be receiving any mail, she had nevertheless written, long and encouraging letters which he had received when the epidemic was over.

He was still staring at the quay when he felt the hand of the boat-yard owner on his shoulder, smiling reassuringly as he handed him a mug of black coffee. He found he could not concentrate. Not even the new samples of wood had been able to engage his attention. He wanted only to see La Sirène making her entrance to the port, or the old-timer rushing to tell him that he had spotted her sails, anything that would finally relieve him of his unease so that he could get back to his normal routine.

The coffee was strong and comforting, as he let its warmth fill his belly and its heady aroma fill his senses. He realised how important it was to be in control at difficult times. To not allow fear and ignorance to cloud his judgement and to be true to the high principles and wisdom which his beloved Danielle had said she loved about him, and which his old Julien has strived so hard to instil in him. Today he needed to justify their beliefs.

At exactly 1.30 p.m., Henri walked through the doors of La Residence and went straight to where Christophe and Genevieve were having their after-lunch coffee.

"I have been to the Harbour Master and I have officially registered La Sirène as missing."

He did not wait for the full import of what he said to sink in, continuing that he needed their approval to launch a search.

There was a rattling of cups and saucers, the hot dark stains of the aromatic drink spilling all over Genevieve's white blouse as her trembling fingers suddenly went numb and she lost control over her beautiful china crockery, sending it tumbling to the floor in pieces. She had been eagerly anticipating the arrival of Louis for lunch, and had been telling herself all morning that La Sirène should be safely in port by now. She was shaking as she tried to get up from the armchair, ignoring the hot coffee that was now soaking onto her skirt, totally oblivious to the scalding skin on her abdomen. But her legs were refusing to obey her commands and she flopped right back into the armchair. Henri rushed to help his mother, opening his arms and holding her trembling wet torso in a manly hug.

Henri wished there had been another way to deliver the terrible news, but deep down he was convinced that his direct approach had been the correct one, blunt and precise. Now that it was done and out in the open they would be able to face this dilemma head-on as a family. Together they would use all the resources which their position offered, but above all they would be able to rely on each other's strength and determination.

As he had focused on his mother, he realised there had been no response whatsoever from his father. He turned to find himself looking into a blank face. His father seemed to be in a trance, his normally expressive face looking featureless. It was obvious that he did not want to acknowledge what he had just heard. He had locked out the outside world.

"Papa, we need you," Henri whispered in a voice which carried a special plea, an anguished and distressed appeal for his father's help. The next few seconds seemed like an eternity but finally, in an almost unrecognizable voice that seemed to come from far away, his father spoke.

"It is just an unforeseen delay but we shall go ahead with the search anyway, starting with first light tomorrow." With that, he got up and left the room.

His fists came crashing down on the polished surface of his *bois noir* desk. He trembled as he leaned on the desk, his elder son's words echoing in his mind. *Officially registered La Sirène as missing…Papa, we need you…*

He felt as though he was trapped in a wicked dream. Then he saw it again, his tempestuous phenomenal vision. Suspended in mid-air, right there in his line of vision, just as it had been when he had been sitting under the veranda, a huge and thunderous cross-section of furious and wrathful menace, trying to communicate with him once more. "Dig deeper!" it seemed to dare him.

It had tried to tell him about his younger son, recognising the special love and bond which existed between them. The intensity and depth of their closeness had transcended space and time and had come to warn him of what was happening out there. The phenomenon in front of him was real.

It was not changing shape, not moving, not wetting the floor and definitely not a figment of his imagination, and it was here to challenge him to see further, beyond the boundaries that normal mortals could perceive. It wanted him to react differently now, to take stock of his own personal power, to erase this overly sensitive and dangerously vulnerable nature. It wanted him to get off his laurels and be a loving husband and father once more, become the force to be reckoned with as he had been born to be.

He blinked, finally understanding the true message.

It was the familiarly confident Christophe who returned to the sitting room a few minutes later. Going straight to where Genevieve was being comforted by Henri and Marie, he opened his arms to her saying, "Do not worry, my love, we shall find him and bring him back home." He turned to Henri.

"We shall go to the Port Office now and make all the necessary arrangements for tomorrow."

"Oui, Papa," he said, relieved at his father's assertiveness. Vivid determination and focused resolution, his father's greatest assets, were back.

The news of La Sirène and her crew missing at sea, and the proposed rescue mission being organised for the next day, spread like wildfire out from Port Victoria. The islanders' shock and dismay at the news quickly turned to concern and sympathy for everyone on board and for their families.

Every man with a seaworthy boat made ready to join in the search; the ladies and everyone else started praying. Genevieve had spearheaded the villagers of Beau Vallon and had left La Residence at the same time as Christophe and Henri were leaving to go to the Harbour Master. She was accompanied by Therese, who had heard the news from Albert, and had rushed down from her cottage to be with her former employer and benefactor in her hour of need, along with an overly-concerned Marie and Agnes, her chambermaid. As they made their way along the length of the beach to get to the church, they had been joined by other villagers who had just heard the news and who wanted to voice their compassion and concern and add their prayers for the safe return of La Sirène and her crew.

It was horribly difficult for Genevieve to walk from her house to the church, and she was grateful for the two arms propping her. She was already convinced that this was God's punishment for her sins. He was going to deprive her of her younger son, just as she had deprived her other babies of being conceived during the past twenty-one years. In Agnes' eyes she could read the same message, for she was having similar thoughts. Her Catholic upbringing combined with her conscience, troubling her deeply for the role which she had played over the long years in assisting her employer to commit such crimes. She had been paid well too, making it even more unbearable.

As they climbed the steps to the church, old Père Valer, having heard the news, was standing on the top step awaiting their arrival. All she could see as she looked at him was the face of God himself, and it felt as though his eyes were reading the content of her very soul, that this was her Judgement Day.

Genevieve did not feel her legs giving way, nor did she realise that she was inside the church until the pungent aroma of smelling salts, thrust under her nose by Therese, awakened her senses. The old priest by her side expressed his regret for the sad turn of events. "Do not lose faith in God's graceful mercy," he said, advising her to put her trust in Him, as He would listen to her prayers.

The deep and penetrating sense of remorse she felt screamed to be released from her tortured heart. She wanted desperately to confess her sin, to be absolved once and for all, because she had been carrying it for too long.

Yet as she looked at Agnes' terrified face, she knew that this was the sentence being imposed on her and she would never be able to tell anyone about this sin. She would have to carry it to her grave. She would never be able to look into her beloved Christophe's eyes again if he ever knew how she had been deceiving him for all those years, and she could never put him through that kind of pain.

This was the agony that she alone had to bear. It was her sin. She would have to find the strength to accept her punishment.

There was a spring in Anna's step as she made her way along the footpath to the oasis, relieved that her work was done for the day for it had been a long and heavy shift. She had left the ward promptly at one o'clock after finishing her morning duties and had gone straight into her afternoon training session with Sister Kent, only to find her in a very strange kind of mood. The awkward atmosphere made it impossible for them to engage in their usual manner, but finally, Sister Kent had come out with what was troubling her. She confided to Anna about her dilemma, how she felt that her loyalties were being divided.

"No matter what I do, I will feel I've let down either one or the other," she confessed, deeply troubled. Then she told Anna about her lifelong friend Charlotte Craddock, who had succeeded her as the Matron of the Royal Herbert Military Hospital in Woolwich.

She explained how she had always been there for her, especially during the terrible years when she had just returned from the Khartoum Expedition, having to face life after losing both David and their tiny baby daughter. She now felt that she was letting down both Charlotte and England by not being in Europe to fulfil her duty to her motherland, whilst Charlotte was working hard and being so active in her war efforts.

As she had listened, Anna was particularly touched by Patricia's care for the Seychelles and the way she had been wrestling with her conscience since the outbreak of the war. Suddenly Patricia stopped. "I'm so sorry. I shouldn't be burdening you with my problems." She knew only too well that Anna had her own far more difficult hurdles to face.

"Please, do not worry," said Anna. Then she told her how the morning was planned to transpire, and how she was still apprehensive that

Louis' parents might not like having the common offspring of their overseer as their new daughter-in-law. Patricia greeted the news with great relief.

"The most important thing is the love between you and Louis. So long as you have your love for each other and your dreams, then you will be able to overcome any difficulties that life may throw in your path."

The silence of the garden was troubling. Anna felt a strange unease as she made her way to the oasis, her heart rate quickening and a cold sweat dampening her forehead. As she approached the final curve around the boulder, she expected to find him sitting there in his usual spot. His absence made her stop in her tracks. She felt her stomach churning once again and it took all her will-power to sit quietly by the pool, to remind herself she should not jump to the worst conclusion.

As she waited, the worrying minutes stretched into half an hour, and then an hour. She was at a loss as to why he had not tried to get to their rendezvous on time. How could he have been so inconsiderate at such a crucial stage in their lives, and what could have been so much more important to stop him from being on time? Could it be that his father had not agreed with his wish to marry her, and had forbidden him to ever be with her again? A work delay? Yes, that was it! Something to do with his trip or the cargo he had carried back from Île du Nord.

To create a sense of stability and peace in the midst of all this worry, she leaned back against the rock where she was sitting and closed her eyes, allowing her heart to reach out to him, and pictured him there next to her with his arm draped protectively over her shoulder. She felt comforted by his warmth and strength. She could smell his manly scent, the firmness of his grasp on her upper arm and the soft thudding of his heartbeat, and it brought a welcome ease and solace to her very soul.

Chantal broke the news to her when she arrived at the cottage. Despite Chantal's torrent of words, all Anna heard was, *La Sirène is lost and they are going to search for her tomorrow.* Those words hit her so hard. She reached out and gripped one of Chantal's arms to steady herself. "Tell me!" she cried. "Tell me!" She wanted to know again and again, exactly what her mother had said. Her own distress made her oblivious to the pain she was causing her sister.

"Anna. Anna. You are hurting her," said six-year-old Joseph, pulling on her arm.

She let go. "Oh my God," she cried, wrapping her arms around her sister. "I'm sorry. I'm sorry. So, so sorry," she said over and over, her body trembling in distress.

Chantal cried too. "They'll find her," she said, her own tears streaking her cheeks. "They will. They *have* to." Then she told Anna that they should join everyone in prayer.

It was only after her tears had abated and she was in the privacy of her bedroom that the terrifying fear fully struck Anna. She could hardly draw a breath, so *physical* was her sense of loss and aloneness. She felt lost. She did not know what to do next. To cry? To pray? To do what? What role did she play in this sudden and frightening drama? *Who am I in all of this?* she wondered, as she paced from the window to the bed and back again. Deep within herself, she feared the answer. She was nobody. Just the overseer's daughter. The love she shared with Louis mattered not. That she was carrying his child mattered not. His intention to marry her...for now, she was a secret. A whisper. A shadow.

The full extent of her emptiness engulfed her. For so long, that chasm had been veiled by his love and reassurance. But now the veil had been ripped away, and only the abyss was there to greet her. *How could I have believed that everything would be all right? What right did I have to believe I'd found a special man who loved me as much as I loved him?* She was angry at herself. She should have known better. Love. Happiness. Joy. What right had she to have thought that she deserved such gifts? And now the truth loomed before her - she would have to face life's cruel reality and everything that comes with it, alone. Oh, it was almost too much to bear. Like a bitter twist, like fate laughing in her face! She wanted to hit out at something, to scream at the top of her lungs. She felt completely engulfed by anger and darkness.

And then she heard a gentle tapping at her bedroom door.

Chantal was there, holding Anna's rosary beads, which she placed carefully on the table next to her bed. Taking hold of her elder sister's hand, she sat quietly on the bed next to her. Despite her young years, she sensed Anna's deep anguish. In the world which Chantal inhabited and in the future which was set out in front of her, God and His merciful blessings were paramount - everything started and ended with Him. She believed completely in His love and compassion. She was therefore certain, as she took her sister's hand, that her prayers would find real consolation for Anna.

"We must ask God for help," she said softly. As she spoke, she was filled with a feeling of being useful, of being strong at a difficult time. For the first time in her short life Chantal felt as though she was the adult. She felt she was about to do something good and beneficial for the elder sister who had always loved her. "Anna, please pray with me", Chantal said softly. "Please let His love and blessing ease your sorrow, and let Him guide La Sirène and her crew safely back home".

Her voice was like a gentle breeze, the kind which you long for without even realising, and which caresses and soothes without being too obvious. The purity and innocence of Chantal's appeal found its way to Anna's troubled heart. It touched her with a startling impact, and as she turned and looked into those clear and innocent blue eyes, she was overwhelmed by the sincerity and beauty of her sister's faith. At that moment, Anna realised what she had lost and the full extent of her actions. God, who had been there for her throughout all the difficult times in her life, was now out of her reach. Her unpardonable sin, its consequences growing within her womb, had taken her away from God's grace, and now that she so desperately needed His help and strength, she was not fit to appeal to Him.

The cruellest twist, which she could clearly see in Chantal's innocent eyes, was the love and hope residing there. Chantal believed she could change the world with Him by her side, right all wrongs and ease her elder sister's pain. Alas, Anna knew it was too late for her. Even Chantal's prayers could not erase her sin. But she could not explain this situation to Chantal, or anyone. Such was her punishment for being a *bad Catholic girl*.

The rest of the evening was a blur. She followed a routine, a ritual, without thought or emotion. She felt only a dull and constant sense of remorse and regret. She had behaved with selfishness at the most difficult moment, when she should have remained faithful and true to their love. She hated that she had been weak and vain, and for allowing herself to doubt the beautiful feelings which she knew he had for her, especially at the one time when he was in dire need of her total faith in him.

Her own feelings of vulnerability and loneliness, which had initially suffocated the life from her, had now dissipated and become suddenly unimportant as though they had never existed. Now she had only remorse and a single focus, the well-being of Louis and the need for him to be found safe and sound.

She had not taken part in Chantal's prayers. God would not be listening to a sinner like her. Yet she clung onto the belief that, somehow, He would be listening to the voice of an innocent ten-year-old who was about to dedicate her life to His service. Whilst a large part of her heart was telling her that this was His punishment for her sin, she could still not quite believe that God would punish her in this way. Surely a God such as He would not punish everybody else for her sin, for there were lots of other crew members on board La Sirène. She tried to hold onto the belief that God would be listening to the prayers being offered all over the island for the safe return of loved ones. Surely it was only an accident, brought about by the heavy storm of the day before, and had nothing to do with God trying to punish her for her sins. Surely, the search party would find them safe and sound tomorrow.

At that moment, Anna's disadvantage of being a young woman governed by the laws of her parents' household was particularly pronounced. She yearned to go to the spot on the beach where she and Louis had shared such happy moments, where she would be able to feel close to him, reach out to him, help him to hold on. But alas, she felt yet again the full force of the problem she was up against, the pain of being a woman and thus having no say whatsoever in her own life.

As she went through the evening, trapped indoors and undertaking the chores ordered by her mother, all she longed for was to be out there. She was still in turmoil as the first cock echoed its dawn call. She had been awake all night, listening from her bedroom window to the distant murmur of the men who had gathered on the beach, her father and brothers included. She had waited in anticipation for a loud cheer from one of them, or a lansiv to sound at any moment, to announce the sighting or approach of La Sirène. But her hopes had been in vain. All those who had been scanning the horizon throughout the night, praying for the sight of that single boat, were now preparing a rescue mission, and the cottage that had been quiet for the past few hours was heard rousing once again.

The significance of fraternity and hope were imperative in the midst of events such as these, and in the dawn on this 27th day of September 1914, both were obvious. Beau Vallon had never before witnessed a flotilla of this magnitude in the security of its bay. Vessels of every size had arrived from all corners of the island, answering the call for the biggest sea rescue mission the Seychelles had ever launched. Some came in the middle of the night, others in the early hours, but all had been driven by the same sense of duty and comradeship towards their own, seafarers just like themselves, in urgent need of assistance.

A spectacle beyond her imagination greeted Anna as she made her way to the beach, accompanied by some of her siblings. Two-year-old Eliane was sitting astride her left hip and she was holding the hand of four-year-old Didier on her right, with six-year-old Joseph clinging tightly to the left part of her skirt. They had never seen so many people, nor so many boats in the bay either, and she could feel them tucking in closer behind her for safety.

Chantal and Maryse, who had been lagging behind, were equally taken aback by the scene, and were now also walking much closer to her. She started to count the number of boats and pirogues in the bay, but gave up half-way through. The impressive Government steam launch, 'Alexandra,' stood out above them, puffing grey smoke into the early dawn sky, a reassuring sign of the strength of official British authority.

At the head of the black pirogue rowing back to shore from the launch, Anna spotted her father. He was waving to her two brothers, Antoine and Maxime, who were standing on the deck of the steamer, next to Christophe du Barré and Henri. What emotion she felt, as she looked at the four of them on deck. She wished she could whisper in her brothers' ears and tell them how much her future depended on their efforts, that she could not contemplate life without Louis. *They just have to find him. Even if it means searching the whole of the Indian Ocean.* She fought back tears as her bleak future stared back at her from across the bay. Her life, her future, was now dependent on the success of the search party. She was at their mercy, completely powerless.

Throughout the previous night she had cried at her window, whispering her love for Louis over and over, hoping he would remember all that they meant to each other. *Stay alive, mon chéri, just stay alive. Help is coming. Hold on...please hold on...*

Now she wished that she was getting onto the steamer with her brothers and going out to bring him back to safety, instead of being made to perform trifling chores such as cooking and caring for her siblings. As she turned away from the boats, she saw genuine concern and fear in the faces of the people gathered on the beach. She saw her mother standing next to the canvas armchair of Madame du Barré, comforting her and applying what must have been *fleur d'orange* water to her face.

Genevieve looked pale and fragile even from this distance, and Anna could feel her heart tightening with sorrow. She wished that she could throw her arms around her, tell her how much she also loved Louis and of the baby she was carrying, and how she felt and shared her pain. But Anna knew that she would have to keep her own feelings hidden from everyone. She was not allowed to show her grief, and there was certainly no one to comfort her.

In the midst of the crowd a tall and distinguished figure stood out, a beacon of hope amidst the anxiety and trepidation. Everyone was looking to him for hope and reassurance. He was staring at the collection of boats in the bay, his eyes firmly fixed on the horizon, and Anna could tell that he was lost in another world. He had transcended the void from the beach to his Master and was now in a place where pain and suffering was unheard of, where perpetual love and hope reigned supreme.

As she fought back tears, she realised that he was her salvation too. The old priest, with a circular bald patch on the top of his head, staring out at the horizon, held the key to her future just as surely as the members of the search party. He was a direct link, offering hope and confidence in the powers of the Almighty, and right now he was all she had, for she had lost her right to appeal directly to God.

The ominous sound of a single lansiv blared out across the expanse of the bay, signalling the start of the search. The distinguished figure in his brown cassock motioned everyone to kneel on the sand and pray, for the success of the search party heading out, and for the safe return of La Sirène and her crew. As his eyes and right hand travelled skyward, imploring his Master's blessing on everyone, it became too much for

Anna to bear. She sank to her knees on the sand, tears streaming down both her cheeks, her heart and soul torn in pain, clutching her younger siblings close to her for comfort.

For the first time since she had heard the terrible news, she begged God for his forgiveness, begged to be heard, begged for Louis' life and for a father for her unborn baby.

The flotilla of white sails headed toward the horizon when the first peal of the six a.m. bell rang out across the bay. Saint Roch was adding his blessing to the search, as well as to the new day. "Oh my," Anna said out loud, brought back to reality as she suddenly realised that she only had forty-five minutes to walk to Victoria hospital, or she would be late for her shift. Approaching her mother discreetly, she handed over her charges and rushed from the scene.

Restored by a fresh hope that the search had begun and that he would be found and rescued safe and sound, Anna rushed from one side of the island to the other, determined that she was going to be strong for him and their baby. It was what he would have wanted and expected of her.

She knew she needed to find the strength to keep going somehow. Memories of their precious, shared moments would have to be her starting point, her one true source of comfort, until his return.

As she walked into the ward, she was aware she was late for her morning shift. She headed straight to the ward sister and, putting aside her anxieties, she explained her reasons. As it was the first time she had ever been late, she got away with only a strong rebuke and some very heavy chores to make up for it.

As she went about her work, she overheard a number of versions circulating the ward as to what might have happened to La Sirène and her crew. Even the most ill patients had their opinions, based on previous stories gathered from seafarers who had been rescued after weeks of being lost at sea. There were some gruesome tales of men having to drink their own urine to keep going, and worse, having to eat the dead bodies of their own friends who had succumbed from the severe exposure to the elements.

Hearing these things made her shiver with fear. The very thought of Louis injured and floating on a piece of wreckage with nobody to help him or, worse still, of other members of his crew waiting for him to die so that they could be fed, pained her.

It was tormenting to have to listen to those comments, to think that the person you love more than anything was going through this, and you could not do anything to help. So, throughout the day, she had to remind herself to remain strong and positive, for Louis would survive this ordeal if only she could retain total faith in him and his safe return. Even her unborn baby seemed to be following the same philosophy – for the first time in weeks her stomach felt calm and normal, as if her baby was also being strong.

Patricia frowned, seeing the pain and worry in Anna's eyes. She was proud of the young woman, and admired her attention to detail and her professional composure. Patricia had learned of the missing schooner and crew as soon as she had walked into the hospital that morning. Realizing that it was skippered by Louis, her first thoughts had been for Anna. She wanted nothing more than to be able to help, but she understood that it would probably be best to let her work it out in her own way. Nevertheless, she kept a discreet eye on her so that her work was not allowed to suffer in the process.

Patricia's frequent visits to the ward that morning had not gone unnoticed by the rest of the nursing staff - they had been kept on their toes each time she had sailed through the wide open doors. But Anna, who shared a very different kind of relationship with her, had gone about her usual duties unperturbed, and that had been a comforting sign for Patricia.

It was only later in the afternoon, as Anna came into her office for their afternoon session, that Patricia decided it was time to give her a shoulder to lean on. She recognized that Anna needed someone to be there for her, someone whom she could trust and who knew about the problems she faced. Her own experience, different though it was, had carried the same pain that she was reading in those emerald eyes. Lessons and lectures could wait for another day. Today, Anna needed a friend, and a confidante.

"It is alright to cry, my dear child," Patricia had said softly, putting her arms around Anna and holding her tenderly in her arms. Anna had allowed herself to be embraced. She desperately needed to be able to lean on someone. She trembled, as the pain and fear poured forth in a torrent of tears.

"You have to believe that he will be found safe and sound, and it is the only thought which you need to keep in the forefront of your mind," Patricia insisted. "Do not worry too much about what you cannot control, just remember that he would have wanted you to be brave and strong and to think about the welfare of the baby, for you must not allow it to become distressed."

This last message got through to Anna, and she found her hand going instinctively to her abdomen in a protective gesture of motherly love.

Back at Beau Vallon, a sombre veil seemed to have settled over everyone and everything. As the sails of the search party disappeared over the horizon, each wondered how and why they were living such a tragedy. How could a brand new schooner with a very reputable captain on board simply go astray?

As the morning progressed and Albert had watched the gathered crowd slowly return to its daily routine, the gravity of all that was happening began to sink in. Accompanying his wife and a trembling and frail-looking Genevieve from the beach to the plantation house, Albert realised he would have to be strong for everyone, for they would now be looking to him for guidance and strength.

It's going to be a mammoth task indeed, he thought as he made his way from the plantation house to the warehouses in the grounds. Without a schooner at his disposal all of the estates products would have to be transported by pirogues, which were very limited in what they could carry. That would mean making many trips around the northern point of the island to reach Port Victoria where the shipping agents were based. *I wish you were still with us my old friend*, he sighed, as he pondered the weight of the responsibility he had just inherited and recalled the strength of his old mentor, Julien.

The task would only become more arduous, for he would now have to take on the work normally done by Christophe, Henri and Louis, make all decisions regarding the estate, whilst all the time retaining a positive morale so that everyone else continued to concentrate on their duties. *At least I will not have to worry about Silhouette's products for a few weeks*, he thought, as La Sirène had brought them all back just a few days before.

He thought about the brand new schooner they had so proudly launched only a few days earlier. It had been such a happy day for the family, so welcome after the heartache of the arson on the Alouette, Julien's murder and the subsequent suicide of Gustave. The launch had been just what everyone had needed to raise their morale.

A feeling of helplessness tugged at his heart then, as he recalled the love and hope in Louis' eyes on the day of his twenty-first birthday when he had embraced him. It was as if Louis had been trying to tell him something very important, something which could not be put into words, but which he hoped could be easily read.

Please God, let the search party find them safe and sound. He drew his palm across his moistening eyes. *What a difference a couple of days can make…*

There had been such happiness and hope on that day. But now, today? There was just the pain and agony in Christophe's eyes as he hugged and kissed him goodbye aboard the Steam Launch. Albert had promised him that he could rely on him to take care of everyone and everything in his absence. He sensed the appreciation that this reassurance had brought to his lifelong friend and employer, who needed to join the search without any worries about what was happening back home.

I know that kind of agony, he thought as his mind drifted back to the terrible months of the epidemic, when his Anna had worked among the sick and dying. Every day, he had lived with the knowledge that she could be the next. He shuddered then, realising the devastation this family would go through if the search was not successful. *Oh Lord, please spare them from that fate*, he prayed as he crossed himself. Then he entered into the first warehouse.

The aroma of dried cinnamon bark wafted through the air, momentarily soothing him as his eyes surveyed the rows of tightly-packed gunny bags ready for transportation to the shipping agent. He mentally calculated the number of trips he would have to make with the pirogues to get the whole lot to Port Victoria, as the next monthly steamer was not due for about three weeks.

To accomplish the task successfully would mean extremely long, hard days, for his rowers and labourers, and for himself. To get the stores to the agent on time, he might have to start as soon as tomorrow to accomplish the task. *I cannot let Christophe down, not now*, he sighed.

As he turned to leave the first warehouse, he almost collided with Marie, carrying two mugs of steaming-hot coffee. She had been in the second warehouse looking for him, and her expression made it clear she needed some conversation as well. She settled herself on the wooden stool next to his desk.

"How will you manage?"

"I have to," he sighed as the strong aroma of the black coffee floated up into his nostrils. He knew it was an impossible task without a schooner but he had no choice but to aim to succeed.

The second warehouse, the larger of the two in the compound, had been constructed a few years earlier. It housed the other export crops like copra, patchouli and sacks of sun-dried salted fish, and shelves full of surplus vegetables, eggs and fruits which were produced on the *mwatye* system by the women living on the estate.

"These will be easy to get to the market," he said, gesturing to the shelves. "It's the other crops I am worried about."

Marie sipped her coffee thoughtfully.

She sought the right words, conscious not to sound as though she was speaking out of turn or, worse still, seen to be interfering in something that was none of her business. She was confident that Albert would respect her seniority if only because of her age. He would never doubt her good intentions, given the difficulty of the problems he faced. Still, he was sure to question her ideas, particularly as they were coming from a member of the inferior sex. She stared at the long rows of gunny sack full of export crops, as she began to speak.

"It's going to be a difficult time. You are going to need all the help you can get. Hard work from anyone and everyone."

She paused to take another sip of the coffee, hoping her subtle hint would make him more likely to listen to her thoughts and ideas.

"Do you remember the ways of the olden days?" she asked softly, very aware this had been a taboo period, one which everyone, especially the black population of the Seychelles, herself included, had tried to put behind them, to forget it had ever existed. "Even though it was not an ideal time and there was too much suffering, they achieved the desired results. Things got done and on time. The labourers did not stop until the task was finished." Her eyes remained on the rows of sacks. His disbelief was evident even in his whispered voice. "What are you suggesting? Surely you know the family's feelings on this subject, not to mention the Government's, and the whole country for that matter."

The olden days had been one of the darkest periods of the Seychelles' brief history, a time when the value of a black man was calculated solely by how much work he could do in a twenty-four-hour day, with little or no rest and on a bare minimum of subsistence. Slavery had been the backbone of the emerging Seychelles economy, the original driving force which had created the prosperous plantations of export crops all over the islands. It had been a time of enormous profit for the white masters. But it was a cruel time. A wicked time.

Albert stared at the old black woman as she sat next to him on the wooden stool, looking exactly as she had when he had first laid eyes on her so many, many years earlier, even then an enigmatic and highly-respectable black lady.

He had been only five or six when his father had brought him to visit his workplace for the first time. Then in charge of the kitchen, Marie was a woman about whom both his mother and his father often spoke fondly. Marie had given him a hug and told him he would make a very good overseer one day, just like his father. He'd felt very proud that day. He had grown up with her presence. She was a confidante and an ally his father always respected, and like his father he had come to value and appreciate her wisdom and insight.

But this? He could hardly believe what he was hearing. How could she?

Before slavery was abolished, nothing had been impossible. Every white colonist pursued enormous profit and riches, acquiring more and more land, and bigger and bigger plantations. The ethos of the times supported them, status and wealth were the twin gods they worshipped. To serve those gods, they needed to demonstrate just how much work and obedience they could demand from their slaves. For some sadistic slave owners, the public degradation of a human spirit and the affliction of severe and humiliating punishments was a source of power and pleasure. Too often, slaves had not known what to expect from one day to the next.

The evil of slavery had begun when the uninhabited islands of the Seychelles were first discovered by the French in 1756, and later colonised in 1778. Under the command of Lieutenant Charles Routier de Romainville, the first French settlers who had disembarked on the island of Mahé on the 15th December 1778, were primarily tradesmen – carpenters, blacksmiths and masons, and a few protégées of the crown – sent to set up what was to be called L'Etablissement du Roi, in honour of the King of France – Seychelles' first town.

Lurking amidst the cargo had been over a dozen black African slaves, soon to be joined by hundreds of others as the small town had taken shape. As the settlers ventured inland, seeking out the potential of the virgin land, they needed extra free labour which, fortunately for them, was abundantly available on the coastline of Africa, ready to be rounded up, chained and transported to the newly-founded colony. It was extremely useful and profitable for the settlers to have the muscle and sweat of this black army at their disposal, but it was a living nightmare for those trapped into slavery.

The dawn of change for the slaves in the Seychelles came on the 1st of February 1835, eighteen months after The Emancipation Act was passed, and they were by then living in a British Colony. By this date the slaves had endured fifty-seven years of captivity.

Knowing this history intimately, Albert shivered inwardly as he contemplated Marie's words. They sat in silence, staring at the rows of sacks. Both relived the pain of those years in their very own way. Marie had been born a slave in 1824 to parents who had been slaves, offspring of two members of the original cargo arriving with the first settlers in 1778. Her parents had not lived to see the sun rise on the liberation of the slaves.

Marie was eleven-years-old when slavery was abolished. By then, she had been an orphan for five years. At the tender age of just six, she was taken in as slave girl to the kitchen of the du Barré family, where she had lived to the present day.

Ninety years, of which she had been a free woman for the past seventy-nine. She had not forgotten for a moment how hard life had been, despite being owned by one of the kindest slave owners on the island. She could still hear the stories that had been told to her over the years, of what happened to others who worked on estates with less gracious owners.

Albert too, remembered the stories. And he was certain that, no matter how difficult the circumstances he was now facing, he had too much respect for his fellow human beings to contemplate such a practice. *I am glad that I am living in a time where there are laws against this inhuman form of barbarism. How dare she?* It enraged him that Marie could even voice the suggestion, let alone think that he would contemplate such an action.

Without a word, he put down his coffee, got up from his chair and left the warehouse, without so much as a backward glance at Marie.

As Albert headed to the pirogue sheds on the beach, his mind wrestling with the transportation problem, elsewhere on the island a pair of malicious eyes was staring at the sea, as Gertrude considered the turn of events and what they could mean to her and her two sons. In her mind, her devilish scheme had actually worked, even if it had come to late to save her beloved Gustave. *This is just what I had hoped*, Gertrude thought. *If only I had found the courage and the will to go there much sooner, then this accident would have happened earlier. There would have been no need for the arson and murder, Gustave would still be with me now, and my son would have a*

clear conscience, and no regrets to live with. Our reputation would still be intact. She shook her head and sighed. *No use crying over spilt milk. What is done cannot be undone.*

Now they had to look to the future. She knew that she would have to do it for her sons, if not for herself. She had played her part, she has been the devoted wife who had always put her husband and family's livelihood first. She had delayed too long but now the time was right to turn things to their advantage by filling the gap that had suddenly materialised in the market due to the disappearance of La Sirène. And this time no one would be able to blame them for it.

She was determined that nobody was going to stand in her way. After all, hadn't they paid their dues with the arrest and death of Gustave? A life for a life? No one would dare question her now. No one would dare stand in her way. In her twisted thinking, she was convinced that her method had delivered the results, and she would deal with anyone who crossed her in the same manner as she has dealt with the du Barrés.

As she stared at the bay and her two schooners, lying idle at their moorings, she thought of the pain and humiliation that she and her two sons had suffered. Since that day when Gustave was charged with the arson and the murder of the watchman, the shame and devastation had been brutal. Their friends and business associates had abandoned them.

At Gustave's funeral, the priest had refused a final blessing. The dead man was a confessed murderer and a suicide, both acts against the teachings of their religion, and therefore not allowed in the sanctity of the church. Only she and her two sons, along with some staff, had carried his coffin and laid him to rest. No comfort. No ritual. No gathering of friends and neighbours. No ceremony in church with prayers and songs of farewell. No procession of mourners dressed in black and carrying bunches of flowers. No one offering her their condolences and saying what a loving man he had been.

He had been buried like a common criminal with only a handful of people around him, and a few flowers which she had picked from their front garden to adorn his grave, next to the lonely-looking wooden cross. The prying eyes had remained behind closed windows as they had carried Gustave quietly along the road to his final resting place. Oh, she felt their burning curiosity but they had not shown themselves!

This strong and lovely man, whose only sin, in Gertrude's mind, had been to defend his family's livelihood, and to whom she would be eternally grateful for giving up his own life so that their elder son could walk free, had been buried with no more ceremony than an animal.

And all her family's pain and suffering had been the fault of one person, Christophe du Barré. It was *his* greed that caused all their suffering, and today, as she gazed upon her schooners anchored in the lovely bay, she was grateful that at least she still had her two sons, safe and sound even if the past few months had taken their toll.

Because of his greed, Christophe and his family would now have to experience the pain of losing a loved one. Even if Gustave had been laid to rest like an animal, at least she could visit him occasionally and bring him fresh flowers. All the du Barré's money and status could do nothing for them now — they would remain forever in mourning, unable to lay their precious son to rest.

Gertrude smiled with the sweet sense of revenge, for she knew that the witch doctor had claimed Louis du Barré as one of his *undead*. Even if she had to live with the pain and sorrow of everything that had happened to them, at least it was in the sweet knowledge that Christophe's son was now beyond anyone's help, not even God himself would be able to save him. *He is a dandosya,*" she chuckled happily, *an undead.*

He was now like one of those with the ghostly eyes which she had seen peering at her from under the bed when she had gone to the witch doctor to have the spell cast. *Their precious son is now a slave*, she sighed, smiling. His soul had been condemned to a torturous sub-human nightmare. He was now but an object, a belonging of the mighty powers of black witchcraft, existing in the limbo world between life and death, partly alive and partly dead, having to endure an eternity of severe pain and hunger, without any hope of rescue or even death.

As she savoured the sense of revenge and victory upon her adversary, Gertrude refused to acknowledge the small lingering doubt about the consequences of her actions. One day she would pay for her sin of course, she knew that, but at least she would be able to tell her Maker why she had been forced to take such drastic action. Had it not been for Christophe's greed her action would not have been necessary. And it *was* greed, because he had wanted to crush them totally, remove them completely from the picture, and this had been the only option left to her, to defend her family and their livelihood.

But the tables had been turned and all she needed now was the strength and determination to pick up the pieces of their lives and start again. She would get her sons back on their feet, get them to move beyond the past and look firmly at the future. Maybe she would pay another visit to the witch doctor, get another spell cast for the success of her new enterprise, get him to open all the doors which had been closed to them. Yes, then people would forget what Gustave had done and see them only as a family trying their best in a very difficult circumstances…

For her hated adversaries, the du Barrés, the reverse was now starting. She intended to be there to pick up the business as they lost it. She looked forward to watching them suffer as they came back from the search empty-handed, their lives torn apart. *You will pay for what you did to my family,* she uttered in triumph.

Even as Gertrude gloated at the misfortune of one poor soul, back at Beau Vallon Genevieve was on her knees, overwhelmed by extreme pain, staring at the crucifix on her wall, agonized tears flowing freely down her pale face. She was certain that this tragedy was all her fault, that God was punishing her.

Please forgive me, Lord, for I was weak. Please, let me pay for my sins. Do not make my son pay. Please hear me, Lord, please do not hurt my family for my sin. Please let me be the one to pay for my sin. Do not turn your gaze away from us.

She had too often taken her good fortune for granted, that her family would always be safe; they had the money, prestige and good name and nothing and no one would harm them. She had been foolish enough to believe that her sacrifice and sin had paid off, for she had been spared from a premature death like her mother. She had believed that God had forgiven her. Not any more. Now she was certain that all she had once held to be true was false. *Is this the price I will have to pay for trying to stay alive? Why, God, why?*

Marie paused before knocking on her mistress' door. Should she be bothering her at such a time? Part of her was convinced that this was exactly what Genevieve might need to keep her going. She had had no success with Albert. He had put his pride before all else.

Now, as she hesitated at the door, she told herself that if someone like her, who had lost everything and everybody to slavery was able to see this solution, then she was going to get her mistress to see it too, and to convince Albert as well. After all, she was only implying that he look at how it was done, and use it as a solution to their immediate problems, without breaking the laws of the land, of course. *I know how lazy they can be*, she sighed. *They will use the absence of Msye Christophe to do as little as possible.* She knew she was right.

They were her own, true. But they were mentally yoked to slavery. They lived from one day to the next, spending all that they earned in a week in a single day, and mostly on alcohol and gambling, as if there were no tomorrow. Life was lived in idleness and promiscuity. Games of *matouloumba* and bottles of baka. They took out their frustration on their children and wives, who were forced to exist on next to nothing, and left with little choice but to beg for scraps, or to pilfer whenever the chance presented itself.

The times when a black man would rise above others were few and far between. The wise ones had gone on to become what Albert called his 'foremen' who had responsibilities for specific tasks. They generally did a good job but Marie was certain that without Msye Christophe, and with Albert having so much demanding his attention, the lazy labourers would run rings around those foremen. *They were going to undo all the hard work that has gone into making this place successful,* she sighed. *Unless I succeed, of course.*

But Genevieve was wholly unreceptive to Marie's approach. Indeed, she wondered why Marie was worrying her with such trifling problems at a time like this.

"Oh Marie, it is not my place to tell Albert how to run the estate. All will be back to normal soon. Christophe and my sons will be coming home very soon. Please do not worry. Just let Albert do as he sees fit."

Sadly, Marie had no choice but to retreat. She came down the staircase into the deep silence and joyless atmosphere of the house, tears filling her eyes as she thought of her beloved Julien and young Msye Louis. *Oh Julien, you would have been able to make them see sense, mon chéri. You would have known what needed to be done. You would have known where to look for my Kinox.*

Huge oil portraits of the ancestors of the du Barré, Baralle and Duval families looked down at her as she descended the steps. She had been gazed upon by these eyes since she was a six-year-old girl, and she remembered the people when they were still alive. It was during the time of the grandfather of Msye Christophe, Grand Msye Ferdinand and his wife Madanm Claudette. She had been a great lady indeed, for it was she who had ordered that Marie should come and live in the main house after she had lost both of her parents.

Grand Msye Francois was just a young boy then. Her sadness was replaced by gratitude for the kindness and sympathy of those surrounding her, and by the beauty and splendour of this house. Indeed, nothing in her parents' thatched hut prepared her for a house like this.

And the atmosphere! There was always laughter and joy, perpetual happiness. Always enough food to eat, always music from the grand piano. Oh how she could still hear the soothing sounds of Madanm Claudette's playing and singing through the walls and doorways between the main sitting-room upstairs, and her makeshift bed under the long table in the kitchen. When she had first nervously set foot in that massive room, Cook had ordered that she would sleep under the table. It seemed everyone was scared of the big, white lady in charge of the kitchen. When she glared down at the young black girl and told her how lucky she was to be there, Marie felt as if she was listening to words from on high, all-powerful and all-mighty. She had trembled with apprehension.

"Girl, you do what Cook says, or you feel the punishment of the cane."

Marie heard the advice and took it to heart. When Cook told her she would be sleeping under the table, she did precisely that. To her pleasant surprise, her new-found home under the kitchen table turned out to be a warm and comfortable spot to sleep.

As she grew older, Marie came to realise that Cook was a very gentle person, as long as her wishes were obeyed. She was also happy to teach anyone who showed any interest in cooking, which Marie did. So they got on well, and forged a warm relationship. Marie soon realised how much she loved the art of cooking, seeing all the different ingredients being turned into tasty dishes. Most of all, she loved the compliments her cooking received, especially from Cook.

It all came back to her as she descended the stairs and ran her fingers over the smooth lacquer of the beautifully-carved banister. In her mind's eye, she could see once again the ladies who had graced the stairs over the years, starting with the exquisite Manmzel Marie-Antoinette Baralle who had arrived from France in 1855. Such a perfect beauty! She had delicate porcelain skin and blue eyes framed by long blond curls that dangled on her shoulders. When she married, she wore the most beautiful wedding dress the Seychelles had ever seen. Marie had been privileged to have been second-in-command of the kitchen for that wedding banquet.

Then, two years later, there had been the baptism of the twins, Msye Christophe and Manmzel Monique. *Such happy memories, and I have seen them all.*

By the time of Msye Christophe's wedding to Manmzel Genevieve from Silhouette Island, Marie had become Cook for the family, and had moved into the nice little room next to the kitchen where old Cook had lived. She smiled as she remembered the birth of Henri and Louis. Oh, how proud Msye Christophe and Madanm Genevieve were of their two sons! How happy!

Msye Louis had occupied a special place in her heart from the moment she laid eyes on him on the equinox day of his birth. Everyone had been fearful that Madanm Genevieve might not recover from the trauma of childbirth and Marie had prayed fervently that the baby would not have to grow up without his mother. Her prayers had been answered two days later.

There has always been happiness in this house, Marie sighed, trying to shake away the sadness and suffering that seemed to envelope the place at that moment. *I am no longer that trembling slave girl. I am too old now, too old for all this, mon chéri. I do not know how to deal with this pain, and I just wish that I could be by your side now. I need you, Julien.*

At the moment Marie was making her way down the staircase, two pairs of eyes were glued to the horizon of the Indian Ocean, seeking the smallest movement, praying to God not to forsake them. At that moment, they bore the hardest cross either of them had ever had to bear; no pain they had ever experienced came close to the intensity of what they were feeling now.

As they had left Beau Vallon that morning, and the Alexandra had headed out towards Île du Nord, both Henri and Christophe searched desperately for signs of a boat coming towards them, perhaps a pirogue which Louis had despatched from Île du Nord to inform them why La Sirène had been unable to make the return trip back to Mahé. But the wide and beautiful bay of Île du Nord remained empty as they made their approach around the tip of the island. No ships anchored in its tranquil waters. No pirogues dispatched with news. They felt only fear and dread.

The Administrator confirmed that La Sirène had left the island two days earlier. "At exactly 12 noon on the 25th of September," he said officiously, shocked to learn the schooner had not reached Mahé. Christophe and Henri accepted the extra supply of water and food which the Administrators and labourers of Île du Nord offered as a gesture of sympathy and support.

La Sirène and her crew had now been missing for forty-eight hours. The Captain of the Alexandra gave instructions to the other search boats to fan out and widen the search in all directions from Île du Nord. The memory of the severity of the storm that had hit Mahé two days previously, just as La Sirène was leaving Île du Nord, had been at the forefront of all their minds.

Occasionally, Christophe and Henri could not help but have their most terrible fears overcome their determination to maintain a positive attitude. The thought that the search could prove futile was so frightening…No!

Christophe could not allow it. Failure was simply unthinkable, too devastating to contemplate, for him and his family. No, he would search every inch of ocean and land mass until he found his son. He would search the world, no matter if it cost him his last penny. He would find Louis somehow, some way.

He would not fail.

For his part, Henri could not help thinking that if only he'd been with Louis none of this would have happened. He should have been there for his younger brother. How could he have been so blind, so engrossed in gaining his revenge? Even after the guilty culprit was dead, still he had sought revenge. He raised his eyes to the heavens and asked his brother for forgiveness.

Among the crew, the atmosphere was no less sombre. Each man went about his duties, avoiding Christophe and Henri, treading lightly around them and remaining respectful of their pain. Despite their wealth and stature, at that moment they were merely two men with an almost unbearable burden, as vulnerable as the poorest crew member. Now, the fate of their son and brother rested in the hands of poor sailors who had come together without hesitation to search for another lost man of the sea.

For some, it was not their first search. They had memories of boats lost at sea, some later rescued on deserted outcrops of land, others managing to make it back to Mahé, or to one of the neighbouring islands. Some drifted aimlessly, devoid of sails or masts, and had to be towed back to Mahé when found, with only one or two members surviving the ordeal. These survivors were frightening to gaze upon, mere skeletons of the men they had been. Dehydrated, emaciated and confused after weeks of drifting around the Indian Ocean in the grip of strong currents, their skin blistered from exposure to the scorching sun. They managed to survive eating raw fish and any seabirds they were able to catch.

They were the lucky ones. Many more never made it back. Many families grieved to the end of their days, never being able to lay their loved ones to rest. But that was history. On this day, the old and hardened sea salts aboard the government launch were all praying that they would find La Sirène and her crew.

Sitting in the soft sand of Beau Vallon beach as the sun hovered on the horizon, Anna shielded her eyes and looked out upon the water. She was determined to remain strong and hopeful and could not allow any other thought into her mind. *They have to find them. They will.*

Thirty days had elapsed since the search was launched. Thirty days of utter misery, sadness, and grief. Even during the darkest moments of the epidemic, she had not known such fear. With each passing day, she lost track of her daily routine. All that mattered to her was her thinking about the terrible ocean where her Louis was. Somewhere out there.

Her moment-to-moment life was a blur, conducted mechanically. She ate because she had to, not because she wanted to. She slept because her eyes closed, not because she sought it. So it was with her every action.

She lived for news, anything. Not knowing was the worst thing of all. What might have happened? Might they have found shelter? In her desperation she listened to anything and everything, any whisper, any bit of gossip. So long as the search continued, it was the talk of the island, but with each passing day the weight of resignation hung heavier; the sadness weighed heavily on everyone. When the smaller boats started to return to Mahé with no news, no Louis, only the empty eyes of those who were giving up hope, Anna wanted to shout at them. *No! They were wrong! Terribly wrong! Her Louis would be found!*

Whatever accurate news there was to be had could be gleaned from the whispered conversations between her parents, who had access to the latest real news. Her mother spent the days with Madame du Barré who received information from the Port Authorities. Her father met each boat as it came to port and learned directly from the crew what they knew.

For her part, all Anna could do was exactly what she was doing that day – praying.

She patted her tummy gently, tracing the contours of the small bump with her palm. This physical evidence of the baby gave her such hope. What's more the terrible morning sickness she'd suffered stopped completely the morning the search began. *We believe in him*, she whispered to her baby. *We know he'll be back soon. I know you are brave, like your father. Like your father would want you to be.*

These past thirty days had been almost unbearable for Anna. The hours she was home were the most difficult. At least when she was at the hospital, she was occupied.

The greatest comfort beyond the baby growing in her belly was the friendship which had been developing with Sister Kent. Since the first day of the search, when she had cried in Patricia's arms, she had felt safe with her.

Their friendship was precious to her, and Patricia had been a tower of strength and comfort at such a difficult time. It seemed that she was always there, watching over her, stopping her from making silly mistakes as she went about her duties on the ward. Then, in their afternoon sessions together, Patricia would speak to her almost as an older sister, reassuring her that she was not alone and helping her to remain strong for her baby and for Louis. Patricia reminded her of the special love she shared with Louis. "You must keep this foremost in your mind. That love is eternal. It can never be taken away."

She found some small comfort at their driftwood for a couple of hours after work every day. The ocean was like a medium connecting her with Louis, although she felt profoundly vulnerable and alone there as well.

What would happen to her and the baby if the worst were to happen and Louis was not found within the next few weeks? Her advancing pregnancy would soon become obvious to everyone. In those dark moments, when she felt most vulnerable, she could sense a reproachful glare coming straight at her from over the trees of Bel Ombre's hill. Saint Roch was condemning her.

In her betrayal of God and the Catholic Church, she had committed an unpardonable sin. With that knowledge, she feared the retribution she and her baby would have to confront if Louis failed to return. Once the truth was known, she would end up completely alone and on the streets. She would be cast out of her parent's house. She would lose her home and family. Most of all, she would lose her self-respect. The utter helplessness of her position tore at her heart. But there was nothing she could do. Not now. She had no one to turn to.

She knew she was being unfair, thinking only of herself as Louis was fighting for his life out there on the ocean. He must be worried out of his mind too, wherever he might be, wishing that he was home now so that he could resolve their problems before it became too late. *Oh, Louis, mon amour, please do not let it be. Please come home to us.*

At that moment, Anna saw the small sail of Jacques Morel's boat set out from the end of the bay, going fishing for the night. She knew Josephine would be alone in her hut. Since she had started work at the hospital, she had not had too many chances to visit her old friend. The months of the epidemic had been one long period, but every now and again she had dropped in for coffee. Josephine loved hearing her news, how she was progressing at work, and of course how things were going with Louis.

She was so happy that Anna had found love! She wasted no more time. She left the driftwood and made her way to the one place where she knew she would be welcome.

As she opened her arms to the tear-stricken girl coming towards her hut, Josephine spoke in a kind and gentle voice *"Mon pov piti.* Do not cry. He will be home soon."

She tried to sound completely sincere, even though doubt had crept into her own heart. She had heard about La Sirène being lost at sea, and she knew the pain Anna was enduring.

It was no matter, Anna did not discern any doubt; she had come for confession not reassurance. Word by word, between bouts of tears, Anna told Josephine of her predicament and of the plans that Louis had made before he left. "Pregnant!" Josephine trembled as she realised the full extent of Anna's plight.

And then, Anna uttered the dreaded words she had not allowed herself to utter for the past thirty days. Her eyes were a pool of sadness and agony and her body trembled as she spoke.

"La Sirène might be lost. I…we…might never see him again". She hugged her baby bump and herself tightly. The awful import of her words cut through Josephine like a sharp blade. She handed Anna a cup of hot, black coffee.

"You must be strong. You have to have faith that he will return, my child. Do not dwell too much on the bad, just try thinking of how happy you will be once he gets home."

Much later, after the sun had dropped from the skies of Beau Vallon and the stars made their nightly appearance over the bay, the black figure could still be seen squatting on the ground next to her little hut as she mumbled softly to herself.

For once in her life, Josephine was determined to find the right answer for this dramatic dilemma. Anna was like the daughter she had always wished for, kind and loving and with a deep sense of true affection for all, whatever creed or colour. It tore at her heart that fate had delivered such a cruel blow to Anna. *I have to help my little girl. I will not see her become homeless.* Her thoughts went back to when things had spun out of control and had become too much for Jacques and herself.

With no option other than to flee from their beloved island of La Digue, they left families and friends and ended up here at Beau Vallon. They could not have stayed, not with the scandal. She knew it to be true then. She knew it to be true now. They had to get away. And with that insight, she had a wonderful idea.

Jacques thought she had lost her mind when she told him. But the look on her face was enough to tell him there was nothing he could say that would change her mind. He had arrived at the hut weary from a long night out in the elements. He had barely sipped the coffee from the mug Josephine handed to him before she regaled him with Anna's story and what they were going to do to help her.

"You have not seen your sister for over fifty years!" he replied, hearing her plan. "Do you really expect her to welcome you with open arms, after everything?"

He was suddenly annoyed. It was too much. Over the years he had tried to forget what happened on La Digue. Abandoning his wife and children had been the most difficult decision he had ever made, but he had done it for the love he had felt for the woman now staring at him. Even today, even after all that had happened, he knew he would do the same again, for he loved her just as much now as he did back then. But now she was asking him to return to La Digue and run the risk of coming face to face with his very own children, whom he had so cruelly abandoned and had missed so terribly for all these long years.

How could he cope with that? Or worse, what if they were no longer living there? It had been difficult over the years to get news of what was happening, his wife had seen to that. But he was not bitter. He knew he deserved her enmity. Josephine, who loved him dearly, knew his pain. Yet she was asking him to return. All because she wanted to help the young girl.

"Please Jacques," she pleaded softly, "I know it will be difficult for you – for both of us – but we are all she has. We must try. Please at least think about it."

Her words were urgent. She knew that Anna's fate lay in her convincing Jacques to agree to her plans.

The next day, as the sun touched the horizon, Anna was once again on the beach. After her work at the hospital, she so needed that break, the peace of her bay, before heading home for the evening. At the far end of the bay, she could see Jacques' boat getting ready to go out for the night, and to her utter surprise, she saw her Josephine climbing on board as well.

Josephine suffered terribly from seasickness and had not been on a boat since her trip from La Digue to Beau Vallon those many years earlier.

Very odd. Seeing the small boat tacking in the breeze made her feel sad and very lonely. As she had made her way from the hospital to Beau Vallon that afternoon, she had looked to visiting her old friend again. Their talk the previous evening had left her feeling hopeful. Josephine had promised to consider things carefully. She had asked Anna to pray that God would guide her thoughts and help her find an answer to her dilemma. With the sail growing smaller and smaller, Anna reflected sadly that tonight she would be alone with her thoughts.

CHAPTER 15

A New Life

It was the 29th of October 1914. As dawn's first light coloured the skies above La Digue Island, a small fishing boat made its approach to the far end of Grand Anse Bay, avoiding the populated west coast side. With their safe arrival, Jacques Morel's gamble had paid off. He had predicted that the early onset of the north-west monsoon a few days earlier, meant that the bay, renowned for its wicked currents and tall waves at other times of the year, would now be easy to navigate.

As the boat sailed in on the mirror-smooth waters, both Jacques and Josephine stared in wonder. Grand Anse Bay seemed completely unchanged after all these years. But, more important, it was the perfect place for a discreet landing. Years of fishing with his father and then fishing on his own made circumnavigating the island simple. Even fifty years after leaving, he felt completely at home in these waters.

"We have to get a move on," he said urgently to Josephine, who had gratefully rested her head against a small boulder on the beach. His own body too cried out for rest, but he knew rest was not theirs to claim, at least not yet. They had to get to the flat terrain on the far side of the imposing mountain range.

The sheer cliffs and deep ravines had been called *Citadelle* for obvious reasons; they stood as protective guard to the island. Indeed, it was four hours of continuous walking that brought them to the midway point.

The path was partially overgrown, and in some places, completely gone. Machetes were needed to hack their way through some areas.

Their path was a long and arduous detour, but one they felt compelled to take. They had to arrive without being seen or recognized. As they walked silently, they each felt the strange sense of retracing their steps from so many years before. With each step they were powerfully conscious of the pain, heartache and hurt they had caused. To venture once again on their home island was both invigorating and a sacrilege.

Fifty years earlier, their legs had carried them lightly as they raced toward a life of love. Now, their legs were less muscular, their hearts less joyful, their mood more pensive. A deep intake of breath signalled their arrival at the top of the small hill overlooking the old, wooden cottage, the home of Josephine's departed mother. This was where she had spent the first eighteen years of her life, together with her twin sister, Norine.

Despite the warmth of the sun overhead Josephine shivered. She sighed, her voice filling with emotion as she gripped Jacques hand tightly.

"It is just as I remember it. Will she forgive me? Will she?"

"It was a long, long time ago," Jacques said softly. "We were young then. Come, we can rest for a while."

He led her to the shaded spot of the old albizia tree, where they sat with his arm over her shoulder. It was the very same tree that witnessed their declaration of love over fifty years before, her virgin blood absorbed within its soil.

From their vantage point, they could see the cluster of thatched huts forming the settlement of L'Union on the west coast. It was always a great hive of activity with plantations of vanilla, coconut, sugar-cane, and maize, plus mills and ox-carts laden with sacks of copra. The very heart of this small island's economy.

"It is as if time has stood still," Josephine sighed. Looking down at their hands, tightly entwined, she could see clearly how many years had passed. Although their love still burned true, their hands were the hands of old people, not young lovers.

Tears ran down Josephine's cheeks. "My beautiful island. La Digue, I have missed you terribly."

They remained quiet for several minutes, each deep in their own thoughts. Then Josephine sighed deeply. "It is time," she announced. "I must face her..."

Her soul quivered and her knees shook. But she was determined to remain strong, to remember why she had retraced her steps to return to the home of her youth. They approached the small courtyard.

"Bonzour, Msye Madanm," Jacques called out firmly, standing alongside Josephine as they faced the tiny outdoor kitchen, seeking the person cooking a delicious-smelling curry.

"Bonzour."

They turned quickly, seeking the gentle voice coming from behind them. They found themselves staring at a fragile old lady who stood barefoot in front of her cottage. She was dressed identically to Josephine, with the traditional loose blouse over a long calico skirt which reached her ankles, and the customary head scarf covering her tight African curls.

Time stood still as the two women stared at one another, as though looking into a mirror and surprised by the image that stared back. Neither sister moved. Josephine and Norine knew each other immediately, intuitively, instinctively. Their eyes and expressions reflected the same emotions – decades of pain, sorrow, sadness, regret, resentment and joy. Neither knew how to act or to react. A fluffy white cat was mewing as it went around the leg of its owner, aware of the tension, wondering why there was suddenly two of the same person. If the two women were uncertain what to do, Jacques was more so. Finally, he found his voice. "I am more to blame than Zephine."

Neither woman paid him any mind.

The cat looked suspiciously at him, sure that he must be the cause of whatever was the problem. Norine was the first of the sisters to speak, her voice soft, still the voice of a young girl.

"I had hoped you would come back to see Manman, and ask for her forgiveness before she left this earth."

Josephine nearly buckled. The regret of not receiving her mother's forgiveness returned with the force it had the day Jacques had broken the news to her.

"I did not know of her illness or death for more than a year after it happened," she whispered, her voice quivering with emotion. "I know that I brought her lots of sorrow and I am eternally sorry for that, but I had no other choice." She continued holding Norine's gaze. "My deepest regret is being unable to tell her why I had to do it and to beg her forgiveness for everything that she had suffered, and that you had suffered too."

Tears streamed down her cheeks. She took a halting step toward her sister, then another. Her voice broke. Her body was wracked with deep sobs.

"Will you ever be able to forgive me?"

She dreaded the thought that Norine would turn away from her. After a moment, Norine reached out and wrapped her arms around her sister.

"Please don't cry. I forgave you years ago, my little Zephine."

As the sisters hugged and sobbed, the white cat circling their legs feared the possible threat on the horizon. Mimi was adamant that she was *not* going without lunch. Drastic measures were required. With a screeching miaow and a loud hiss, she launched herself at Jaccques, scratched his leg with an angry paw, then bolted into the house.

"Oh no, my curry is burning," said Norine, dashing to the kitchen.

After they had enjoyed a dinner of octopus curry accompanied by La Digue's saffron rice, all three sat on the small veranda, sipping small cups of strong black coffee and reliving everything that the day had brought them. As Josephine looked at Norine, sitting contentedly in her canvas armchair and stroking the cat lying next to her, she thanked God for giving her this chance to make amends with her sister. Earlier in the day, Norine had taken her to visit her mother's grave. As they stood and looked at the fresh flowers they had placed around the wooden cross, Norine squeezed her hand. "Manman told me before she died that if I ever saw you again, I was to let you know that she understood why you had to leave, and that she never stopped loving you."

Norine looked at her sister and smiled. "It has made me so happy to see you again. I still cannot believe that you are here having coffee with me, and I hope that soon Anna will be coming here to live with me for a while."

For this was Josephine's plan, to bring Anna to her sister for sanctuary and safety.

Two days later, after a journey that saw Josephine suffering constant seasickness, the small fishing boat came slowly around the tip of Bel Ombre. Despite her illness, Josephine smiled with contentment. She was almost home.

It was the first day of November 1914, five weeks to the day from when La Sirène left Beau Vallon. On the same day that Jacques was anchoring his boat, out in the vastness of the Indian Ocean, far from the island of Mahé, two extremely tired men scanned the beach of the island they were approaching, praying that this was the place where they had been sheltering. For five long and terrible weeks they had traversed the vast waters around Mahé and many of the islands of the Seychelles. They circumnavigated those which were obviously uninhabited and then moved on, disappointed when nothing was found.

Leaving Île du Nord on the first day of the search they had gone straight to Silhouette, three miles south, on the route back to Mahé, the most probable place which Louis would seek if his schooner was in any trouble. It was the only island before reaching Mahé, and owned by the du Barré family.

After a tearful goodbye to the shocked Administrator of Silhouette, the Alexandra had made haste to the two most northerly islands of the Seychelles - Île aux Vaches and Île Denis. The smaller boats in the search party had gone north-east, around the inner islands close to Mahé.

Please God, let them be here, Christophe prayed as they approached the low-lying coral island of Marie Louise, the last one in the Amirantes, the outer islands of the Seychelles. Lying some ten miles from its nearest neighbour, Île Desnoeufs, the oval-shaped Marie Louise was a beautiful island, with a verdant hue fringed by powdery white beaches.

She was very different from Île Desnoeufs which was almost barren and used solely for commercial exploitation of guano, seabirds and eggs, because of its very large seabird population. They had only circumnavigated Île Desnoeufs as it did not have a resident population outside the nesting season of June to August, but they had found no sign of life, nor any floating debris.

The small welcoming committee that had gathered on the beach of Marie Louise were mostly labourers and fishermen. They had used their own pirogues and expertise to get them ashore from the Alexandra, as landing was always very hazardous on Marie Louise. When they heard about the plight of La Sirène and her crew, they were just as surprised and upset as everyone else Christophe and Henri had met over the past five weeks, and had only been too happy to offer any support and provisions they could spare for the search party.

It was heart-rending in some ways because when they had left Île aux Vaches on the third day of the search and decided to venture further south, it was because there were more Seychelles' islands in that direction. They had decided that with more traffic in these waters, they would stand a better chance of finding some clues. They had all been full of renewed enthusiasm and confident that it was the right way to take the search, and had headed for The African Banks, the first island in the Amirantes group lying on the south-west of Mahé.

The Amirantes was the largest group of the outer islands totalling some ten atolls and sand cays, some with year-round residents and well over 170 miles from Mahé. This had greatly increased the scope of the search and after having visited every island in the group and having found no clue, by the time they got to Marie Louise they felt beaten and disheartened.

Henri dared not look his father in the eye since setting off from Marie Louise, tracing a south-easterly route which was taking them to the island of Coetivy, lying some 250 miles from Mahé. The debate with the captain of the Alexandra the night before had been quite heated, as Christophe had been unable to agree on the next course in the search. Prior to heading for the Amirantes, it had been the general consensus that they would return to Mahé from there and at the time Christophe had agreed, positive that they would have found La Sirène by then. But now, Christophe was adamant they needed to go a bit further to the south-east. "It has only been five weeks," he had yelled in desperation. "We have to search some more!" He could not bear to give up. Not yet, not ever.

Sensing someone approaching, Henri turned from the railing to find Maxime Savy next to him. At fourteen, he was the youngest member of the search party, but a born sailor nonetheless. Henri had marvelled at Maxime's enthusiasm and dedication over these past difficult weeks. He had been a tower of strength for his elder brother Antoine who had found out that he did not have any sea legs, and for whom the journey had been agony. But observing him had also caused Henri deep pain. Maxime reminded him of Louis when he had accompanied Captain Francourt and himself on the Alouette.

"How are you today Msye Henri?" Maxime asked, his bright eyes studying Henri. "It looks like we are going to have good weather now," he added, keen to engage Henri in conversation. Looking into the innocent young face surrounded by a mop of curly black hair, Henri could not resist the brotherly urge to pat the younger man on the head.

"I am fine, Maxime," he replied, his lie not fooling Maxime nor himself. He forced a smile. "I think you are right, we have seen the last of the bad weather."

Just then, he looked up to see his father watching them and Henri's heart sank. In his eyes he could see the last rays of hope, as if they were telling him that this is it - we have to find Louis now or we have to go home…having failed. Henri understood his father's pain but he was powerless to comfort him. In his certainty of the success of the mission he had built such a fortress around himself that even now no one could manage to breach its walls.

A week later, on the 8th of November, Patricia performed another prenatal examination on Anna. "All is going well," Patricia said reassuringly. "It should be an early April birth," she added, as she helped Anna get up to rearrange her clothes. Anna calculated that she was now four months pregnant. Soon, she would be showing and at that point there would be no hiding her sin or her shame.

"Have you given some thought to the near future?" Patricia asked. "If the search continues for a long time…" She sighed. "You will be unable hide the pregnancy for much longer."

Anna remained silent. Then she shared the plan that she had discussed with Josephine only two days earlier. "I have decided that it will be best if I leave Mahé." She drew a weak breath. "There is a lady living on her own on La Digue island, the sister of a friend of mine, and she has kindly offered to take me in for a while."

This news stunned Patricia but she managed to remain calm as she listened.

"I had thought telling my parents the truth, and maybe even telling the du Barré family too. But on deeper reflection, I think it would be best for me and for my baby if I go away for a while. Girls in my position are not welcomed in their parent's home, and their babies are taken from them to be raised as bastards by others." She lowered her head. "I could not bear it if my baby was taken away."

"But…" Patricia began.

Anna interrupted her. "La Digue will be a temporary solution. When Louis is rescued he will come for us, and we will return to Mahé together."

Patricia studied her young friend's face. "Are you sure this is for the best?"

Rather than answer directly, Anna said, "I do need to ask you for a very big favour though. Will you write and let me know any news about the search, no matter how small or trivial? I will be desperate to know what is happening."

Patricia got up and hugged the younger woman. In that gesture, she had given her reply. Then she looked at Anna. "And you must write a letter for Louis to tell him where you are staying. I will make sure he gets it the moment he lands on Mahé." Tears filled their eyes. They were going to miss each other badly.

Anna visited the hospital chapel, her regular refuge since the launch of the search. There, in the cool shadows, she asked God for forgiveness and guidance, just as she had during the long months of the epidemic when she had offered her life to His service in exchange for keeping Louis safe. But as well as forgiveness and guidance, she prayed for God to allow the search party to find Louis alive and well. *Please forgive me for my sin and for taking the coward's way out*, she implored the small crucifix at the altar. *I could not allow my child to be taken away from me. Please forgive me.*

During her discussions with Josephine, she had had her worst fears confirmed. Her child would indeed be taken from her, and worse still, if she was to approach Madame du Barré she might be seen as an opportunist, naming Louis as the father of her bastard child in an attempt to get money from the du Barré family.

As Anna was on her knees in the chapel, Patricia was in Matron's office reviewing their conversation. She felt sad and powerless. How she hated those stupid rules and laws of society now rendering her helpless. *I have to find some way to help her, to help them. Oh David, my darling, please help me.*

She opened the brown envelope that had landed on her desk that morning. Charlotte Craddock's handwriting was as neat as ever, although her news was sombre indeed. The gloom and fear of war seemed to have settled over England, with recruitment posters adorning walls all around and great numbers of men signing up, filled with the fervour of a patriotic glory.

It is all so very sad, Charlotte wrote, *some of the men are so young, so young. They think this is some kind of game. Those who should know better, such as the government, are content to create the illusion there will be an early end to the fighting and that all will be well, perhaps even by Christmas.*

She also wrote of women mistreating their young men simply because they did not want to become soldiers. *Cowards they called them! Handing them a white feather as a sign of weakness.* Imagine - their own children and husbands!

Such a mad rush to war. Groups of young men from farms, factories and universities were joining up together, forming what was known as 'Pals Battalion.' Then of course, there were all the ones without jobs who saw this opportunity as both exciting and lucrative, Charlotte had added. 'Your King and Country Needs You!' She told of Lord Kitchener's recruitment poster message that seemed to have had the desired result.

To be honest I have the premonition that this war is not going to be a short affair at all. It is disturbing to be so at odds with everyone else, to be in the pessimistic minority, but I cannot help how I feel. It is all just so troubling.

As she read the letter Patricia tried to imagine what it must be like in London at that moment, with posters adorning streets and public places, and all the talks in the inns and taverns focusing on the latest news from the frontline.

She could imagine early November in her beloved Woolwich, with the last leaves falling from the trees. The crisp morning frosts would cover the branches in a soft white glaze, while the prevailing winds whistled their chilly arrival from the expanse of the River Thames, a cruel reminder to everyone that autumn was definitely over.

These were always busy times at the Royal Herbert Military Hospital, preparing for those long and bitter winter months ahead. It was a hard task for the Matron and staff alike, but now with the added enormity of the country at war it was surely an even greater nightmare. Of course, the Royal Herbert being the main orthopaedic centre for the British Army, would be receiving the majority of the casualties straight from the battle fields.

And in combination with the huge numbers of civilian volunteers without any formal army training, it would make for very high casualty figures indeed. "What a tragedy," Patricia sighed.

The images from the Khartoum Expedition returned to her, gripping her heart. Such horrifying and brutal wounds inflicted on all those innocent young men. She had cradled them in her arms, when she could do no more to help. All those lost hopes that she had read in their eyes in their last moments. *Poor Charlotte! What a horror for you and your staff.*

She felt an overwhelming urge to return to England, but then she remembered that the Seychelles needed her too. *And my poor little Anna. I will have to be here for her if, God forbid, the search for Louis is unsuccessful.*

It was all so terribly sad. She sat with her hands on the side of her head, staring at Charlotte's letter as the dark and brutal images of war kept coming. It was all so hard and painful. Amidst her sadness, she felt a presence stirring.

A fleeting image of his radiant smile and sparkling blue eyes came to her from the office door. Tears welled in her eyes as she stumbled out of her chair and rushed to the open door, but the veranda was empty. *David, my darling, oh my darling*, she murmured softly as she gripped the door frame for support. She trembled as her tears flowed. *You came to me to give me strength and hope. I will always love you, my darling.* Then she turned and made her way back to her desk, back to her duty and responsibilities. She sat down, comforted, yet sad with emptiness. *One day I know you will come for me, when my time is done, and I will be ready and waiting, my darling.*

*Two months. I cannot bear another moment...*she cried, staring at the haggard, pale figure of this emaciated woman looking back at her from her bedroom mirror. Eight weeks. Eight impossible weeks. All unbearable days, each ending with the hope that maybe the next would be *the* day, when her family would be whole again. Meanwhile, she stared at the strange woman in her mirror, the one who bore almost no resemblance to the image that used to greet her. *Please God, let it be today*, her soul cried.

It was early evening on the 22nd of November 1914, when Genevieve du Barré left her bedroom and slowly made her way to where Therese and Marie were waiting. Even though the change had been gradual, the two women had to stifle a gasp when they saw the figure of their beloved mistress. How the past eight weeks had destroyed her! Her beauty, her vigour, her joy! All gone…

"Tonight will be a special vigil," Genevieve said in a low, barely recognisable voice. She looped her arm with Therese and walked slowly across the sitting-room, heading for the wide double doors leading onto the veranda.

Eight weeks. The search to be called off soon. Too painful to even contemplate. So, so horrible.

The skies were tinted with the rays of the sunset and the golden globe of the sun seemed to hang motionless on the horizon, alongside Silhouette Island. "I do not know how I would have managed without you both," Genevieve said softly. Neither had the strength to say anything. They gripped their mistress tightly and continued along the beach to the church, the soft breeze blowing in from Silhouette, soothing their faces.

Three hours into the vigil, the night felt heavy and warm with the burning heat of the candles. The church was filled with worshippers, all on their knees, all praying for the safe return of La Sirène and her crew. Suddenly, Genevieve felt a massive, lightning-bolt impact, as though she had been struck in her heart and soul with a hot blade. Over miles of empty ocean, it was the echo of a terrifying cry of agony – a father's despair, pain and torment.

It punished her, as it did him. She saw his face flash before her, the hurt and pain made him age decades beyond his years. As much as she felt the agony of their loss herself, she could not bear to know the pain he felt. A man of such incredible power rendered completely helpless. He was beaten. Defeated. Lost.

"Non, non, mon Dieu, non!" she screamed. She tried to get up, to rush towards the priest at the altar. "My fault! All my fault!" she cried as she threw herself on the floor at his feet. "Mercy! Ask Him for mercy, I am begging you. Do not let him take our son! I am begging you. Have mercy on us! Please!"

The anguished cry echoed over the steamer, the torment and devastation of this great man touching everyone. His knuckles were white as he held the metal rail of the Alexander, his grip the only thing stopping him from jumping into those turbulent waves and joining Louis. Henri's strong arm gripped across his father's shoulder, holding him tightly against his own torso. The younger man tried not to think of his own feelings. He only wanted to be strong for his father. He had no words to say; the sure grip of his arm was all he could give...

The lights of Île Plate, their last port of call, were still visible. The search was now officially over, and they were now heading north on the last 100 miles back to Mahé.

As he held his father close, Henri felt himself drowning in guilt and remorse. He had failed. Failed in his duty as the elder son and protector of his younger brother. Because of him, a beautiful young man had lost his life. He had taken his mind from his responsibilities because he had been blinded in his quest for revenge. *Justice is mine,* the Lord had said, *Justice is mine.* Henri had wanted his own justice. He had not been satisfied to leave it in God's hands. As a result, his father and mother were robbed of a precious son, and he had lost his brother, a brother whom he had loved and adored.

"We are still a very long way from Mahé. There is a lot of sea to cover. Maybe they are just drifting, close to home." The voice was distant. It was a moment before he realized that it was his own. "Let's not give up hope, Papa," Henri said. "Not yet."

His father had admitted defeat, but something within him would not allow Henri to do so. He prayed, gripping his father tightly. *Please help me, Lord. Help me to keep him safe. I cannot lose him as well.*

At Beau Vallon, the *fotey brankar* with its fragile occupant was almost at La Residence. The four fishermen who carried Genevieve had been surprised how light she was.

At the church, the vigil continued but with a disturbed air of questioning. The old priest did not feel that it was pressure and pain alone that had affected Genevieve. There was more to it, something in her eyes and in her voice when had she cried out that it was 'her fault.' Her ambiguous confession weighed on him. He prayed for strength and wisdom deep into the night as he stared at the candle casting its dim glow on the crucifix above the altar. Long after all his parishioners had left, he was still lost in prayers. He needed his Master's guidance, for he had seen the weight of the cross she was bearing. He had seen her soul.

For her part, Genevieve had regained just enough strength to sit on the veranda of her upstairs bedroom, gazing out at the small slit of moon casting its gentle glow over the island of Silhouette. As she sat, she was able to contemplate the fullness of her sin which had claimed the sacrifice of her young son and the soul of her husband.

She had decided when she got home earlier that she would not entertain anyone now, not even the old priest, no one. She would remain in her room until her husband and Henri were home again.

Why did it have to be so harsh, Maman, she asked, facing the direction where her mother and father laid buried. *Why did it have to happen to me?*

All her privilege and status had been for naught. Her arrogance in going against the laws of God and the Church had cost her dearly, and she was now paying the penalty for her cowardice and weakness. All those poor lost souls on board La Sirène with Louis. Her own beloved family. They were now all being punished for her sin. She should have toed the line just like any other woman – she was no exception in God's eyes.

For the next two days she stayed on her veranda, reliving again and again the agony she had heard in her husband's cry. The pain of losing her younger son crushed her very soul. She had lost all faith in her God and she ordered Therese to remove all religious memorabilia from her house. "Please make sure that Père Valer is not allowed to visit me", she instructed a sad and tearful looking Therese. "I do not want anything to do with the Church any more."

It was almost 6 a.m. on the 24th of November and Anna was on her way to work. Walking down the small footpath from her home, her thoughts were on Louis. Was he staring at the horizon now, waiting to be rescued and wondering what had been happening here on Mahé? It seemed an eternity, but it was only two months since they last met at the botanical gardens, and he had held her in his arms, reaffirmed his love, and reassured her that all was going to be fine. But it was not all fine. Not fine at all. The past few days had seen her secretly taking a few items clothing every day to Josephine. She was getting ready to leave Mahé.

Genevieve sighted the steamer first, seeing it as it came around the tip of the northern coast. "Marie!" she screamed, leaping from the veranda.

She rushed through the bedroom and down the staircase. "Marie! They are here!" A moment later, blasts from the siren echoed across the waters. Anna stopped in her tracks, the unfamiliar sounds of the siren piercing her very soul. She trembled as she realised that it could only be the steamer. "Louis, Oh Louis," she cried as she ran down the foot-path.

Marie ran to her mistress. "Madanm!" she cried, stopping her from going out dressed only in her thin night dress. With Marie's intervention, Genevieve was properly attired and waiting on the beach with Therese and Marie at her sides as the first pirogue from the steamer headed towards the beach, with the imposing figure of Albert standing at its bow.

Soon after, the others followed. The beautiful bay of Beau Vallon was bathed in the soft light of sunrise as soft, sweet breezes blew gently. A perfect day, but for the unstated truth of the steamer's arrival. They had failed.

The pirogues were met by silence. Christophe's legs felt like lead as he disembarked and tried to stand on the sand next to the craft. The waves drenched the bottom of his white trousers. His eyes searched wildly until they captured the one person he sought in the silent crowd. And in Genevieve's eyes, he saw that she had heard his message, had heard his cry and felt his anguish. In the cruel silence, all he could hear was the sound of his own wet footsteps in the sand as he moved up the beach toward the emaciated figure of the person who had been his beautiful wife. The agony of seeing what had happened to her tore at him.

He felt the first impact across his chest. A heavy, punching blow that radiated and travelled upwards to his neck and his head. It squeezed his chest in a giant grip, but it was naught compared with the agony his soul was enduring. He took the blow like a man – a man who had failed. His eyes held Genevieve's gaze.

Just then the bells of Saint Roch tolled, breaking the deadly silence and stopping Christophe in his tracts. Henri appeared next to him, with Albert flanking his other side. Christophe was looking at all the other faces then, at all the men and women who had come to greet the search party. Most of them were his employees and people he had known for years; people who had previously worked for his father, men and women he had known as he was growing up, good hard-working people. Behind them, overlooking the bay, he could see the imposing façade of La Residence — his house, his home. A place that had been filled with joy and laughter, with love. A place where his beloved had given him the greatest of blessings, his two sons.

The bells continued to toll. He turned and looked at the old church. Its walls had stood witness to the best and worst episodes in his life, but it had always been there for him. Those same bells which had sounded two months earlier, when the search party left. Then, he had lifted his eyes to the heavens and prayed to his God as he never had before. He offered to sacrifice himself, to lay down his own life, for the return of his son.

He knew now that God had not listened.

As he stood motionless in front of this new dawn, the blows came from all directions. His head pounded, the bones of his skull felt ready to explode. He had failed. Failed as a husband, failed as a father. As these harsh realities tore through his tormented body, he realised that Louis was gone. His beloved son was gone forever. Albert and Henri took his arms, urging him on, but he could not move. He tried to call out Genevieve's name, to beg her forgiveness, but nothing came forth. There was no more oxygen…it was too late…

And then only blackness.

The Alexandra looked big and impressive in the empty bay as Anna got to the beach. She was breathless as she held onto the pillar of the pirogue shed for support. *Oh Louis, mon chéri, you are back!*

She watched as the first pirogue from the steamer came to a standstill. Her father got out of the pirogue first, then helped Monsieur du Barré and Henri to disembark. She had wanted to scream, *Help my Louis as well!* Instead, Albert had stood next to Monsieur du Barré and along with Henri, assisted him up the beach. She could not understand why no one had helped Louis.

The bells of Saint Roch startled her then, and she trembled as Monsieur du Barré stopped. He seemed to be staring at Madame du Barré, trying to speak. She could not read his silence any more than Madame du Barré. But she could read his face and saw the agonising pain and defeat etched there. And then the awful truth dawned on her.

"Non, oh mon Dieu, non!" Her head started spinning. She couldn't breathe. "Louis, oh Louis," she tried to cry out, but the intensity of pain had taken her voice away. Her legs started to give way, and she held tightly onto the pillar of the shed as she went down, hoping her baby would not feel all of the pain surging through her body. *Oh, my poor little one. You are an orphan even before you are born.*

Her father's voice broke through her tears. "Anna, Anna, we need your help!"

She looked up and she saw that Christophe du Barré had collapsed on the beach. That vision, that horrible moment! It all happened so quickly. She had no time to think. She could only react the way she had been trained to react. She managed to get herself up and began to run down the beach, wiping her tears.

In that moment, all the hours spent in the confinement of that hospital, all the teaching and the knowledge drummed into Anna's mind from Patricia's years of experience in hospital, flowered then. Anna found herself on her knees on the sand, reading all the signs first, just as she had been taught.

She felt Patricia's presence next to her. "Please tell the crowd to move away. He needs fresh air," she said to her father and to Henri, as she laid Christophe on the sand. She started loosening the shirt buttons around his neck, working her way down his chest. "Get me a blanket, or some other warm clothing, and please fetch the doctor," she added. Then, seeing the panic in Henri's eyes, she said reassuringly. "Do you trust me?"

He remained still.

"Will you let me try and do what I have been taught to start his heart and breathing again?" she pressed on. He blinked and nodded. "Yes. You have my permission to do whatever you can to help him. I trust you."

Drawing a breath, Anna covered Christophe's mouth with hers and emptied her breath into his lungs. Once. Twice. Again and again. She raised her hand and brought it down sideways on Christophe's chest with all her strength. Then she returned to breathing into his mouth, repeating the procedure over and over, until at last she was able to feel a faint pulse. A moment later, the doctor came running down the beach towards them. Exhausted, she fell out of the doctor's way as he tended to Christophe and a stretcher was brought over.

"Merci," Henri silently mouthed to Anna, making his appreciation clear. Then he scooped his father in his arms, and started to walk up the beach to La Residence. Meanwhile, Doctor Haggart attended to his second patient on the beach. Genevieve du Barré also had been unable to bear the intensity of the pain and torment.

Josephine was hopeful when she saw the arrival of the steamer. She was sure that all was well and that Louis was to be reunited with Anna. But that was not to be. No matter that Anna deserved such a reunion, it was not what God or fate had determined.

"Oh no," she cried, as the harsh reality dawned. "Oh God no, please spare her from that." The realization tore at her soul. Her legs gave way and she fell down to the sand, trembling in sorrow and hurt.

She knew that Anna's future would be hard indeed. She would be alone. Josephine's exile was a small heaven on earth because she was with her beloved. But Anna would not know that blessing. Worse, the innocent child would bear the stigma of her parent's illicit love. Tears streamed down her wrinkled black face as she hugged her body for support.

She did not manage to climb from the sand until she heard the sounds of sobs coming closer. She looked up to see a young girl, her hair flying wildly as she ran towards her. Josephine scrambled to her feet and opened her arms, holding Anna as she took refuge in the older woman's girth.

As Josephine comforted Anna, back at La Residence the doctor reassured Henri and Albert that Christophe was out of danger. He would need full-time nursing care for the foreseeable future, but a recovery was quite possible, given time. He was less certain about Genevieve, as her case was more complex. But for both, it was not just their physical bodies that needed healing, and it would be a long process.

"You will need to be very patient and take one day at a time."

Henri listened attentively, focusing on his beloved mother and father rather than his own sorrows. "I would be grateful if you could make all the arrangements," he said,

Doctor Edward Haggart was more than ready to serve.

As a number of decisions clearly fell to him now, Henri also moved to make sure that the estate would be managed well. He turned to Albert.

"I would like you to continue with the running of the estate, just as you have been doing. We will try to keep things just as Papa would have wanted, but to succeed, I need you."

Albert nodded. It was clear that Henri was using an incredible amount of energy just to keep from breaking down. It was so painful for Albert to see, but this was life and it was necessary to keep moving forward. Albert leaned toward Henri and took his hands into his own. "I watched both of you grow up. I have loved you both like you were my own, and I know the pain you are now going through. You have my total dedication and promise that I will always be here for you and for your family."

Albert's heartfelt words were too much for Henri, and he threw himself into Albert's arms. "Why did it have to happen to my Louis?

Why my little brother? Why my father and my mother? What have we done to deserve this?"

Even as Albert tried to comfort Henri, so Josephine tried to comfort his daughter. "You have to think of your baby now," she said, putting her arm around Anna's shoulders. "Louis would want you to be strong for the baby."

Anna nodded sadly. "You are right." She tried to be brave but she couldn't keep it up. "I am scared, so scared!"

All Josephine could do was hold her closer. She could taste the salt of her own tears as she answered. "Try not to worry. You are not going to be on your own. Jacques and I are going to help you. You will live with Norine on La Digue. She has been alone for a long time now and she is looking forward to your arrival." She wiped away her tears and tried to sound reassuring.

"I promise that I will visit when the baby arrives, even if it means getting seasick. So, no more worrying now. Just rest and let me look after you today. When you go home tonight, you have to pretend that everything is alright. Do not let anyone see that you are upset, because no one can know of your plans. It will be easier if no one knows until after your departure." Anna nodded.

"I will make sure that you are all right, my little one," Josephine whispered. "Norine will defend your honour at all costs, and she will look after you both. So be calm now, drink the infusion and lie down. Everything will be all right."

She watched pensively as Anna curled into a foetal position, cradling her abdomen. Josephine felt helpless and angry. Angry at a God who was ready to condemn this young girl and her innocent baby to a life of hell and rejection. *Why do you have to be so cruel, Lord? Was two months of pain and trauma not enough punishment for her sin?*

As Anna walked home at sunset, she managed to regain some composure. It had been the most horrible day of her life. Despite the sedative effects of Josephine's herbal infusion, the agonising pain within her heart and soul had surfaced again and again, tearing at her with its intensity. The bleakness of a future without Louis was just too heavy and painful.

"Calm down my little one, calm down," Josephine had comforted her each time she had cried out, forcing her to have more of the infusion. She wanted to believe that he might still be alive out there somewhere, and would one day be rescued, but she was also tortured by the vision of Louis injured and in great pain, with nothing to eat or drink and with no way of getting any help.

As the soft sand of Beau Vallon cushioned her bare feet, Anna thought about Josephine. The seclusion of her friend's little hut had been a much-needed sanctuary, and she knew she could not have managed without her. *I will never forget your kindness today, my old friend.*

The beach was deserted now. Only deep silence remained, only hazy memories of what had happened there that morning lingered on the breeze. The whole place looked like an empty shell, as though its heart and soul had been ripped out. That special something was gone, everything was now bare and vacant. Even if still beautiful in the magnificence of the sunset, it was somehow meaningless.

As she crossed to the main road, she saw a solitary black flag floating over the roof of La Residence. She sighed as she was taken by the poignancy of its message. *Oh, mon Dieu.* A male voice interrupted her thoughts. "Anna, Anna."

Oh, that voice! So like Louis! It sent shivers throughout her body. She whirled around, almost losing her footing, as Henri approached, extending his hand in a formal greeting.

"I want to say thank you for all your help with my father this morning. The doctor said that your efforts saved his life. My family and I will be forever indebted to you."

Anna needed all the strength she could muster to stop herself trembling as she shook his hand. The pain of standing so close to someone who looked and sounded so like Louis, was just brutal; it was like fate playing a cruel game with her feelings. She answered him in a voice that was soft and controlled, praying that Henri could not read the pain in her eyes.

"It was my privilege to attend to Monsieur du Barré today. I sincerely hope he will make a quick recovery, and please accept my heartfelt condolences for your sad loss."

By mid-afternoon, news of Alexandra's return had reached the hospital, and Patricia's worst fears were realised. She suspected something was wrong — Anna had not made her shift that morning. She spoke a silent prayer.

Memories of the day that David was taken from her re-surfaced, and she knew the pain Anna would be experiencing. *Hold on tight my child* her heart pleaded, promising to help both Anna and her baby. She owed it to her young charge and to the memory of her David.

Meanwhile, as she continued her work, she subconsciously persevered in her determination to find the best way to help her. Then, at the end of the day, just as she was getting ready to leave for home, came her epiphany. Her heart rejoiced as she realised that all was not lost. For the first time in weeks she smiled a wide, genuine smile. Anna was going to make her proud!

In the days that followed, and in her own way without betraying her secret, Anna began the process of saying her farewells to the people and island she loved. Each time she said goodbye, a goodbye the recipient did not realize they had received, she felt a pang of guilt.

She could not remember the walk from Saint Louis to Beau Vallon two days later. The painfully poignant picture of her old grandmother standing waving under the veranda had been too much to bear. It had clouded everything else along the way, and knowing that she would never see Monia again in this lifetime was more painful than she could have imagined.

Oh, Memer, I am so sorry for everything. I am so sorry for all the pain and shame that I have caused to our family. Please forgive me. Please do not hate me for one mistake.

She carried her guilt and sadness to her beautiful, natural sanctuary. She would miss this greatly too. As she gazed at the familiar beauty, she inhaled the sweet air and deep peace that surrounded her. She implored its magical soul to soothe her heart one more time. She was so desperate for one final chance to feel the mystical powers of this special place. *How will I live without you?*

One last time she stripped off her clothing, her small baby bump visible, and stood under the sprays of the waterfall…her waterfall. The delicate softness and deep coolness of the water slowly worked its magic, releasing her if only for a moment from her sadness. She found it hard to say goodbye to this place, for it had shared such difficult parts of her life and her past.

In the days since the return of the search party, she had adopted a new perspective. The plan she had set in motion had to be honoured. There was no going back now. No more hoping that Louis would return and that she would not have to go to La Digue. No more miracles, just harsh reality. Now, as she looked around for one last time at the comforting density circling the waterfall, she wished desperately that it had all been just a bad dream. But she knew differently.

She had to be strong now, strong for herself and her baby. Louis was gone, her one and only love, cruelly taken from her. The past was a sad trap. She had to look forward now. But even as she said all this to herself, she just wanted to break down and cry. Cry and mourn the loss of Louis, cry for her family, and cry for her baby who would never know its father's love.

Anna knew only too well the pain her sin would cause her family. She desperately wanted their forgiveness. But she also knew that, given the chance, she would not have changed a thing. Her love for Louis was eternal. It was true. She could never regret their love, never regret their night of passion that sealed that love. But now she bore such a heavy burden because her *sin* was going to be the downfall, dishonour and shame of her family – for every single member of her beloved family.

She prayed fervently, with the images of her siblings, her very proud mother and father, and her grandmother filling her thoughts. *Please forgive me, Lord, please, I am begging you. I never meant for them to suffer, please Lord.*

The last day of November, the day she had dreaded. With the distant sound of the cockcrow, she opened her eyes and she saw her nurse's uniform, hanging in its usual place on the hook on her bedroom wall. She felt such regret. This would be the last day she would work at her beloved hospital, signalling the end of her nursing career and the end of the life she had lived and loved. She thought of her patients, her colleagues, everyone there. Her second family. And another family she would have to deceive by saying goodbye in a way they could not understand. And then simply leaving...

Anna's legs felt weak as she climbed the last steps leading onto the veranda of Victoria Hospital. She turned round to admire the view one last time. *My hospital, my beloved hospital. I will never forget you, never.*

"Nurse Savy."

She recognized Patricia's familiar English accent.

"Good Morning, Sister Kent."

Patricia smiled. "Will you come and see me after your lunch break? We have a lot to talk about, and I am confident that you will like what I have to say." A mischievous glint sparkled in her blue English eyes.

During the morning, Anna held her emotions in check though it pained her when she left the ward and heard her patients say 'See you tomorrow.' Only one of her favourite patients, old Madame Dupres, seemed to sense what was really happening. She was big lady, a larger-than-life character, who suffered from diabetes, obesity and any number of other ailments, and unfortunately was a regular in the ward. Anna was extremely fond of her.

Today, while Anna attended to her, she had been very quiet, most unlike her usual jovial self. When everything was done, Anna said, "All nice and fresh now, just in time for that cup of tea." As she readied to pull the screen away from the bed, Madame Dupres grabbed her hands and looked straight into her eyes.

"One day the pain will ease, I promise. You have a magnificent gift, a great talent for healing, never forget that. Next year, my child, those two hands will behold a very special gift," she said, as her plump fingers traced the lines on Anna's hands. "*She* will bring you enormous joy and lots of happiness. *She* will help ease your pain."

Anna's eyes widened...

"Yes, my child. Only a special little girl can do that – *your* special little girl."

Anna had struggled to remain composed as the old, wrinkled black face gazed at her. She felt this old woman was looking straight into her soul, as though she knew everything Anna had tried to conceal, everything that was going to happen in the future.

After lunch, Patricia found Anna in the chapel. They walked together along the length of the veranda to her office. Patricia sat her down and outlined her plan – *to have Anna head a clinic on La Digue!*

"I will of course have to get the approval of Matron," she cautioned, as she outlined her thinking. As La Digue has no clinic and the sick have to be taken by boat to Mahé, it would be a great help to have a nurse out there. Someone capable of treating the minor ailments and only sending the cases that need hospitalisation out here.

"And of course, I will have to oversee the initial stages of the project myself, which will be an incentive for me as I need to get something new going, to help me avoid stagnation."

Anna was dumbfounded.

"I…I don't know what to say," Anna replied. "Are you sure I am capable of taking on such a project?"

Patricia's smile widened. "I have complete confidence in you and in your abilities my dear. I have trained you myself and I know exactly how you work, even in the face of extremely grim and difficult circumstances. Believe me, the residents of La Digue are going to be very lucky to have your services. You are the best candidate for this post. Never doubt your capability, not for one minute." Then she laughed softly and winked at Anna. "You didn't think I was going to let all your hard training go to waste now, did you?"

"How can I ever thank you?" A sudden stab of fear hit Anna. She shook her head. "Oh no, it will not be possible."

Patricia looked alarmed. Taking Anna's hands, she leaned closer.

"Calm down, my dear. Tell me why you think it will not be possible."

Trembling, with tears streaming down her cheeks, Anna stammered. "The rule about unwed mothers…Matron will never allow it."

Patricia patted her hands. "I have already thought about that and I know what to do. So, do not worry yourself about it. I will make sure that Matron and everyone else concerned see things my way. Trust me, Anna, everything will work out just as I've planned it. Trust me."

It was sad and painful when it was time for them to say goodbye, but Patricia quickly brushed their emotions away. "I will be on La Digue on my fact-finding mission soon and we can discuss all the plans then. But now, before you go home, please write down the list of things I have instructed you to do when you get there." Patricia knew the next twenty-four hours were going be painful and distressing for Anna. Leaving her family and her home was going to be traumatic. She had to ensure that Anna remembered and followed her every instruction.

As Patricia watched Anna preparing the list, she inwardly rejoiced in the knowledge that all was not lost and that Anna would still have a career in nursing. She unlocked the top drawer of her desk, brought out a large brown envelope and placed it next to the three leather-bound books on her desk top.

As she went over Anna's meticulous list, Patricia looked at her.

"As the first point said – over the next four months you have to continue with your studying and you will do a written test every month." She then gestured to the books and the brown envelope. "This will keep you going. Until you start earning again."

Anna remained silent, gazing at the envelope and wondering how she was ever going to repay such a debt. "This is a gift, not a loan." Patricia had said, reading her mind. She reminded Anna that she would be accomplishing a great ambition of hers by making a success of this new project, that it had been her ambition to change the Seychelles' healthcare system. "Now my dear, we are going to do it together. You are going to make me proud".

Anna did not look back at her hospital as she went down the long driveway, but she sensed Patricia's gaze. Tears filled her eyes as the weight of the books and the obligation of the promises she had just made reminded her of what her future now held. *Thank you, Lord, for sending her to me.*

She was dreading the next twenty-four hours, but worst of all she was dreading this final visit, this final goodbye to their oasis. Everything looked vacant and soulless as she arrived by their little pool. Tears streamed down her face as she sat for one last time on his favourite rock. *Oh Louis, mon amour, why did it have to be this way, why did I have to lose you? I will always love you, mon amour, always. I promise that I will bring up our child with all the love and care I can give.*

She picked up her bags and looked around their sanctuary for one last time. *Please pray for us, mon amour, wherever you are. We will always need you and we will always love you.*

Anna did not remember much about the walk back to Beau Vallon, the pain was too intense. But she was happy to see Josephine outside in her kitchen as she approached her hut. Josephine smile broadly as slowly Anna relayed the details of Patricia's plan to establish a medical clinic on La Digue, and then later branch out to the other neighbouring islands.

"She is a true guardian angel, this Patricia," Josephine said.

For her part, Patricia knew how fortunate she was to have someone as dedicated and intelligent as Anna to further her plans. The unfortunate demise of Louis had made it possible for Anna to devote her time to the clinic. She had provided money for Anna to live on while she continued her studies. She had promised to protect her and the baby.

I did not plan any of this, she thought with a twinge of remorse. *I am only trying to do what is best for her now.* She wanted to preserve Anna's talents and gifts, and make sure she did not end up as one of the Catholic Church's taboo victims – a disgraced, unmarried mother bringing up a bastard child.

As Patricia contemplated her master plan, at Beau Vallon, Christophe du Barré opened his eyes and stared at the ceiling of his bedroom. He felt dead inside, an empty shell. The heart attack and seizure had robbed him of both his speech and the use of his limbs. The shock from the emotional and psychological traumas had been too tragic to cope with, and his body had gone into meltdown. His doctor's only hope now was that he could find the courage to face what had happened and the will to fight once more. In a cruel twist of fate, his brain was still functioning, so that he went on suffering. All the bad memories of his loss, his pain, his failures, would continue to gnaw at his soul. Everything was now meaningless. He had lost it all. He wished he was dead.

Whilst Christophe stared at the ceiling, in the next room Genevieve was holding Therese tightly by the hand, wishing she did not have to leave so soon. She had become so dependent on her presence. Life and fate had robbed her of a beautiful son and husband and she felt so alone.

Worse still was the remorse she felt each time she saw the pain in Christophe and Henri's eyes. All her fault. She was to blame for everything. In an attempt to distance herself from them, she kept to her bedroom. It was one sure way of not seeing their distress. She wished it could all stop. She wished she was dead.

Outside La Residence, in one of the warehouses, two people sat quietly sipping their last coffee for the day, contemplating all that had happened. It was extremely hard for both Albert and Marie to witness all the pain and devastation this family was enduring. They had both done what they knew was the best way to help, given the circumstances. This had meant extremely long hours for Albert, but he was starting to get the desired results. And despite her earlier cruel suggestions, Marie had been a tower of strength too, very keen to engage positively with the labourers and show them how much the plantation and the du Barré family needed their support.

Her courageous endeavour had resulted in everyone pushing in the same direction and getting as much work done as possible. Albert was very pleased with her and her efforts.

It was coming up to 5 p.m. that evening when Anna got home. Chantal relayed Therese's message that Anna should get dinner ready, as Therese was attending to Madame du Barré. Anna was pleased. She wanted to spend time alone with her siblings.

As they stood together preparing the vegetables, Anna asked Chantal how things were going with her tuition with the nuns. A jubilant Chantal had needed no further prompting and regaled Anna with the details of everything that had happened over the past months, and how happy and fulfilled she felt to be soon embarking on her new life as a nun and teacher. "I feel blessed Anna," she concluded with tears in her eyes.

Anna hugged her sister tightly, and kissed the top of her head. "You will be a wonderful teacher and a great nun. I am so happy for you, Chantal, so happy that you are going to find this great fulfilment and true happiness".

A small voice at their feet interrupted their special moment. It was their brother Didier, wearing a big beaming smile, and holding little Eliane's hand.

"May we also have a hug please?"

As Anna prepared the farewell dinner with her family, Henri Du Barré walked barefoot on the soft sand of Beau Vallon beach, trying to come to terms with all that had happened to him and his family. The branch of driftwood imbedded in the sand had been a comforting refuge for those past seven nights since they had returned from the search. Seven nights since they had given up on Louis. His heart agonised as he watched the sun ready to submerge into the ocean. *I should be out there...out there searching for you. I am a coward. A coward and a failure.*

In frustration his fist pounded the sand next to the driftwood. The small white sand crab stopped and stared at him, dumbfounded. His house had been flattened yet again!

It was 6 p.m. and Saint Roch's blessing echoed over the bay. Henri stared. He had lost all faith in his God. He had lost his one and only brother. His father and mother were now just empty shells. He felt cold and dead inside.

That evening at dinner, Anna gazed at her family seated around the table. She had to summon all her strength to keep from breaking down. The three younger members of the family were enjoying the special dish of pumpkin and fried fish fricassee, which Anna had lovingly prepared for them. Everyone else, including her mother and father, were enjoying the delicious vegetable curry and a large charcoal-grilled *vyey babonn*, which was accompanied by an equally peppery aubergine *satini* and lots of steamed rice. Albert spoke suddenly.

"I have a special announcement to make. After discussions with Monsieur Henri today, we have agreed that Antoine will start his overseer's training when he finishes school at the end of December."

Antoine beamed. He had always wanted to follow in his father's footsteps. "Thank you very much, Papa."

"What wonderful news," Therese said with a broad smile, "I know you will make your father proud, my son. It is so nice to see you continuing in the family tradition."

Anna listened quietly, with a heavy heart. She knew her own impending news would diminish the happiness of her whole family. "You will make a very good overseer Antoine," she said softly. Without thinking, she then turned to fourteen-year-old Maxime. "What would you like to do when you finish school, Maxime?"

"I want to be a sailor and train to be a skipper, just like Monsieur Henri!"

Therese glared at him. "You have two more years at school yet. It is still rather too early to decide what you will want to do," she said sharply. Given the events of the past couple of months, she had no desire to hear of her child seeking a career at sea.

Albert had remained quiet, omitting to mention to his family the other part of his conversation with Henri. "Your Maxime is a born sailor," Henri had told him. "He has shown great potential. Why, even the Captain of the Alexandra was impressed." Albert decided it was judicious not to tell Maxime about the praise, but to change the subject instead.

"Anna, my dear," Albert had addressed her directly. "You should be very proud of yourself." Anna froze. "Doctor Haggart told Monsieur Henri that your nursing care on the beach saved his father's life." He spoke with pride in his voice and in his eyes as he looked at his first born. Anna could not breathe. She dreaded the inevitable pain and anguish that would be in her father's eyes tomorrow.

"I am so proud of you my dear," her mother had said, smiling at her. A beaming Chantal joined in. "We all are. It must be such a wonderful feeling to know that you have saved someone's life – what a blessing Anna," she said, reaching out and squeezing her elder sister's hand.

Later that night, in the privacy of her room, Anna thought about her family and found comfort in the events of the day. Her brothers, she was sure, would be successful. Chantal would make a wonderful nun. She knew she would miss them all terribly. And she hated that she would not be there to celebrate their successes with them. But there was no use thinking that now. All she could do was pray that they would be able to find it in their hearts to forgive her. Pray that they would still remember some of the good things she represented.

Standing at her bedroom window, she looked at her favourite view of the valley of Beau Vallon under the soft moonlight for one last time. The gentle fragrance travelling up the hill in the breeze soothed her face, kissing her goodbye. Her heart ached from the approaching solitude.

On her bedside table, an envelope held the letter she had written for her mother to read the following day. She felt like a coward, but she did not know another way. She hung her head, once again shamed by the consequences of her actions. *Please forgive me, Maman. Forgive me for leaving in this cruel way.*

Deep down Anna knew that Therese would never forgive a sin of this magnitude. She had lived her life by the rules of her faith and her God – and this was the ultimate sin. Anna was also aware that in order to move on, her family would have to be seen to be merciless to her, to completely disown her and the bastard child. Only then might they stand a chance of being reintegrated into the fold of their society and their church – after a good period of shame, humiliation and suffering, of course!

The first day of December 1914. The 'Advent' season in preparation for Christmas had started a few days before. But instead of anticipation and jubilation, the island was veiled in apprehension and pain. Morale had never been lower.

The return of the search party had signalled the acceptance of the tragedy. La Sirène was lost, her crew had perished. Still many questions remained. How could it have happened to a new and sturdy boat? Why couldn't the experienced Captain have prevented it? Families of crew members wearing mourning badly needed answers, but none was forthcoming. Masses in churches across the island had replaced daily vigils for their safe return. They now prayed for all their souls to rest in peace. It was all so sombre and sad. The Seychelles had known this kind of tragedy before, but each time it happened anew, the pain was harder to bear.

As well as acceptance, speculation was rife too. Could 'The War' have had anything to do with the disappearance of La Sirène and her crew? Were German war ships attacking and destroying defenceless boats in their waters? Was it safe for fishermen to go out fishing?

The veil of uncertainty, apprehension and general malaise seeped into every nook and cranny. It covered the islands, allowing the pain to fester. It registered on every single face. The start of Advent did nothing to raise morale. It would be a sad Christmas indeed.

The sea was calm on that day, as Anna sat sipping a last coffee with Josephine. They had been silent for a while now when Josephine suddenly broke the stillness. "Do not worry too much about it. Things are out of your hands now. You have to think of yourself and your baby."

Anna nodded her head, knowing she was right. The day before, Patricia had said to her: "You have to believe in yourself wholeheartedly, believe in your strength and your intelligence, and know that from now onwards you are standing on your own two feet, and you are the master of your own destiny." Bold words. Hard words. But words she had needed to hear.

But she was having difficulty in focusing on the advice. She was thinking of her mother leaving the cottage around lunchtime. Before going, Therese had turned to her and said, "Anna, will you prepare the vegetables and fish for dinner before you leave for the hospital this afternoon? I should be back from Madame du Barré by around six, and I will finish the cooking then."

"Yes, Maman," Anna answered. Half-way to the front door, Therese turned suddenly, and said inquisitively to Anna, "Why are you working night shift again?" Anna froze, scared her plan was about to unravel. "It will only be for a few nights, Maman," she heard herself saying softly. Nodding and shrugging, Therese left the cottage.

Anna trembled from the blatant lie. It was the last time she would ever see, or speak to her mother again. And she had had to lie.

Her final farewell to her siblings was the hardest. She nearly broke down as she hugged and kissed them tenderly, especially Chantal. "Take good care of them."

She had took a final look around her bedroom then moved discreetly into her parent's room where she left the dreaded letter on her mother's dressing table to be discovered later. Then she rushed straight out of the cottage, looking back only when she was half-way down the hill, imprinting in her memory a final picture of that small cottage perched among the trees, her real true home and the home she would never again see in this lifetime.

The soft sand of Beau Vallon caressed her feet as she walked towards Josephine's hut. The spire of Saint Roch seemed to stare straight at her, its silent message condemning her. It was as though she had been found guilty of a hideous crime and was on her way to a prison sentence. It was all so brutal, so final.

Half-way to Josephine's place she stopped. Her whole body trembled as she leaned heavily against the driftwood, a heart-rending sob escaping her tortured soul. She could see images of Louis, she could see him smiling at her. *I will miss you terribly, mon chéri.* Saying goodbye to their special spot had been both poignant and excruciating. She said farewell to the wonderful memories she had shared with Louis when he had found her sleeping on that fateful night of her sixteenth birthday, and where exactly two years later they had made love, that one and only time…

Why had it all had to happen to them and their perfect love? Why was she being condemned to a life of exile?

Josephine seemed to read these thoughts and images in her young friend and she wished there was a way to take some of the pain from her. "At least you now have a way to continue working and do what you love best," she said softly, trying to persuade Anna to look to the future and leave the past where it belonged.

"It is the only way, my child," she added tenderly. "The only way."

Josephine knew this truth well, recalling her own hasty exodus from La Digue. She could only hope that, once Anna held her baby in her arms, she would know it was all well worth it, and that the pain would ease.

She reached out and touched Anna's hand. "Thank you my child, for all the joys and pleasure your friendship has brought me over the years. You have made a big difference to my life. And it gives me great comfort now to know that my Norine will not be alone anymore, but that you will be keeping an eye on her."

Anna patted her old friend's hand. "Our friendship has meant everything to me too. I will always keep its memories close to my heart."

Therese's feet plodded the familiar footpath, forging her way uphill. She felt drained and helpless. Those past hours with Madame du Barré had been heart-rending and very sad. *Please help them, Lord* she heard her heart whispering. Witnessing the misery and pain this proud family was enduring, without knowing how to help them, was truly devastating.

"I have killed my own son. My beautiful Louis is dead because of my sin. It is all my own fault," she could hear Genevieve's words echoing once more. She had tried reassuring her then, telling her that it had all been just a tragic accident, but to no avail. Over the past week, all of

Albert and Therese's well-rehearsed reasoning had fallen on deaf ears. The three members of the du Barré family needed to blame themselves for this tragedy – they felt guilty for being alive, whilst Louis and his crew were dead.

The cheerful voices brought her out of her reverie as she approached the cottage. Therese was happy to be home. Picking up Eliane she gave her a big cuddle, smiled at Didier as she held his hand, and together they climbed the steps leading onto the veranda.

Meanwhile, in Christophe du Barré's room, Albert was spending some of the last hours of his working day with his best friend. Even if the seizure had robbed him of his speech, Albert treated him with a genuine respect and dignity, given the circumstances. Events of the day were recapped. Reassurances were given. Christophe communicated by blinking, and then closed his eyes when he wanted Albert to go.

An eerie silence greeted Albert as he made his way down the staircase. This once lively and joyful home was now but an empty shell. He stopped and stared around, the pain visible everywhere. He trembled, holding the banister firmer still, as the enormity of the tragedy that had befallen this family stared back. He looked back in the direction of Christophe's room. *May God help you, my friend.*

At that moment Albert realised just how blessed he was. How proud and happy he was of his family, his children. How fulfilled was his life.

At the same time, in the church of Saint Roch at the end of the bay, the lonely figure on his knees in front of the altar was also praying for a revelation.

He badly needed guidance and help from his Master. He had failed in his duties. His heart was heavy. Members of his flock were lost. Pain and tragedy had taken them away from their faith, turned them away from God, and he had been unable to reach out to them in their darkest hours.

Please forgive me, Lord. I have failed. Please guide me. Show me how to bring them back to the safety of your love.

This balmy early evening also saw Henri du Barré on the veranda of his upstairs bedroom, his heart and mind in bitter turmoil. He was about to make the biggest decision of his life. The small bundle of unopened letters with Mauritius postmark on his coffee table looked forbidding in the glow of the approaching sunset. *What right do I have to happiness and love? I am a failure. A coward and a failure.* Images of his beloved Danielle flashed momentarily. *She deserves someone better than me. She deserves an honourable man.*

Henri du Barré wrote two letters that evening. The first, to Danielle de Ravel and her father, Fernand de Ravel, in Mauritius. He expressed his deep regrets and great sadness at this decision, but respectfully asked to be released from the bonds of his proposal of marriage. The second letter was more formal. It was addressed to Sir Terence Hastings, Governor of the Seychelles. He expressed his wish to join the British Forces mobilised in France, and to help in the war efforts on the frontline.

"It is time." Anna took a deep breath and looked at Josephine. "I will never forget you, nor everything you have done for me. You have my promise that I will look after your sister." Anna whispered, kissing the top of Josephine's head. They both cried as they hugged one another.

Josephine finally broke away and looked at the young woman. "Promise me you will be strong. Promise to look after yourself properly. In return, I give you my word that in exactly six months, I will brave those waves and come back to La Digue to see you and your little one."

Anna did not look back. Not once. She told herself to concentrate on what lay ahead.

When she arrived at the water's edge and boarded the small *saloup* which would take them to Jacques's fishing boat, she felt a shudder of fear. She had never been in a boat before and quickly discovered that she disliked being tossed from side to side. She held tightly to the sides, staring at Silhouette Island, as Jacques rowed out.

Boarding the fishing vessel proved trickier. She thought she might fall into the sea but for Jacques's strong arms lifting her up into the boat. She settled onto the pile of old sails in the corner of the craft, next to where her two bags lay side by side. There she was, with all her worldly possessions, her entire life packed into just two vakoa bags. She grabbed them and held them tight, fearful they might fall overboard and disappear, like the rest of her life.

She closed her eyes tightly. She wanted to think only of what lay ahead. An eerie silence seemed to reign over the bay. She trembled, as suddenly, the boat slid out further into the waters. This was it. The moment had truly come. She was leaving her beloved Beau Vallon forever. Her chest tightened with emotion and fear, a truly frightening sensation. Her heart skipped and raced madly. She was breathless. It was as though her entire world had collapsed beneath her, and everything that she had ever treasured lay in shambles.

The chime of the church bells echoed across the waters, startling her. Her eyes flew open. Then her jaw dropped, but no words came forth. She was speechless.

Therese heard the first chime of the bells too, but was not startled. She was past that point. Her whole body was trembling and she held onto the bed post for support. The pain she was experiencing was horrendous. It charged mercilessly throughout her body. It felt as though an enormous weight was pressing on her chest, and her rib cage was about to crumble under the pressure, as though there was no more oxygen left in the room.

She tried to speak, but no words came forth, the pain was just too intense. She stared at the holy image on the wall. *Why, Holy Mother, why? Why did she do that to us?* All she could see was the humiliation and devastation heading their way.

The stigma and black stain that could never be washed clean. Everything she had strived for, everything she cherished, they were now all in a shambles.

The second chime of the church bells was more audible. The echoes seemed to fill the bedroom. It told of retribution…punishment…shame…the downfall of her family. Therese stared at the crumpled letter in her hand, then suddenly, a gigantic surge of anger and hatred erupted within her. It consumed her totally. She could feel the room closing in on her, getting smaller and smaller. She wanted to scream, yell at the top of her voice.

She held tighter to the bed post, her body ablaze with rage and bitterness. Her life, her perfect life, has been totally destroyed. It was all ruined. She was livid as she threw the crumpled letter to the floor

You little slut! May you rot in hell, both you and that bastard of yours. I hate you…hate you…

Just then, she felt a sharp contraction tearing angrily at her uterus. She gasped in shock and pain. *Oh Lord, no.* Her arm instantaneously cradled her abdomen, trying to shield it from the inevitable. She realised immediately what was happening, and also knew she was beyond anyone's help. Her whole body trembled fiercely as the horror of this new ordeal took hold, but she knew she had to remain focused. She had to stay in control.

A second massive contraction, followed almost immediately by a third, shook her inner core. A flood of uterine liquid gushed down her trembling legs. She felt the baby's head crowning her birth canal. *No, Lord, no. It is too soon! Too soon! Please have mercy, Lord. Do not punish me in this way. Please do not take my baby from me as well!*

But on this the first day of December 1914, the Lord had clearly decided otherwise. As the beautiful sun dipped into the turquoise waters of the bay, illuminating everything in a kaleidoscope of vibrant colours, a five-month-old foetus slid smoothly from the warmth and protection of her mother's body.

Anna was mesmerized. She had not seen the bay of Beau Vallon from the sea before and she was stunned by its beauty. The glow of the sunset was caressing everything in front of her eyes, creating a picture of unimaginable artistry, colour and elegance. She felt a great tightening feeling in her chest, realising this was the last time she would see the beauty of Beau Vallon bathed in the sunset.

The second chime, even more intense than the first, rang then. In the chiming of the bells, Anna heard of the terrible retributions that were to be visited upon her, the black stain, the stigma that her child would have to bear all of its life.

This more than anything, tore at her very soul. She hugged the two vakoa bags tighter still against her body. She was very scared. Scared of the future, and scared of the pain and hardship her family would have to endure.

As the small sail-boat glided further out to sea, she stared at the beautiful bay and all she had lost. At one end of the bay, the tall roof of

La Residence dominated the landscape. Such grief that image brought to her heart! But then she reminded herself it was only a big house now. Without Louis, it meant nothing. *Why Lord, why. Why did you take him from me. Reduce me and my baby to nothing. Why Lord, why?* She knew that life without Louis, without his love, was going to be a meaningless journey.

What did have meaning was something in the middle of the beach that suddenly caught her eye — a branch of driftwood. The memories came cascading in a rush that overwhelmed her. Every beautiful image of what they had shared. *Why? Why did it have to end this way, mon chéri? Why did I have to lose you?* She sobbed uncontrollably.

Her pain and anguish were so intense that she was left breathless as the third and fourth chimes of Saint Roch's evening bells resonated on the evening air. She turned her gaze to the other end of the bay, to the proud spire standing tall among the trees of Bel Ombre, dominating the landscape with its mighty presence. *Did I really deserve such punishment, Lord?*

Therese's tears streamed down her face, and ran over the tiny, lifeless body she cradled to her breast. The words of her prayers accompanied its soul on its way to heaven. She was grateful, at least, that in the rush of emotion she had not forgotten to perform this most important duty for her new born baby boy. As she gathered the little foetus from its pool of blood, she baptised him to ensure his soul a safe passage to heaven. This to protect him against the Church's teaching that all babies are born in mortal sin, *Le Pêche Originel.*

Thank you Holy Mother. Thank you for reminding me, for giving me a chance to save the soul of my little boy, my little Jean-Paul.

Therese stared at the mat around her then. Bright red blood mingled with all the afterbirth. She had landed on the bedside mat when her legs had given way, when she had felt her baby being born. Reaching out, she picked up the crumpled letter, her heart aching. *Why Anna? Why did you have to do that to us?* Folding the letter, now blood-smeared, she placed it next to the lifeless body of her little boy. The poignancy of that image tugged at her heart as she realised that tonight she had not only lost a son, but a daughter too. Anna was dead to her now. Dead to this family. Never again would her name be mentioned in their house.

And still the small sail-boat continued on its way, the detail of the beach beginning to fade in the approaching evening darkness. Anna was on her own now. Her pain grew more intense, more brutal. She had lost everything. Her past and her future. The only thing that she could still make out on the shore was the spire of Saint Roch's church. *Why have you forsaken me Lord? Why?*

Then, in the failing light, that Anna saw the reflection of a saintly face, an apparition, hovering over the roof of the church. Her eyes widened as she stared at the image. It was so vivid, she was tempted to ask Jacques if he could see it too. Her heart raced and she felt breathless.

This image with its gentle, kind eyes looked into her heart, penetrating her soul, and she felt suddenly frightened. She brought her legs up to her stomach and hugged her body into a small ball, oblivious to the two bags that were bruising the sides of her abdomen.

She shook her head and closed her eyes. *I'm imagining it. The emotions of the day have affected me. It is only my grieving soul feeling desperate.*

Meanwhile, the waves grew. The boat rocked from side to side, a breeze filled the sail. Suddenly, she felt a big kick, as though the bottom of the boat had hit something. Panicking, she opened her eyes. There was Jacques, sitting in the same spot.

He had obviously not felt the impact. Then she saw the saintly face once more, but this time it was not only looking at her, but was communicating with her. In a magical voice that filled her heart and soul as it travelled across the expanse of the empty bay, she heard clearly the words: "I have not forsaken you my child, and you will never be alone. Remember that always."

Its gentleness was like a balm to her aching soul. Tears streamed down her face. *Thank you, Lord. For your mercy, thank you.* She could feel a genuine love and warmth surrounding her, appeasing the intensity of her pain and anguish.

Another kick. Hard and pronounced. No, the boat had not hit another obstruction. Anna realised it was her baby kicking. She knew then that she would never be alone. She knew God had not forsaken her. She knew that a part of Louis would always live on.

Epilogue

April 1916

*I*t was a sight to behold at sunrise. An opulent farmhouse with its neatly manicured rows of vineyards basking in the peace and beauty of the Bordeaux countryside. A difficult picture to imagine at this time in history when other parts of France were in such terrible turmoil. As Henri du Barré stared from the tall window where he had sat all night with his injured leg elevated, the beauty and peace escaped him. He could not hear the melodious singing of the rossignol as they welcomed the new dawn, nor see this late spring's early morning frost glistening in a white tinge on the vines, for he was still back there...back in those muddy trenches. He shuddered as he remembered the foul taste of the poison gas and his own warm urine, and the decaying stench of the battlefields. One by one the horrifying images of death and mutilation circled, and he trembled as his Nemesis surfaced, and he came face to face with Verdun...

Much later that same day, far away from Europe, two women strolled slowly along the soft white sand of Anse Union beach on the Island of La Digue, enjoying this late afternoon respite and the impending sunset. As they walked they held the tiny hands of the 'birthday girl,' one-year-old Catherine Savy, who was beaming with excitement and grinning from ear to ear at having just discovered the 'use' of her legs. While witnessing her happiness, it was hard for both Anna and Patricia not to dwell on the significance of this day, on the tragic absence of the important father figure, and the ugly stain that Catherine would eventually have to confront...when she was old enough to understand her predicament. As they shared a meaningful glance, both women wished they could keep the child at the happy innocence of this tender age, and spare her from that cruel fate...

Around the same time, in a tiny fishing village on the southern coast of India, the sun had already disappeared for the night, but the lone figure staring out at the horizon was still in deep meditation. This sunset vigil had become his only respite and they did not begrudge him that, only disappointed that he always kept himself to himself rather than try to integrate into their culture and their way of life. It had been hard for them to accept this at first, but his kindness, obedience and respect had carved a special place in their hearts in a short space of time. As they watched him, they realised it was only a matter of time before he found the answers he sought, before meditation and his strong will overcame that overshadowing cloud. But for now, he was the son they had never had, the special gift offered by the mighty Indian Ocean, and that was all that really mattered.

Glossary

Albizia-*type of tree*
An nou ale-*let's go*
Baka-*a home-made alcoholic drink*
Baka kann-*home-made alcoholic drink made from sugar cane*
Bake-*galvanised iron washing tub/bath tub*
Baravan-*a screen used in a hospital*
Ben mare-*cooking with steam (bain-marie in English dictionary)*
Betal-*a dark red snuff*
Bilenbi-*a tree producing a sour-tasting fruit used in cooking*
Biskwi sale-*salted biscuit*
Bodanmyen-*type of tree*
Bonnonm dibwa-*sorcerer/magician who uses black magic*
Boulangerie-*bakery*
Bourzwa-*a fish; red snapper*
Bred mouroun-*a type of spinach that grows as a big bush*
Bwa gadyac-*type of tree*
Cassava galette-*hard breakfast bread/biscuit made from cassava*
Casuarina-*type of tree*
Coco rouge-*type of coconut used for its drinking water only*
Dandoysa-*the undead, or zombie*
Dife-*fire*
Dwat-*the right side*
Etensel-*first spark/first flare*

Fideles-*Christians*
Flamboyant-*type of flowering tree*
Fotey brankar-*a canvass armchair with two poles, carried by four men*
Gardkor-*amulet or talisman*
Gardyen-*a watchman / security man*
Gato piman-*deep-fried small balls of chillies and lentils cake*
Gos-*the left side*
Granm-*chickpeas cooked with onions and chillies*
Granmoun-*elders*
Grigri-*sorcery / black magic*
Kalis di pap-*a tree of light-coloured wood*
Kalorifer-*a distillation / processing plant*
Karang-*a fish*
Katiti-*name of a bird*
Kazak-*loose-style ladies top, worn over a printed ankle-length skirt*
Kinox-*nickname for equinox*
Krinol-*a 'posh' lady's hat*
Kriz-*screams – particularly after a death is announced*
Ladal-*bamboo system for water collection / distribution*
Laliyan de me-*a creeper with tiny white flowers*
Lalwa-*a tree used for making ropes*
Lans-*beach*
Lansiv-*cone-shaped shell used as horn to announce boats' arrival*
Larap koko-*metal coconut grater bolted onto a small wooden stool*
Laso-*burnt coral lime used for disinfecting*
Lavann-*a circular, flat-woven basket*
Lespatil-*a wooden cooking spoon*
Let demann-*a letter of wedding proposal*
Lev lasanm-*the ritual to ascertain a bride's loss of virginity following the wedding night*
Malbar-*Indian shopkeeper*

Mangliye-*a nut-producing tree – nut used as floor polish*
Manmzel-*Miss*
Marmit lafont-*cast-iron cooking pot with three legs / big cauldron*
Matapolanm-*white cotton fabric used for bedsheets / shirts*
Matouloumba-*clandestine card game involving money*
Memer-*nickname for grandmother*
Mon pov piti-*my poor child*
Moulouk-*a home-made crispy fried snack*
Moutay-*small, sticky cake in brown caramel sauce*
Mwatye-*a 50/50 system of sharing production between landowners and tenants*
Myse-*Mister / mister*
Paroisse-*the parish and the church*
Patatran-*a ground creeper that grows near the edge of a beach*
Penpen-*a type of heavy bread made with cassava*
Priz taba-*chewing tobacco*
Reso-*open charcoal burner used for cooking*
Rezizer-*administrator / overseer on a small island*
Rougay-*a Creole dish similar to a ratatouille or stew*
Sak kitouz i trouv son brenzel-*every salted turtle meat find its aubergine - in the olden days this dish was a delicacy. All turtles are now protected species*
Sal ver-*wedding marquee made from bamboo posts*
Saloup-*a small boat used to access a bigger one*
Samousa-*a deep-fried triangular pastry filled with fish / curry*
Sandragon-*a tree producing a reddish-coloured wood*
Satini-*a way of preparing a vegetable or fish dish*
Senbou-*apparel worn by an Indian man*
Servyet latet-*headscarf worn by old black ladies*
Sikredos-*boiled sweets / candies*
Takamaka-*type of large tree*

Tante-*aunt*
Tonton-*uncle*
Troutwel-*a bird*
Vakoa-*palm tree whose leaves are used to make hats and bags*
Vellu-*an Indian nick-name*
Vvey babonn-*a white-fleshed fish*
Vyev-*a fish*
Zanberik-*pulse / lentil*
Zanmalak-*type of tree*
Zouven-*expensive shoes*

About the Author

 A.R. Tirant was born in the Seychelles in November 1958. The daughter of a policeman and the eldest in a family of four brothers and four sisters, she grew up in the tiny seaside village of Beau Vallon on the northern coast of Mahé island. Her working life started in 1975 as a nurse at Mahé's Victoria Hospital, followed by a long career in the Hotel Industry.

She emigrated to England in 1995, and lives in West Sussex with her husband. She has two grown-up sons and a granddaughter.

'Echoes from the Oasis' is her debut novel, to be followed by other titles in the same series.

For author interviews, features and events visit
www.seychelles-author-in-cuckfield.com
Email: **a.r.tirant@gmail.com**

www.ingramcontent.com/pod-product-compliance
Lightning Source LLC
Chambersburg PA
CBHW021115300426
44113CB00006B/161